HUMANE MUSIC EDUCATION
FOR THE COMMON GOOD

COUNTERPOINTS: MUSIC AND EDUCATION

Estelle R. Jorgensen, *editor*

HUMANE MUSIC EDUCATION FOR THE COMMON GOOD

Edited by Iris M. Yob and
Estelle R. Jorgensen

INDIANA UNIVERSITY PRESS

This book is a publication of

Indiana University Press
Office of Scholarly Publishing
Herman B Wells Library 350
1320 East 10th Street
Bloomington, Indiana 47405 USA

iupress.indiana.edu

Manufactured in the United States of America

Cataloging information is available from the Library of Congress.

ISBN 978-0-253-04690-1 (hardback)
ISBN 978-0-253-04691-8 (paperback)
ISBN 978-0-253-04694-9 (ebook)

1 2 3 4 5   25 24 23 22 21 20

CONTENTS

HUMANE MUSIC EDUCATION
FOR THE COMMON GOOD

INTRODUCTION

Education for the Common Good in a Diverse World

Iris M. Yob

A QUIET, BOOKISH YOUNG MAN WALKED INTO ALISON Beavan's honors chorus at Nauset High School on Cape Cod, Massachusetts, back in 2002. The moment was the beginning of a transformation. In his own assessment of the experience, Julian reports that he gained confidence and poise, his self-esteem grew, and he found his voice—literally and figuratively. Then word came down that the Nauset Regional School District had a $1.8 million budget gap. If left unfilled by voters at the Town Meeting, forty teaching and staff positions would be cut, including Alison Beavan's. Confronted by the likely elimination of his favorite teacher and the music department, Julian mobilized a student-led effort to persuade voters at four town meetings to fully fund the budget with a Proposition 2½ override. He and his classmates wrote a brochure to taxpayers outlining what would be lost to quality education if the cuts were sustained and mailed it to thousands of households; he and his peers made impassioned speeches about the vitality of a quality education, one that included music and the arts. Their efforts were successful, and the budget override was passed at all four town meetings.

Today that young man, Julian Cyr, is a member of the Massachusetts State Senate, where he works hard on issues around clean water, affordable housing, the impact of changing climate patterns, employment opportunities, substance abuse, education, the value of music and arts education, and other issues that can improve the lives of people in his district and across the commonwealth. At the heart of this good-news story is a music educator, Ms. Beavan. Her work with the young people in her school chorus exemplifies the double-pronged influence teachers can have on the greater public welfare: first by the positive and humane impact they can have on the lives of individuals in their classes and then by giving those students the confidence and imagination, along with the skills and knowledge, to contribute to the common good.

This is the vision guiding the recent United Nations Educational, Scientific, and Cultural Organization (UNESCO) report, *Rethinking Education: Towards a Global Common Good?*[1] It suggests how education can respond to the challenges of our day in purpose, policy, and pedagogy in a way that respects and nurtures all members of the human family. Against this backdrop, the humanities and the arts have an important and even unique role to play, for it is in these arenas of endeavor among others that the human spirit finds expression and can be nurtured. The contributors to this collection explore, analyze, apply, critique, and expand these ideas as they relate to music education. More precisely, the contributors investigate how the music classroom, studio, rehearsal space, performance venue, religious site, and wherever else there is music making and music taking can be centers for contributing to the common good. The central question addressed by our writers in this collection is the following: How can music education, by adopting a humane approach across its many contexts and for its variety of learners, contribute to the common good?

The UNESCO Reports

The 2015 report *Rethinking Education* follows two preceding reports from UNESCO: *Learning to Be: The World of Education Today and Tomorrow* (1972), also known as the Faure report, and *Learning: The Treasure Within* (1996), referred to as the Delors report.[2] The writing teams, made up of "Senior Experts" in the field of education, were commissioned to analyze the challenges to education around the world at the time of writing and the educational practices responding to those challenges, and then offer recommendations for aligning education more closely with the realities of the day.[3] It is interesting to follow the development of ideas and the continuities/discontinuities across time and across these successive publications with the same intent and from the same source.

In one instance of discontinuity among the reports, the Faure report was written and presented by an all-male team and, not surprisingly, couched in the male-dominated language of the day, suggesting to readers a very masculine view of education and its role in the world, with talk of the complete man, his nature, his potential, his progress, his technology, and his genius. The report, however, did lament higher illiteracy rates among women and girls and their lower participation in schooling as one indicator of a developing nation compared with an industrialized one.[4] The Delors team, which included a better balance of men and women, also addressed the topic of the education of women and girls, strongly and explicitly encouraging greater focus on their development. *Rethinking Education* adds the violence against women and girls around the world and the lack of educational access afforded to them as explicit areas of social concern and action in the world of the twenty-first century.

Another discontinuity from report to report is the striking way in which they move successively away from a modernist understanding of the role of education to a more postmodernist stance. In the first of the series, straightforward assertions were offered on a number of topics and data sets, leading directly to announcing goals and processes for education. This confidence was bolstered even more by the second report, which unabashedly saw the right kind of education leading to "utopia" for all, and words such as *universal* are found throughout—although even in this report, the modernist bent is somewhat ameliorated by acknowledgement of "the value of a cautious measure of decentralization."[5] By 2015, however, the certainty in tone is diminished. The world is seen much more for its complexity and diversity. Even the subtitle of this last publication suggests less assurance about providing a unanimous and comprehensive plan for the future of education world-wide, concluding with a question mark—*Towards a Global Common Good?*—where "towards" suggests adaptability and flexibility going forward, and the very idea of a "common good" is questioned. Addressing this latter point, the writers significantly propose that the "diversity of contexts and conceptions of well-being and common life" help frame what we mean by "the common good."[6] In fact, this report sidesteps the term *public good* to avoid the impression of supporting some universally applicable goal.[7]

It is interesting to note, however, that even in the discontinuities, it is possible to see the gradual development of the basic principles that underscore all three reports. By moving away from a more paternalistic, patriarchal, universalistic account to a more gender-neutral, inclusive, and adaptable one, the series represents a growing sense of what participatory inclusiveness and diversity actually mean.

Each of the reports was published in response to a time when the world seemed to be changing, technology was burgeoning, international connectedness was becoming more apparent, and educational practices needed to be renewed to meet these challenges. All three reports promoted education-al methods and content believed to be more in keeping with the times and extended learning across the lifespan.[8] While underscoring the importance of accountability, *Rethinking Education* affirms the importance of "multiple learning pathways" to reinvigorate "the relevance of education that is life-long and life-wide."[9] It identifies "open and flexible . . . learning systems" as critical in the "validation and assessment of knowledge and competen-cies."[10] It further identifies "keys" that can transform learning to meet the challenges in the early twenty-first century: "an ethical foundation, . . . crit-ical thinking, independent judgement, problem-solving, and information and media literacy skills."[11] It envisions moving away from traditional edu-cational institutions and methods toward "networks of learning," "mixed, diverse and complex learning landscapes in which formal, non-formal, and informal learning occur through a variety of educational institutions and third-party providers."[12]

Humane Education for the Common Good

One of the most obvious continuities across all the reports is that each takes a humanistic approach and proposes a humane education, although how those views are expressed takes on the flavor of the time in which they were written. Throughout the series of reports, the term *humanistic* is not spelled with an uppercase *H* but rather a lowercase *h*, because it does not refer to a narrow philosophic tradition. Rather, the humanism spoken of in the reports is to be understood to mean a human-centered, human-focused, science-based approach to education. Humankind, writ large, is meant to be the object, purpose, and focus of educational endeavors, and humanity in all its varieties is to be taken into account, regardless of whether particu-lar humans live in poverty or affluence, in underdeveloped, developing, or developed countries, or have present access to good schooling or not. It is the welfare of the whole human family that motivates the contributors to this series of reports.

The humanistic theme is introduced in the Faure report. One fear of the writers of this report was that the human race would continue to fracture apace into "superior and inferior groups, into masters and slaves, supers [*sic*] men and submen" because of differences among peoples in their ad-vantages and privileges. They worried that the human family could lose its "unity" and "future as a species" and even "man's identity" if educators among others did not intervene.[13] Interestingly, they noted that education itself contributed to the disparity among peoples for learning had benefitted from the technological and scientific advances of some societies, advances which had "affect[ed] man's most profound characteristics and, in a manner of speaking, renew[ed] his genius,"[14] while other societies had not experienced these advances and concomitant developments in economics, politics, and health and well-being. The suggestion was that for some a process of "dehumanisation" ensued from the lack of these advantages, which should be addressed by a humanizing education that occurred across the life span and by "learning societies" wherever human beings happen to be.[15] The humanism adopted by the writers of the Faure report does not subscribe to idealistic, subjective, or abstract views of what a human being is. Rather, their focus was on "a concrete being, set in a historical context, in a set period. [This conception] depends on objective knowledge, but that which is essentially and resolutely directed towards action and primarily in the service of man himself."[16]

While these humanistic notions were laid out in the Faure report, the Delors report made them even more explicit and central. This began with the title of the report: *Learning: The Treasure Within*, which immediately draws attention to the potential of the human learner. In the opening paragraph, the Delors report stated, "Education is . . . an expression of affection for children and young people, whom we need to welcome into society, unreservedly offering them the place that is theirs by right therein."[17] He added that when the members of the UNESCO Commission accepted their mandate, they also accepted that "while education is an ongoing process of improving knowledge and skills, it is also—perhaps primarily—an exceptional means of bringing about personal development and building relationships among individuals, groups and nations."[18] Early in the document, the Delors report introduced a theme that develops later: education is the "continuous process of forming whole human beings," later reformulated as the "four pillars of learning": "learning to know," "learning to do," "learning to live together," and "learning to be"—the latter two pointing directly beyond the acquisition of knowledge and practical skills to education's additional tasks in developing the whole person.[19] This formulation has found particular resonance with several of the writers in the present collection as they argue that music education can have a vital part to play in promoting development in all areas of human potential, especially in living together and being fully human.[20]

Rethinking Education is clear about the humanistic approach it is built on: "Sustaining and enhancing the dignity, capacity and welfare of the human person, in relation to others and to nature, should be the fundamental purpose of education in the twenty-first century."[21] The writers acknowledge that humanism, narrowly understood, has been criticized by "postmodernists, some feminists, [and] ecologists" for its exclusive and limited focus on humankind and more recently by "trans-humanists or even post-humanists" who would improve the human species through "natural selection" or "radical enhancements."[22] Nevertheless, they remain firm in their commitment to a humanistic approach to education for it takes a wider moral vision that values human beings not because of the part they might play in economic development but because they simply are, and hence it values all human beings without exclusion or marginalization.[23] Under this rubric, the purpose and foundation of humane or humanistic education for these writers lie in these ideals: "respect for life and human dignity, equal rights and social justice, cultural and social diversity, and a sense of human solidarity and shared responsibility for our common good."[24] In the light of these ideals, they reaffirm and reinterpret the four pillars of education enunciated in the Delors report, giving a particular nod to learners with disabilities, gender equality, multicultural learning societies, and consequently alternative learning spaces and teaching methods, each of which is explored in the context of music education by contributors to the present collection.[25]

Integral with the notion of humane education, the "common good" or more particularly, "a global common good," is another central continuity among the three UNESCO reports. Given the mandates of the three task-forces that produced the reports—that they should address the challenges and opportunities facing societies and education across the world of their times—this is not surprising. Education for the common good is a theme that has persisted in educational thought and has, in some instances, even become an assumption that no longer needs justification.[26] In the Faure report, the writers did not use the expression, "the common good," but they nevertheless adopted it in spirit by taking the view that the right kind of education can contribute to the transformation and progress of society.[27] For its part, they suggested, "education may help society to become aware of its problems" and, by a holistic training, prepare people who "will consciously seek their individual and collective emancipation, . . . [and] may greatly contribute to changing and humanizing societies."[28] The focus of the Faure report was not narrowed to European or Western society but took a global perspective, and the influence it envisioned embraced the whole world, as it pointed to "gaps" between societies, addressing directly such issues as environmental degradation and the need to imbue students with the principles and skills of democracy.[29] The report closely tied the issue of learning democratic principles and skills to the notion of the common good, describing the close connection between the two in the following words: "an individual comes to a full realization of his own social dimensions through an apprenticeship of active participation in the functioning of social structures and, where necessary, through a personal commitment in the struggle to reform them."[30]

The Delors report took up this idea and expanded on it.[31] Apart from the image of "four pillars" of education, it used a number of other metaphors to capture the sense of the global common good in what the authors pictured as an increasingly "crowded planet."[32] The notion of a utopia was introduced in the first chapter. The writers did not intend to conjure an image of a world where all problems are solved and all ideals are realized, but rather an idealistic vision of the goals of education as the "principal means available to foster a deeper and more harmonious form of human development and thereby to reduce poverty, exclusion, ignorance, oppression and war."[33] Such a vision was not to be limited to privileged societies but was for all societies as they partnered together to bring about this worldwide harmony. The writers applied "the global village" metaphor to capture this idea and implied this vision could be realized through international cooperation in sharing monetary resources; aiming for an inclusive education that would embrace everyone, across the lifespan, giving special attention to neglected women and girls; and bringing the technology of the information age to all.[34] Another metaphor the Delors report introduced was that of the "learning society" in which all are learners, regardless of position or age, and more significantly, where ongoing learning enhances society and society embodies and supports learning in a reciprocal relationship.[35]

Building on the primary sentiments of the earlier reports, *Rethinking Education* is the first to name the connection between society and education (of the Faure report) or the idealistic vision of education (of the Delors report) as a movement toward the common good. They identify the common good, reframed at times as "common goods," as education and knowledge, and provide three dimensions of the common good (as opposed to simple public good): it is related to "the goodness of the life that humans hold in common"; it is "defined with regard to diversity of contexts and conceptions of well-being and common life"; and it is a "participatory process" where "shared action is intrinsic, as well as instrumental, to the good itself." In other words, it implies "an inclusive process of public policy formulation" and aspires "towards new forms and institutions of participatory democracy."[36] In these descriptors, a couple of tensions appear: between what is common and what is responsive to diversity and between what is a common good and what are common goods. By not explicitly resolving these tensions, the writers of this report allow for multiple interpretations under their general principles of humanism, education, democracy, and development.[37]

It is apparent that the notions of humane education and the common good are inseparable in these reports. A humane, humanistic, or human-centered (terms that seem to be interchangeable in this account) education enhances, nurtures, and promotes the highest development of every individual. This is true whether the individual is an immigrant child in a boat that washes ashore in Greece, a transgender individual in the choir, a nonsinger and nonmusician in the learning community, a differently abled participant, or a learner whose culture and values portend a different kind of music and music production—as writers in this present collection argue. In a humane (inclusive, responsive, participatory) education, the humanness of humankind is enhanced, nurtured, and promoted. And that in essence is the common good. By the same logic, the common good is better understood as common goods, indicating that it is made up of what is good for each individual. And what is good for the individual is a humane education that promotes and nurtures his or her human potential. This account assumes a codependence between humane education and the common good, and so the two notions can be readily conflated.

Furthermore, whether one is talking about the individual or the larger society, the promotion of human good is to be done without regard to where that learner is found, whether in a school classroom, a teacher-education seminar, a prison, a religious setting, or a private studio, as other writers in this collection show. So both notions—humane education and the common good—have a social justice edge in that they would activate teachers, curriculum builders, policy makers, and in fact all of us to dismantle the barriers that would prevent anybody from full participation in these lofty aims of democracy, development, and a holistic education.

And yet, there is a distinction between the two notions, humane education and the common good. Educators should aim for both, but humane education points more to the means of achieving the common good and the common good more to the ultimate goal of humane education. In essence, although they are inseparable, humane education is the foundation of the common good, and the common good is the outcome of a humane education. There can be no service toward the common good if that service is not inclusively humane through and through. No common good is possible if the welfare of any single member of the human family is not humanely understood and their needs, context, and personal potential addressed. It is the concern for each individual that modifies "common good" toward "common goods" because individual needs, possibilities, and challenges are not reducible to a single good unless that common good is understood in a most encompassing way. The larger welfare of humankind depends on the humane education of every member of the human family.

Reduced to these basic premises, the vision of *Rethinking Education* is radical, maybe even too radical. It conveys the sense that a humane education, conducted in various ways, times, and places across the lifespan, is the sole means toward the common good. In some fundamental, inescapable way, it alone will eliminate inequality, violence, poverty, and destruction of the environment and create peace between nations, democratic institutions, and prosperous societies. Realistically speaking, however, we know that much more needs to come together for this dream to be fulfilled, and several writers in the present collection point this out and even question its absolutist claims. Nevertheless, however we might modify and adjust the vision of *Rethinking Education* in the light of lived realities and alternate understandings, the right kind of education may yet remain pivotal in making the world a better place: reaching for the common good rests at least in part on a humane approach to learning and learners.

In the chapters that follow, the writers respond to *Rethinking Education: Towards a Common Good?* in the context of music education. The first and last sections are more reflective and bookend the two middle sections that are more practical in their focus. "Part I: Critique and Clarification" examines the premises of *Rethinking Education*. Iris M. Yob analyzes the tensions inherent in talk about both the *common* good and common *goods*, between focus on the individual and the whole human family. Randall Everett Allsup raises the specter of whether there really can be an international humanism and whether a common good can be realized when rational beings, at the personal or public level, cannot agree. Hanne Rinholm and Øivind Varkøy warn music educators against the kind of hubris that would lead them to expect more than music education can deliver in making the world a better place. Kevin Shorner-Johnson raises significant questions about the linear notion of progress exhibited in all three of the UNESCO reports and proposes that educators consider instead a diversity of temporalities and alternative experiences of the flow of time and what that might do for individual and community development toward the common good. Ebru Tuncer Boon, recounting the Gezi Park uprising in Istanbul, explores the nexus between political activism and the creative arts and how the former can lead to an explosion in the latter and vice versa, casting the arts in a central role in activism for the common good.

"Part II: Principles and Practices of Music Teaching" explores some of the practical applications of *Rethinking Education* to the work of preparing music educators. Betty Anne Younker builds on the legacy of progressive education and makes the case for inquiry-based learning as an essential pedagogy for moving toward the common good. Christine Brown draws on the humanistic writings of Abraham Maslow and Carl Rogers to suggest principles for teaching in the piano studio. Emily Howe, André de Quadros, Andrew Clark, and Kinh T. Vu share what they have learned as music educators by working in diverse settings outside of the traditional classroom, specifically with inmates and disabled learners and with issues faced by people of another cultural heritage and location. Joseph Shively explores the qualities of music teacher preparation that is based on humanistic principles.

"Part III: Educating Others for the Common Good" suggests how specific contexts of music education or the needs and interests of particular learners can be addressed to enact the vision of *Rethinking Education*. Luca Tiszai describes the social benefits of bringing together people of different ages and abilities in community music making, benefits that are mutual and boundary-shaking. Emily Good-Perkins helps us see how cultural diversity in vocal music education is manifested and can be included to expand students' understanding and appreciation of difference. Blakeley Menghini draws parallels between the principles outlined in *Rethinking Education* and the Suzuki Method and draws on her practical experience to show how those principles can be maximized. Mary Thomason-Smith describes a particular case, set not in a traditional classroom but a sacred community, as an exemplar of where music education can promote an understanding of and involvement in addressing a pressing global issue of our times. Jacob Axel Berglin and Thomas Murphy O'Hara illustrate a variety of approaches open to the music educator in providing a hospitable place for the transgender student.

"Part IV: Elaborations and Expansions" points to some areas for continuing and future development in music education beyond what is gleaned from *Rethinking Education*. Johnnie-Margaret McConnell and Susan Laird outline the very human need for musicking and the benefits of reaching out to satisfy the musical hunger of those who are not in traditional music classes. Deanne Bogdan picks up on the theme of holistic education by describing the chronic dissociation of thought and feeling and how they might be reintegrated in literature and, by comparison, music, and how music itself might be integrated into a whole when it brings the Other into a place where there is no Other. Alexandra Kertz-Welzel, Leonard Tan, Martin Berger, and David Lines, representing Germany, Singapore, South Africa, and New Zealand, respectively, illustrate cultural diversity in music and how education systems in these countries are addressing these differences and developing inclusive music education programs. Eleni Lapidaki addresses an omission in *Rethinking Education* by describing and illustrating intimacy and trust as key features in inclusive and humane music education.

In the conclusion, Estelle Jorgensen gathers together the themes of the collection across critiques and clarifications, pedagogies and approaches to music educator preparation, the diversity of learners and sites for learning, and elaborations and expansions as we think about the future of music education. She connects these again to the central ideas of *Rethinking Education* and shows how they promote a clearer, more realistic, and imaginative understanding of how music education can be humane and directed toward the common good.

At this point in time, the 2015 UNESCO publication is prescient in many respects but strikes one as out of date in others, so fast-paced are the social, political, economic, technological, and musical worlds we live in today. Because of this, this present collection does not give a comprehensive plan for what music education should be going forward, for that would limit its vision to what we can imagine now. The writers included in this collection responded to a call for papers for the journal *Philosophy of Music Education Review*, announced on the Facebook page of the journal. The response was so immediate and so broad that the journal could not publish them all even over the course of multiple issues. So the idea of publishing them as a book collection was conceived. The editors thought the set of proposed papers as a book would do more justice to the topic of humane music education for the common good. The writers of this collection are from New Zealand, South Africa, Norway, Cambodia, Singapore, Turkey, Hungary, Greece, Germany, the United States, and Canada. They include graduate students at the beginning of their careers and retiring professors at the end of theirs and every stage in between. They come from the ranks of studio teachers, K-12 teachers, professors of music, choir conductors, curriculum specialists, administrators, philosophers and theoreticians, and exponents of Kodály and Suzuki. And yet, clearly, there are voices left unheard in this collection and perspectives and applications unexplored. The best this collection can do is to begin a conversation and open possibilities to new thinking and doing in music education that would make it humane in service of the common good.

IRIS M. YOB is Faculty Emerita and Contributing Faculty Member in the Richard W. Riley College of Education and Leadership at Walden University, Minnesota.

Notes

1. UNESCO, *Rethinking Education: Towards a Global Common Good?* (Paris: UNESCO, 2015), http://unesdoc.unesco.org/images/0023/002325/232555e.pdf.

2. UNESCO, *Learning to Be: The World of Education Today and Tomorrow* (Paris: UNESCO, 1972), http://unesdoc.unesco.org/images/0000/000018/001801e.pdf (hereafter referred to as the Faure report); UNESCO, *Learning: The Treasure Within* (Paris, UNESCO, 1996), http://unesdoc.unesco.org/images/0010/001095/109590eo.pdf (hereafter referred to as the Delors report).

3. UNESCO, *Rethinking Education*, 5.

4. UNESCO, Faure report, 52.

5. Ibid., 27.

6. UNESCO, *Rethinking Education*, 78–79.

7. Ibid., 78.

8. For instance, the Faure report encouraged the development of multimedia skills for communicating, social studies along with sciences and the study of subjects relevant to human living, the arts as well as technology, manual training as well as physical education (UNESCO, Faure report, 61–69). The Faure report advocated for teaching practices based on cognitive science and psychology and promoted the positive impact of individualized learning programs (chap. 5). Twenty-four years later, the Delors report picked up many of these same themes and translated them to the various levels of schooling, from elementary through university, and in continuing education throughout life (UNESCO, Delors report, chap. 6).

9. UNESCO, *Rethinking Education*, 64.

10. Ibid., 65.

11. Ibid., 38.

12. Ibid., 48.

13. UNESCO, Faure report, xxi.

14. Ibid., xxi, xxii.

15. Ibid., xxi, xxxiii.

16. Ibid., 146.

17. UNESCO, Delors report, 11.

18. Ibid., 12.

19. Ibid., 20, 21, chap. 4.

20. See for instance, Joseph Shively, "Navigating Music Teacher Education toward Humane Ends"; Blakeley Menghini, "Rethinking Education: The Four Pillars of Education in the Suzuki Studio"; and Johnnie-Margaret McConnell and Susan Laird, "Nourishing the Musically Hungry: Learning from Undergraduate Amateur Musicking," in this collection.

21. UNESCO, *Rethinking Education*, 36.

22. Ibid., 36, 37.

23. Ibid., 36, 37.

24. Ibid., 38.

25. Ibid., 39, 43, 47–53. See Luca Tiszai, "Friendship, Solidarity, and Mutuality Discovered in Music"; Jacob Berglin and Thomas O'Hara, "Working with Transgender Students as a Humane Act"; Emily Good-Perkins, "Rethinking Vocal Education as a Means to Encourage Positive Identity Development in Adolescents"; Alexandra Kertz-Welzel, Leonard Tan, Martin Berger, and David Lines, "A Humanistic Approach to Music Education: (Critical) International Perspectives"; Eleni Lapidaki, "Toward the Discovery of Contemporary Trust and Intimacy in Higher Music Education"; Betty Ann Younker, "Inquiry-Based Learning: A Value for Music Education with Aims to Cultivate a Humane Society; Mary Thomason-Smith, "Music Education in Sacred Communities: Singing, Learning, and Leading for the Global Common Good," in this collection.

26. This assumption can be seen, for example, on the website of the American Association of University Professors, in the essay "Education for the Common Good," posted with the subtitle "The goal of education needs to be more than individual success" (Marcus Peter Ford, "Education for the Common Good," *Academe* 102, no. 5 [September 2016], https://www.aaup.org/article/education-common-good#.WcE6_8iGMtI); in Amy L. Watts, *Education and the Common Good: The Social Benefits of Higher Education in Kentucky* (Frankfort, KY: Long-term Policy Research Center, 2001), http://e-archives.ky.gov/pubs/LPRC/education_and_the_common_good(2001).pdf; and in the "core values of equity, quality, transparency, accountability and community" professed by the North Carolina State Board of Public Education at "Public Education for the Common Good," NC State Board of Public Education, accessed September 19, 2017, https://stateboard.ncpublicschools.gov/resources/public-education-for-the-common-good-1.

27. UNESCO, Faure report, 55.

28. Ibid., 56.

29. Ibid., chap. 4.

30. Ibid., 151. This theme was taken up again by the National Taskforce on Civic Learning and Democratic Engagement, *A Crucible Moment: College Learning and Democracy's Future*,

accessed September 20, 2017, https://aacu.org/sites/default/files/files/crucible/Crucible_508F
.pdf, first published in 2012.

31. UNESCO, Delors report, chap. 2.

32. Ibid., chap. 1.

33. Ibid., 11.

34. Ibid., 31, 32.

35. Ibid., chap. 5.

36. UNESCO, *Rethinking Education*, 78.

37. For a further discussion of these tensions, see Iris M. Yob, "There Is No Other," in this collection.

PART I

CRITIQUE AND CLARIFICATION

1

THERE IS NO OTHER

Iris M. Yob

IT IS RARE FOR THE TITLE OF A publication to end with a question mark, but the 2015 UNESCO document *Rethinking Education: Towards a Global Common Good?* does just that.[1] In this case, the question mark captures the central tension in simultaneously thinking globally about the welfare of all while valuing diversity and individual differences. Can one speak of a *common* good or a single common *good* when rethinking an education that is appropriate across worldwide contexts, challenges, and opportunities? In this chapter, I will explore whether the tensions can be resolved and, if so, how. I will do so by exploring the apparent conflict between the concept of "the Other," which recognizes the individuality of each member of the human family, and the concept that there is no Other, which embraces everybody regardless of their differences.

The Other: Humanity Up Close

A significant reality faced by teachers and educational policy makers for every age group is the substantial diversity among learners. Individual readiness, abilities, interests, and needs present themselves to teachers who want to do their best for each student. Then there are personal histories and inherited differences to take into account, which can determine if the match between the individual learner and the official curriculum is a good one or a soul-destroying mismatch that imprisons the student in an educational environment that saps his or her curiosity and discourages active engagement in learning and personal development. Teachers have long recognized these differences, and many experiment with ways to meet the individual needs of each learner in their care.

Of course, this diversity manifests in more than learning readiness and inherited and cultivated abilities. A recognition of multiculturalism has become standard in referring to diversity in society and in the classroom. Racial and ethnic backgrounds help form our self-understanding, perception of the world, and values and belief systems, as well as shaping how others see us and respond to us. These backgrounds give us language and the words we use to communicate and make meaning. Across our communities, there are others whose skin tone is different and who dress in different clothes, eat different foods, sing different songs, play different instruments, enjoy different games, speak different languages, and worship different deities in different ways and in different sacred places. Add to this mix the range of differences in gender and sexual orientation and identity, age, physical ability and appearance, political affiliation, family background, geographic location, life experiences, loves, hopes, dreams, and fears. Getting our heads around the "booming, buzzing confusion" of the world around us is a formidable task.[2] It is a task that teachers in both formal and informal educational settings need to be responsive to in ways that promote the well-being and personal development of each individual in their care.[3]

The apparent diversity in our communities and educational institutions has compelled us to examine the notions of equality and fairness. Equality demands that everyone has the same opportunities and access to resources. Fairness acknowledges that equality cannot be determined by quantity alone but may mean differences in the kinds of offerings we provide. For instance, a differently abled learner may need a one-on-one caretaker, mentor, or teacher's aide to participate in classroom exercises with everybody else; a Muslim teenage girl may be better served by a girls-only swim class; the choice of repertoire or performance venue for a school choir may need to be chosen with sensitivity to the different affiliations and belief systems of the choir members and their parents.[4] Such accommodations may challenge the notion of "equality" if understood rigidly or simplistically; they demand creativity in conception and practice to maximize fairness for all. The fundamental goal of equality and fairness is inclusion. No one is to be left out despite his or her differences, even if inclusion requires accommodations.

Postmodernism shares with multiculturalism a number of key premises: "a valuation of marginality, a suspicion of master discourses, a resistance to empty conventions."[5] It allows different interpretations of shared facts and even the existence of facts that may have been automatically filtered out by one's assumptions and beliefs. It does not, however, support propaganda created to convince others of a particular account or ideology, such as "alternative facts" and "fake news," because they lack evidence, reason, and integrity in any shared system of meaning making. Postmodernism challenges our self-understanding and worldviews by acknowledging the existence of and validating the Other, including even the "nomads" or "schizophrenics" in our society.[6] For instance, a person may be white and, therefore, mainstream but also a woman, making her a nomad in a man's world, just as an old person is a nomad in a young person's world. Someone who is gay, wheelchair-bound, and an immigrant may hold multiple senses of self. When followed through to its logical conclusion, we become increasingly aware that we too are Other—we may be multiple Others within ourselves or may be nomads out of the mainstream. And we are certainly Other to others.

Postmodernism has opened the door to new words and concepts as we respond to this growing awareness of the Other. Poststructuralism is one natural companion of postmodernism, with its fundamental premise that the interpretation of texts, how one reads and understands something written by another, or even something enacted, played, or sung, is not necessarily what is intended by the author or performer but is determined by the reader/watcher/listener's personal history, context, intentions, and values. So, multiple possible interpretations and meanings can be ascribed to every text and act. For teachers, this means that each learner can be seeing and hearing and viscerally experiencing something different in a shared learning event.

Deconstruction is another companion of postmodernism. Its basic premise is that words are not reality but signifiers and therefore notoriously unreliable. Claims made in a modernist mode are taken as certain, universally applicable, and stable; claims seen through the lens of postmodernism can be questioned because they are individually or locally understood and, therefore, changeable and open to interrogation. In other words, what one individual takes as inalienable truth is possibly just one truth among many possible truths at any particular moment in time—or possibly even an untruth for some. Failure to acknowledge the possibility of multiple truths can result in policy actions, teaching approaches, and communal relationships that are inimical and violent to some Others.

In an extreme form, deconstructionist ideas are nihilist; that is, they lead to the conclusion that there can be no certainties. In a less extreme form, deconstruction is a critical approach to what we know. It encourages us to interrogate and problematize key concepts, assumptions, and truisms that we might have taken for granted and that might alienate us from others or at some level do harm to others by violating their very way of thinking and being. This approach can open us to new possibilities and alternative worldviews, or at least to the very real possibility that there are alternatives.

Understanding the Other—and there are grave concerns about whether this is even possible—or at least acknowledging to ourselves that there are Others requires us to take a close-up view of the human family. It has given added impetus to the various rights movements: civil rights, women's rights, LGBT rights, and the rights of the differently abled, for instance. Each of these movements has taken as fundamental that the differences exhibited by individual groups should be protected and included in social policy, access to resources, and fair treatment. "Politically correct" language, or how we talk about the Other, and the inclusiveness and sensitivity to differences that we demonstrate in our discourse has grown out of the same root, no matter how disparaged it may have become.

When mishandled and incomplete, however, the close-up view can also tempt us into classifying and stereotyping, sorting and dividing, identifying and separating. The rifts between different others can promote wariness and even fear of the Other—fear of losing one's own identity in a morass of legitimate othernesses, fear of the challenges others might pose to one's cherished way of being and the sharing of resources that might be required, fear of an implicit requirement to change. Because of these fears, schools may assume the responsibility, tacit or explicit, to move the Other toward being more mainstream and therefore more "acceptable"—to moderate and dominate, rather than include and smooth the sharp edges of exception, to create a sameness (that can end up being dull and monochromatic). So, the close-up view must go deep, pushing through any initial fear and reticence to a fuller acceptance and celebration of the differences within the human family. This is where a humane music education takes place.

There Is No Other: The Wide-Angle View

While the close-up view of humanity is a preferred option for all of us living effectively in today's world and mandatory for teachers who must respond to differences every day and in every learning event, the wide-angle view is equally compelling. As our view zooms out to encompass increasingly wider sweeps, from individuals to classrooms, communities, nations, and the world, human beings begin to merge into one, differences become fuzzier, and commonalities across all individuals emerge. If we zoom out far enough, we begin to see the common humanness, the shared history and potential futures, and the common ecological system in which that humanity exists, to which it contributes, and by which it is nurtured. The wide-angle view is also a preferred option.

The expression "There is no Other" both acknowledges the existence of the Other and simultaneously affirms something more than otherness.[7] It is an iteration of much moral philosophy and the fundamental ethic of the world's religions: "Do unto others as you would have them do unto you."[8] The Golden Rule, as the statement is best known, invites one to see the Other in oneself and oneself in the Other. It blurs the differences that might exist among us as human beings and encourages us to reach for a common humanity that collectively knows pains, fears, needs, hopes, aspirations, and dreams. This goes beyond empathy for others to embrace a oneness with others.

With public discourse that seems dominated by extremists on all sides and entrenched partisanship that stalls politics and governance, healing the rifts among and between people calls for this wider view. In pointing out how we are different from others, we can also be aware that we are in the same human family. Mahatma Gandhi is on record as saying, "I am a Muslim, and a Christian, and a Buddhist, and a Jew."[9] Reminiscent of this are the banners waved at the time of the terrorist attack on the *Charlie Hebdo* offices in Paris that read "Je suis Charlie" and the tweet of former US secretary of state Madeline Albright that said "I was raised Catholic, became Episcopalian and found out later my family was Jewish. I stand ready to register as Muslim in #solidarity."[10] These Shylockian pronouncements indicate our togetherness despite our differences—and for good or ill, as Shakespeare's character illustrates.[11]

The stance of "no Other" is deeply connected with morality. When we allow some members of the human family to become invisible to us and to exist outside our imaginative and empathetic world because they speak a different language, are a different color or socioeconomic status, or possess different intellectual or physical abilities, we are treating those people immorally. John Dewey makes this point in *A Common Faith*, when he pictures "all in the same boat traversing the same turbulent ocean."[12] This is also the central argument of Raimond Gaita's *A Common Humanity: Thinking about Love and Truth and Justice,* although Gaita expresses this same idea more positively: "Treat me as a human being, fully as your equal, without condescension—that demand (or plea), whether it is made by women to men or by blacks to whites, is a demand or a plea for justice."[13] This succinct statement goes beyond simple justice, however; Gaita opens the possibility of love for others without reservation. This is where he describes a "goodness beyond virtue" for it goes beyond fairness and equal rights to respect for and acceptance of the full humanity of all others without condescension.[14] For him, it is an unconditional acceptance of the "preciousness of others" that disregards anything we might feel uncomfortable with or dislike. It involves loving others "beyond reason, beyond merit and beyond what moralisers might say about them."[15] His stance includes, for example, even a Hitler or an Eichmann, because Gaita accepts as fundamental the interconnectedness and interdependence of all human beings. This allows him to conclude that as there is goodness beyond virtue, so there is "justice beyond fairness," one that deeply accepts and is built on the full and shared humanity of all.[16]

Gaita echoes a similar argument made earlier by Philip H. Phenix concerning the essential morality inherent in recognizing our shared humanity. This morality is bound to the notion of democracy in which all are equal. Individuals are equal, Phenix elaborates, not because they have the same "abilities, wants, interests, needs, qualities, or circumstances" but because they are "human, mortal, possessed of body and mind." Consequently, a single "standard of worth" applies to all.[17]

Systems theory gives us an important perspective when we take the wide-angle view of humanity, for it sees the whole human family and its environment as connected and interrelated. This web-of-life or ecological view brings every individual into the picture in a dynamic way, for the bonds that tie us together make us one; whatever impacts one has a ripple effect throughout the whole. It is easy to see this on so many levels: when a tsunami in Japan brings flotsam to the shores of North America; when greenhouse gases contribute to melting icecaps and shrinking glaciers; when a monetary policy in one country sends a shiver through economies worldwide; and when poverty or greed drives people to cut down a rainforest, upsetting the water cycle and contributing to drought in other parts of the world. On a social level, an authoritarian and militaristic regime can raise the threat of nuclear armament so that nations begin to fear other nations, perceived slights can enrage terrorists, unsanitary and impoverished conditions can start a pandemic, ignorance and powerlessness can make people vulnerable to exploitation by others, and tyranny can produce waves of refugees desperate enough to climb into flimsy boats and cross treacherous seas to safer havens. When one child is abandoned to street life or one family is homeless and hungry or one enemy combatant is tortured, we are all diminished.

On the other hand, when the knowledge gained in a literate society is used in the service of all, individuals reap the dividends that come from an improved economy, better access to health services, government stability, and improved status for women and minorities. When we nurture the best in ourselves and our children locally, we contribute to humanity as a whole. In an important sense, despite the overwhelming magnitude of the problems facing this planet and its inhabitants, systems thinking can give us courage and resolve.

Many forces impinge on us today, threatening to drive us apart. Populism and nationalistic ideologies would build walls, real and ideological, around groups who feel rightly or wrongly beleaguered and endangered, isolating people from each other and severing bonds of caring and mutuality across borders and boundaries. Hyperpartisanship divides liberals from conservatives, capturing people in echo chambers, where they hear only their own kind talking, making cooperation for the common good almost impossible. The entitled, the rich, the exploiters, the "one-percenters" are accused of losing touch with the struggles of ordinary people, the poor, the exploited, the other 99 percent. The secure and comfortable are afraid of refugees, often without any good reason and without offering positive solutions to their plight. Economies are pitted against each other, so they cannot agree on responses to carbon emissions, fair trade practices, or worker safety and protection standards. Racism, misogyny, and homophobia too often go largely unchallenged in public and private discourse.

All this is happening at a time when humanity needs to unite and find realistic, long-lasting solutions to environmental degradation and the increasing gaps between rich and poor people, communities, and nations. Violence, both local and international, calls for collective action, as does exploitation of women, children, and the vulnerable. Educational opportunities, health care and safe living conditions, preservation and support of the family, and peace at home and abroad cannot be accomplished by a single individual or group of individuals. These are concerns for all human beings, and they require the collective effort of all to see them accomplished. This is where the cutting edge of a music education for the common good can contribute.

The *Common* Good and the Common *Good*

More than the UNESCO reports preceding it, *Rethinking Education* expresses the force of the tension between the Other and no Other. Its humanistic vision encompasses both, for its basic principles include, on the one hand, "equal rights and social justice" and "respect for cultural diversity," which represent a response to the Other, and on the other hand, "respect for life and human dignity" and "international solidarity and shared responsibility," which point to a shared humanity that operates as though there is no Other.[18] This report accepts with little modification the tensions identified in the 1996 Delors report from UNESCO, including that "between the global and the local; the universal and the particular," which we have identified as the wide-angle view and the close-up view of humanity, respectively.[19] If anything is favored in *Rethinking Education*, it may be the wide-angle view that there is no Other, given what the writers identify as "the central concern" of the world: sustainability of life on the planet.[20] Even in this discussion, however, they note that human rights campaigns, awareness of growing disparities in wealth, reports of escalating violence and disconnectedness and rising vulnerabilities among people, and a greater awareness of diverse worldviews draw our attention back to the plight of the Other.

We find here the beginnings of a resolution of the tension between the Other and no Other, for maybe they are inseparable. What is common about the common good, as far as education is concerned, is first stated in the conclusion to the report's second chapter. Announcing that a sustainable existence must acknowledge the variety of social, economic, and environmental dimensions of human development, the writers state that "an empowering education is one that builds the human resources we need to be productive, to continue to learn, to solve problems, to be creative, and to live together and with nature in peace and harmony."[21] Nurturing the development of each individual human being across the life span, wherever that individual is located and whatever his or her circumstances, is what is required to live meaningful lives, in dignity, and this will contribute to the "collective quest of well-being."[22] There is a common purpose implied here, but not necessarily a common means and method for achieving it.

The distinction between the Other and no Other may tempt us into a false dichotomy. However, the Other exists in our shared humanity, and the no Other includes those who are Other. I saw a metaphor for this when visiting the archaeological site of the terracotta warriors near Xi'an, China. The scale of the various pits where the figures have been unearthed is astonishing (like the scale of so many things in China): row after row, column after column, in pit after pit of standing life-size soldier figures stretched out before us. But even more astonishing is what you see when you look more closely: each figure is unique as evidenced by the variety of beards, moustaches, hairstyles, buttons on jackets, sleeve styles, boots, buckles, the placement of the hands, and the tilt of the head. Even the horse figures stand differently, wear different saddles and bridles, and have their own distinctive tail and mane plaits—such diversity in military figures where uniforms and uniformity are ideals! When you take a wider view, however, these individual soldiers make up a single army, unified in their dignity and purpose to serve the emperor. Their differences make up the whole.

This fusion of the Other and the no Other is also illustrated by several writers in this collection. We see it, for instance, in the purposeful variety of music cultures that make up the New Canadian Global Music Orchestra in Toronto; in the multiple types of voice production, representing various singing cultures, learned and practiced together in the same voice class; in the elimination of differentiating roles for music educators in the Boston area engaged with prisoners, the differently abled, or people embedded in a different ethnicity as they engage in music making together; in Hungary with severely disabled young people performing with a community of other musicians; and in the hospitality shown the transgendered Other in a college choir.[23]

In these examples, the Other is both not present and present. These principles apply equally to all lifelong learners—all lives are respected; all have equal rights and are entitled to what is fair and just; cultural diversity everywhere is respected, and all participate and share in a community of human music makers and music learners. Yet, throughout, the Other does not lose his or her otherness. This is not a case of either-or, where our attention to the Other or the no Other is taking its turn on center stage or waiting in the wings for its turn. It is essentially a case of "this with that," where both are always center stage.[24] The writers of *Rethinking Education* express this central idea in these words: "We must recognize the diversity of lived realities while reaffirming a common core of universal values."[25] In other words, we validate the Other by cultivating the humanness that connects us all as though there is no Other.

This basic resolution also helps answer the question, what is good about the common *good*? The basic good is "sustainable human and social development." It is a goal of education that takes the wide view of humanity. At the same time, it must be "both equitable and viable."[26] Later in *Rethinking Education*, the writers speak of "common goods": "the goodness of the life that humans hold in common," "defined with regard to the diversity of contexts and conceptions of well-being and common life," undertaken as a "participatory process" involving "shared action . . . intrinsic . . . to the good itself."[27] The common good can be best, or perhaps only, understood when we focus on the human being—not some idealized, theoretical being, but real people living in actual contexts in our time, as the 1972 Faure report from UNESCO report indicates.[28] This means seeking the development of the potential of humans in all their capacities for good, as the Delors report proposes.[29] It is bound up with "the right to meaningful and relevant learning," which is explained in *Rethinking Education* by both the close-up view of humanity—that there are "many different ways of defining the quality of life"—and the wide-angle view—that education and knowledge are common to all "as a collective social endeavor."[30]

Formal and informal educators, policy makers, curriculum builders, administrators, teachers, and community music makers are called on to nurture the human family in all its diversity. Being humane is understood not simply as being kind to others but more rigorously and radically as acknowledging the essential value of each individual with common human needs and to whom we are inseparably bound both now and in the future that we create together. It is a way of thinking and being that not only promotes the "good life" but nurtures the goodness in the life humans share. The way forward is by recognizing and validating the Other, the individual who is different from us, and at the same time, fully appreciating the commonalities and the wholeness of humankind, as if there is no Other.

IRIS M. YOB is Faculty Emerita and Contributing Faculty Member in the Richard W. Riley College of Education and Leadership at Walden University, Minnesota.

Notes

1. UNESCO, *Rethinking Education: Towards a Global Common Good?* (Paris: UNESCO, 2015), http://unesdoc.unesco.org/images/0023/002325/232555e.pdf.

2. Here, I am borrowing a phrase that William James used to describe the sensory stimuli we must learn to process, one that seems just as apt when describing the social stimuli we must learn to process. William James, *Principles of Psychology* (1890; Cambridge, MA: Harvard University Press, 1983), 462.

3. See, for instance, some of the work of one of the most creative music educators, June Boyce Tillman, who sets up choirs for dementia patients and people who self-identify with the statement "I can't sing" and stages musical productions that bring in every age, religious group, and ability level. See June Boyce Tillman, "The Dignity of Difference" in *Stories of the Great Turning*, ed. Peter Reason and Melanie Newman (Bristol: Vala, 2013), 169–177; June Boyce Tillman, "Music and Well-Being—Music as Integrative Experience," *Journal of Urban Culture Research Art Access and Advocacy—Promoting Creativity and Innovation for the Development of Participatory and Happy Communities* 7 (2013): 48–71.

4. See William Perrine, "*Bauchman vs West High School* Revisited," *Philosophy of Music Education Review* 25, no. 2 (Fall 2017): 200–204.

5. Rafael Perez-Torres, "Nomads and Migrants: Negotiating a Multicultural Postmodernism," in *Cultural Critique* (Winter 1993–1994), 161, https://www.peacepalacelibrary.nl/ebooks/files/Nomads-and-Migrants-Negotiating-Postmodernism-Perez-Torres.pdf.

6. Gilles Deleuze and Felix Guattari, *A Thousand Plateaus: Capitalism and Schizophrenia*, trans. Brian Massumi (Minneapolis: University of Minnesota Press, 1987), celebrate these terms, which are meant to describe not a pathological condition but rather the act of putting oneself outside the "normal" to allow a creative and more just engagement with the world and others. I am somewhat hesitant to use the term *schizophrenic* even as a quote because applying *schizophrenia* to an individual who is not mentally ill but is culturally nonconforming perpetuates a demeaning stereotype ("That's crazy!") and does not promote creativity, given that the term "schizophrenic" is still a pejorative in the general population.

7. For introducing me to this expression, I am grateful to Jan Hively, who has been an activist for good causes all her life and is one of the wise women I am better for knowing.

8. Comparative statements from religious groups can be found at the following websites: "'The Golden Rule' a.k.a. Ethics of Reciprocity, Part I," Religious Tolerance, accessed January 17, 2017, http://www.religioustolerance.org/reciproc2.htm; and "'The Golden Rule' a.k.a. Ethics of Reciprocity, Part II," Religious Tolerance, accessed January 17, 2017, http://www.religioustolerance.org/reciproc3.htm.

9. See, for instance, "Mahatma Gandhi," Goodreads, accessed July 7, 2019, http://www.goodreads.com/quotes/361107-yes-i-am-i-am-also-a-muslim-a-christian.

10. Madeleine Albright (@madeleine), Twitter, January 25, 2017, 1:18 p.m.

11. Shylock, who was different from other merchants in Venice because he was a Jew, claims a common humanity with his Christian counterparts: "Doesn't a Jew have eyes? Doesn't a Jew have hands, bodily organs, a human shape, five senses, feelings, and passions? Doesn't a Jew eat the same food, get hurt with the same weapons, get sick with the same diseases, get healed by the same medicine, and warm up in summer and cool off in winter

just like a Christian? If you prick us with a pin, don't we bleed? If you tickle us, don't we laugh? If you poison us, don't we die?"

He also reminds us that this commonness is for good or ill: "And if you treat us badly, won't we try to get revenge? If we're like you in everything else, we'll resemble you in that respect." William Shakespeare, *Merchant of Venice*, 3.1.52–58. So, while we can joyfully claim our oneness with the human family, like all families, there are dark spots and shady implications to be aware of as well.

12. John Dewey, *A Common Faith* (New Haven: Yale University Press, 1934), 84.

13. Raimond Gaita, *A Common Humanity: Thinking about Love and Truth and Justice* (London: Routledge, 1998), xx.

14. Ibid., 17–27.

15. Ibid., 27.

16. Ibid., 73–85.

17. Philip H. Phenix, *Education and the Common Good* (New York: Harper, 1961), 7.

18. UNESCO, *Rethinking Education*, 14.

19. UNESCO, *Learning: The Treasure Within* (Paris, UNESCO, 1996), 20, http://unesdoc .unesco.org/images/0010/001095/109590eo.pdf.

20. UNESCO, *Rethinking Education*, 19–33.

21. Ibid., 32.

22. Ibid., 33.

23. In this collection, please see Deanne Bogdan, "Dissociation/Reintegration of Literary/ Musical Sensibility"; Emily Good-Perkins, "Rethinking Vocal Education as a Means to Encourage Positive Identity Development in Adolescents"; Emily Howe, André de Quadros, Andrew Clark, and Kinh T. Vu, "The Tuning of the Music Educator: A Pedagogy of the 'Common Good' for the Twenty-First Century"; Luca Tiszai, "Friendship, Solidarity, and Mutuality Discovered in Music"; and Jacob Axel Berglin and Thomas Murphy O'Hara, "Working with Transgendered Students as a Humane Act: Hospitality and the Other."

24. Estelle R. Jorgensen, "This with That: A Dialectical Approach to Teaching for Musical Imagination," *Journal of Aesthetic Education* 40, no. 4 (Winter 2006): 1–20; Estelle R. Jorgensen, "A Dialectic View of Theory and Practice," *Journal of Research in Music Education* 49, no. 4 (2001): 343–359.

25. UNESCO, *Rethinking Education*, 29.

26. Ibid., 31.

27. Ibid., 78.

28. UNESCO, *Learning to Be: The World of Education Today and Tomorrow* (Paris: UNESCO, 1972), http://unesdoc.unesco.org/images/0000/000018/001801e.pdf (also known as the Faure report).

29. UNESCO, Delors report.

30. UNESCO, *Rethinking Education*, 80.

2

ON THE PERILS OF WAKENING OTHERS

Randall Everett Allsup

TEACHERS ARE OFTEN ASKED TO THINK ABOUT EDUCATION as a common good. It is, as Iris M. Yob puts it in the introduction to this collection, the means, sometimes "radical" means, with which the common good is attempted.[1] A humane education, more specifically, functions as an interconnected endeavor that fosters mutuality among and across cultures, languages, and traditions. The common good in education is "inherent in the relationship that exists among members of a society tied together in a collective endeavor."[2] This collective endeavor, conjoined by means and ends, is what Yob gestures toward when she describes the relationship between a humane education and the common good as "codependent."[3] In solidarity, our lives are mutually productive, producing and sharing knowledge, understood in the UNESCO report *Rethinking Education: Towards a Global Common Good?* as "the way in which individuals and societies apply meaning to experience. [Knowledge] can therefore be seen broadly as the information, understanding, skills, values and attitudes acquired through learning. As such, knowledge is linked inextricably to the cultural, social, environmental and institutional context in which it is created and reproduced."[4] Indeed, we hold out hope that the individual's pursuit of knowledge cannot be understood apart from the "Other," which is a way of knowing that sees humanity, as Yob contends, both "up close" and through a "wide-angle view," tangled up in all its vagaries such that distinctions are lost and magnified all at once. Yob claims that self-knowing has something to do with both difference and togetherness, even oneness, and this makes sense to me.[5]

As we search for ways to understand the place and purpose of education in a global context, we might pay special attention to the UNESCO proposition that "the common good can only be defined with regard to the diversity of contexts and conceptions of well-being and common life."[6] This normative claim calls to mind the tension between the identity that one has locally secured and one's potential to change as we live with others. Worldliness, arguably, becomes a necessary achievement, a disposition "to recognize and nurture [a] diversity of contexts, worldviews and knowledge systems."[7] I am reminded of Michel de Montaigne, an early globalist. "Mixing with the world," he writes, "has a marvelously clarifying effect on a man's judgment." He continues, "We are all confined and pent up within ourselves, and our sight has contracted to the length of our own noses. When someone asked Socrates of what country he was, he did not reply 'of Athens,' but 'of the world.' His was a fuller and wider imagination; he embraced the whole world as a city, and extended his acquaintance, his society, and his affections to all mankind; unlike us, who look only under our own feet."[8] I like this cosmopolitan sentiment, one that embraces difference in the humanist pursuit of a better self and a better world. As it relates to the UNESCO report that forms the starting point of this collection, the sentiment is outcome, precondition, and method all at once. We must live with others and change with others, refusing the parochial and familiar all while pursuing a Montaigne-like "fuller and wider imagination." Few other options seem available, at least as presented in *Rethinking Education*. So I wonder about the inevitability of this idea. I wonder about the self-evidence of travel and the creative coexistence of "Other" and "no Other." This condition is new, I think. Neither Socrates nor Montaigne lived in a world of such incredible diversity and interconnectivity.

Neither did they live in a world in which invisible and unaccountable actors in, say, Frankfurt or New York push down growth and well-being in, say, Athens or Bordeaux. Being awake, stung by a gadfly, or being stung by the absence of well-paying jobs means exactly what, in terms of a common good? What "good" has education done if so much of the world is angered and getting angrier? Lately, with the resurgence of nationalist populism, I have begun to ask myself just who is wide awake and who is not. Who gets to render an education to another? On whose behalf do we awaken the sleepy and unaware? More prosaically, who benefits from difference (understood here as the world) and who does not? Where do we travel (the search for truth), and what or whom do we avoid? I contend that Trump voters in the

United States, Le Pen supporters in France, and now Bolsonaro followers in Brazil are wide awake to the proposition that values related to the "common good" are not doing them a whole lot of "good."

Is worldliness an uncontestable norm? Who exactly is "the world" good for? This essay is both a departure from and a response to UNESCO's *Rethinking Education: Towards a Global Common Good?*—a document in which the basic tenets of progressive education are advanced against the vicissitudes wrought by violent global change (educational principles, I might add, that are hard to argue against). Like Yob,[9] I appreciate the tentativeness with which the UNESCO authors approach the very notion of a common good, rendering the concept open with the title's startling question mark. *Rethinking Education*, following the Faure and Delors reports,[10] shifts in language and tone away from modernist platitudes about education's inevitable contribution to the universal good to dwell in new arenas of what Yob calls a kind of postmodern tension. Although newly cautious, *Rethinking Education* retains a certain hubris, as the following chapter will explore: a tension between the obligations of capitalism (a word that was not mentioned once in *Rethinking*) and the recognition that something has gone wrong with our new world order.[11]

It is not that I doubt the report's sincerity. But what did the authors—the report's senior experts group—suffer in the course of its creation? As the sine qua non face of a new intergovernmentalized world, were they haunted by the viciousness left in the wake of democracy's worldwide retreat or the very fact of globalism's untethered inevitability? The report's discourse comes from a world far from the everyday classroom, a panoramic pre-Brexit world where there is multilateral agreement about what is good for others, authored by invisible philanthropic committees that are purported to represent—who, exactly? Would I be better served, contra Montaigne and the stoics of old, were I to return to the length of my own nose and look at who is nearby and what is underfoot? Such misgivings place me in unlikely solidarity with Trump supporters. Is this collective mistrust what the experts at UNESCO imagined when they offered up the word *common*?

Educational humanism is a method of teaching that focuses on the growth of the rational subject. Reasonableness is the goal of John Rawls's socially just liberalism, just as deliberative consensus is the working ideal of a pluralistic democracy.[12] A person can be taught to act intelligently in changing conditions—to self-identify as an individual who sees that her self-interest is tied to the creation of a common good. Maturity of judgment is achieved through agonistic encounters with difference, often midwifed by a teacher who (to mix my metaphors) is also a gadfly. Clarity results from what John Dewey calls scientific thinking. "The word *logical*," he writes, "is synonymous with wide-awake, thorough, and careful reflection—thought in its best sense."[13] Teaching for wide-awakeness leads liberal humanists to no small degree of righteous anger when reviewing the choices made by Trump, La Pen, and Bolsonaro voters. "Asleep, asleep," we say, "like bumpkins on a hayride!"

I have not met many people who sleepwalk through their lives, and rational lives free of self-deception are hard to locate. But there is something more insidious at stake, I believe. The liberal humanist educator may be selective in how he understands and applies multiple ways of knowing, a norm that is at the heart of *Rethinking Education*. We may assume a stance that accepts diversity, except when it does not align with a particular set of values. Thus—in our own form of sleepwalking—we avoid encountering difference with those who are too differently different or who think too differently.

With most of my family having voted for Trump, my life intersects closely with the French writer Édouard Louis, who grew up poor among France's abandoned working class. Gay, bullied, and self-hating, Louis provides a cautious defense—no, a cautious understanding—in his postmodern biography of what it means to be white, unemployed, and poor: those people, in other words, for whom we hold universal scorn; those people on whom we place blame when we talk about Trump, Le Pen, and Bolsonaro; those people we seek to awaken. Speaking with derision about his mother and the ways she "thinks," Eddy (the autobiography's main character) writes, "It took me a long time to understand that [my mother] wasn't being incoherent or contradictory, but rather that it was I myself, arrogant class renegade that I was, who tried to force her discourse into a foreign kind of coherence, one more compatible with my values—values I'd adopted in order to construct a self in opposition to my parents, in opposition to my family—that incoherence appears to exist only when you fail to reconstruct the logic that lies behind any given discourse or practice."[14]

Rationality projects a posture of somnolence on those who reach conclusions that *we* know are wrong or faulty. Clarity of vision is promised if I, as your humanist music teacher, can just keep bothering you about what you believe. Rather than grappling with the idea that all thinking is modal, local, and intersectional—that discourse comes into existence in ways that are relational and thus contingent—we choose, when confronted by an epistemological field that does not fit nicely with our own, not to engage in thoughts wherein the possibility holds that "differently different" stories can attach, transmogrify, or even momentarily align. This is what Virginia Woolf asks at the beginning of *A Room of One's Own* when she insists that the reader's story must commingle with her own: "Lies will flow from my lips, but there may perhaps be some truth mixed up with them; it is for you to seek out this truth and to decide whether any part of it is worth keeping."[15]

New agonistic philosophers such as Chantal Mouffe and Nadia Urbinati both claim that once the politics of liberation are characterized as a quest for "truth," our attentiveness to difference is lost.[16] When the "awakened" act as if only one political group is right, those citizens who deviate from a so-called self-interested political view are necessarily placed with those with whom Hilary Clinton derisively labeled a "basket of deplorables." From a teacher's standpoint, it is important to emphasize that if we continue to characterize education as a search for truth, its forms of inquiry must be diverse (the humane education) and its findings must be open (the common good). We get into trouble when aims and means are characterized as worldly, I think. What exactly does "worldly" mean? We have often heard that the local is global and the global is local, but what kind of truth is that? Is the virtual experience worldly or internal? Is Facebook global or local? And can we please stop using the word *glocal*?

It is also common to conflate the concept of education with clear thinking, as Wayne Bowman and Anna Lucia Fraga do in their philosophy of music education: the "business of making, refining, and clarifying meanings."[17] The moment when clarity and truth intersect is surely consummatory, to borrow from Dewey, but as an educational end, it is also ideologically constructed (*ideology* defined here as false obviousness). Clarity and truth are different manifestations of searching, and my search is different from yours. Indeed, I might argue that clarity of vision is a perilous starting point for an educator, as one might be tempted to awaken others on their own behalf—to teach *my* truth to you or to assume a course of travel *by* me *for* you. Channeling Maxine Greene, I see wide-awakeness as (yes) an agonistic encounter, but one that leaves you awake to questions—not only answers—to more searching, not less. Wide-awakeness is the awareness of polyphony, rarely a space of cognitive convergence. Are we awake when we all agree?

I cringe when I hear people say that Hilary Clinton voters must engage in dialogue with Trump voters. There is an assumption that Trump voters will come around to our point of view if we just keep talking. I would rather we make art together. If art privileges interpretative divergence (reading versus knowing; searching versus travel), I would rather compose a song or share a story. In such a setting, I guarantee that the contested notion of "nation" or "family" would arise, as would words like protection, safety, fear, and need. I would like to know how Trump makes art, a thought experiment that I do not offer facetiously. How would we hear the same song? A Toby Keith anthem? An early work by Taylor Swift? What kind of reading would ensue? Question: In our rush to include popular music in the American public school music curricula, why is contemporary country music not included? Answer: Because it falls outside a liberal humanist epistemological field. It might produce, in other words, "wrong" insights about nation, family, protection, safety, fear, and need.

Nonetheless, I contend that it is in the classroom, not the world, that we might discover that we share some of the same fears and frustrations, even though the possibility looms there might be very little shared ground at all. Missing in the UNESCO report is the word *art*. The Senior Experts Group and their external experts long for a commonality that includes a vision of diversity and contingency that might best be experienced through art. In a space of interpretation and critique, our contradictions could coexist—my lies, your truths, and vice versa. A critique of capitalism might ensue. We might create something critical together and enjoy nearness more than revelation, as Eleni Lapidaki suggests at the end of this book.[18] It is a better posture to allow for the simultaneity of difference—prolonged and patient—than to persuade one side that the other is wrong, I think. Discussions, insights, and opinions are not permanent epistemological states. This insight gives me hope. Like Panos Kanellopoulos, I have found that composing and improvising are activities of becoming more than of clarifying—of liminality and emerging criticality.[19]

In this spirit, I would like to share my experiences teaching in China, where I believe some kind of experiment in a global "humane" music education took place. I offer my description as an antidote to TED Talk–style "big thinking," making a humble case for intimacy and proximity as emergent educational values. For three summers, I mixed American and Chinese students together to invent small one-act operas. Hosted by Xiamen University in Fujian Province, we worked for three weeks, practically all day, every day, to compose and perform original music. In thinking of these experiences, I recall most profoundly the physical intimacy of our time together. Classes took place in our poorly air-conditioned dance studio, and creative assignments were worked out collaboratively in practice rooms or outdoors in a state of near 100 percent humidity. Feelings of exhaustion and constant stimulation were omnipresent.

Students were divided into four groups, and each group composed its own work; all the works were performed on our last day together. Each opera was made up of about five songs that came out of class assignments. I asked students to remix two folk songs from different traditions, for example, or to create a musical prelude using environmental, digital, and acoustic sounds. We took inspiration from Meredith Monk's *Atlas* and created duets without words; we attended local Chinese opera and deconstructed archetypes and tropes from East to West. The classroom setting was multilingual, with little translation. The American students studied basic Mandarin in the late afternoon, and all students were encouraged to learn a new instrument or vocal style.

In an indirect way, our work became political and possibly critical. Three summers ago, the Supreme Court decision on gay marriage created many informal discussions in our classes about LGBT rights; two summers ago, the Orlando shooting was traumatic; last summer, the American students were processing issues of immigration and what it mean to be a refugee. Many Chinese students were agnostic about the proclaimed obviousness of democracy and confused by Trump's election. Operatic themes, necessarily, emerged from these informal cross-cultural conversations. One summer, two operas dealt openly with same-sex attraction. Another addressed the right of the individual to choose who to love, even when it inspires parental objections. Challenged to think about the role of nature in art, the creators of one opera dealt with cell phone addiction; another group told the story of survival after someone young had died.

Many operas were about the pleasures of friendship, and that's interesting to contemplate. Can friendship be political? Is love—or admiration or infatuation—critical? I do not know the answer to the latter question, but a case can be made for fellowship as a political act, where there is physical contact with difference—physical togetherness, involving all the senses. This notion of proximity included the requisites of eating together, sweating together, and composing in tiny practice rooms amid the pungent smells of bodily odors and takeout noodles. The sounds: a mix of Mandarin and

English everywhere, Chinese music blending with Western art, pop, and jazz. How *is* difference encountered? This is the great question of our time. How is difference experienced and rendered meaningful? This question is especially timely as communities around the world continue to self-select and as we sort ourselves into enclaves that reinforce the familiar and like-minded. Safe and sorted out, we are taking the *strange* out of living.

I am wondering about the untapped intersection of creativity and physical proximity and whether traditional explorations of diversity allow for too much distance between object and examination. Traditional studies of diversity often start with an *anti-* position, in which terms and conditions that define, for example, anticolonialism predate a live encounter, the same way that musical norms and standards of practice predetermine how we perform Mozart. I worry that criticality can be learned in ways that produce rote responses to the very particularities of life and the vagaries of (sub)cultures or that teachers place well-intentioned boundaries around the practice of becoming. I worry that we do not meet difference where it hurts us, or shocks us, or exhausts us, where it can result in some aspect of beauty, pleasure, or heartbreak. My point is rather simple. Proximity—physical proximity with a living other—produces something electric, something uncontainable. Proximity in the service of a shared creative endeavor does something even more (or *can* do something even more): it produces fellowship, friendship, admiration, even love, which in turn triggers curiosity and wonder—those kinds of openings that are uncontainable and unfinished.

Teaching for proximity meant that I could not use terms like *global humanism* to describe my teaching goals, even as a strong sense of mutuality occurred in spite of, or because of, vast differences in culture, ideology, and location. I had to refuse a totalizing discourse. I had to suspend even cherished educational beliefs in favor of relational and emerging norms. For example, I used to think that it was my job to bring democracy to China, though now I prefer to teach there in ways that are nonhierarchical and inclusive. This turn is a subtle but important difference. Classroom change (societal change, personal change) takes place, but its effects are fractal or prismatic. I keep thinking about the surprising number of student-written operas that have dealt directly and indirectly with gay and lesbian relationships. Why was this topic—at this time and at this place—so important to these students? I have come to appreciate that criticality is not an antecedent proposition but must always remain precarious in both its emergence and submergence.

One summer, for example, two Chinese men came out to me at the course's conclusion. Communicating through a messaging app, they tell me their lives are now better, though not necessarily happier. One has found a lover. The other has decided that he will have a wife and child, but unbeknownst to his future wife, he will keep a steady boyfriend. Here is new knowledge, new truth, provoked by a shared classroom experience—one in which I bear responsibility. Confronted by the "wrong" kind of difference, I must will myself to suspend my beliefs about human flourishing as an explicit practice of openness. Still, I hope this young man's conception of family is not an ending. I hope that this new conception of family is his beginning. Even as I attach myself to his confusion (to a small part of his journey), I can decline to make it *my* beginning. Understanding that he is imagining a future life and thus not hurting anyone in the immediate, I refuse to force him to travel along the "right" epistemological field. Like the Trump voters in my family, I can wait. Just as importantly, I can examine myself.

In the end, *Rethinking Education* is difficult to argue against on principle. The report is alarmed, like all the authors in this book, by climate change, the unfair and inequitable treatment of migrants and minorities, and rapidly growing resource and income inequality. The UNESCO authors remain committed to a concept of public schooling and teacher professionalism, and they rehearse well-trodden bromides to the power of *Education* with a capital *E*. But the narrative they offer seems unequipped to deal with the notion that an education as self-formation must contain within it all the prerogatives of diversity and difference. Throughout the document, they conflate "identity-based political mobilization" with cultural chauvinism and violence, not understanding that strategic and embodied essentialism is a space within the common where a dominant epistemology can be refused. Those who form identity-based affiliations know that knowledge can be co-opted, marginalized, or delegitimized. An apology for Trump, Le Pen, and Bolsonaro voters? No. An awareness, perhaps, that life is interpreted and precarious.

Returning to Montaigne, if someone were to ask me what country I belong to, I would not reply New York or Athens or even the world. I would reply *the classroom*. I am with you, in this moment, an ineffable and irrevocable present. I have found that the greatest possibility for mutuality occurs through an open curriculum, one that is enacted, which means that it is local and immediate, but foremost actively creative. In such a setting, epistemological fields need not cohere or align. Criticality, its emergence and handling, its submergence and reappearance, will be delicate and require patience. Clarity will be foresworn in favor of searching—not travel, *searching.*

RANDALL EVERETT ALLSUP is Associate Professor of Music and Music Education at Teachers College Columbia University, New York. He is author of *Remixing the Classroom: Toward an Open Philosophy of Music Education.*

Notes

1. See Iris M. Yob, "Introduction: Education for the Common Good in a Diverse World," in this collection.
2. UNESCO, *Rethinking Education: Towards a Global Common Good?* (Paris: United Nations, 2015), 78.
3. Yob, "Introduction."
4. UNESCO, *Rethinking Education*, 16.
5. Iris M. Yob, "There Is No Other," in this collection.
6. UNESCO, *Rethinking Education*, 78.
7. Ibid.
8. Michel de Montaigne, *Essays*, trans. John M. Cohen (London: Penguin Books, 1958), 63.
9. Yob, "Introduction."
10. UNESCO, *Learning to Be: The World of Education Today and Tomorrow* (Paris: UNESCO, 1972), http://unesdoc.unesco.org/images/0000/000018/001801e.pdf (also referred to as the Faure report); UNESCO, *Learning: The Treasure Within* (Paris, UNESCO, 1996), http://unesdoc.unesco.org/images/0010/001095/109590eo.pdf (also referred to as the Delors report).
11. Hanne Rinholm and Øivind Varkøy, "Music Education for the Common Good? Between Hubris and Resignation—A Call for Temperance," in this collection.
12. John Rawls, *A Theory of Justice* (Cambridge, MA: Harvard University Press, 1971); Jurgen Habermas, *The Inclusion of the Other: Studies in Political Theory* (Cambridge, MA: MIT Press, 2005).
13. John Dewey, "How We Think," in *The Middle Works of John Dewey, 1899–1924*, ed. Larry A. Hickman, vol. 6, *1910–1911* (Carbondale: Southern Illinois University Press, 2003), 224.
14. Edouard Louis, *The End of Eddy*, trans. Michael Lucen (New York: Farrar, Straus and Giroux, 2017), 58–59.
15. Virginia Woolf, *A Room of One's Own and Three Guineas* (New York: Houghton Mifflin Harcourt, 1927), 4.
16. See Chantal Mouffe, *Agonistics: Thinking the World Politically* (London: Verso, 2013); Nadia Urbinati, *Democracy Disfigured: Opinion, Truth, and the People* (Cambridge, MA: Harvard University Press, 2014).

17. Wayne Bowman and Ana Lucia Fraga, "What Should the Music Education Profession Expect of Philosophy?" in *The Oxford Handbook of Philosophy in Music Education*, ed. Wayne Bowman and Ana Lucia Fraga (Oxford: Oxford University Press, 2012), 17.

18. Eleni Lapidaki, "Toward the Discovery of Contemporary Trust and Intimacy in Higher Music Education," in this collection.

19. See Panagiotis A. Kanellopoulos, "Freedom and Responsibility: The Aesthetics of Free Musical Improvisation and Its Educational Implications—A View from Bakhtin," *Philosophy of Music Education Review* 19, no. 2 (2011): 113–135; and Panagiotis A. Kanellopoulos, "Problematizing Knowledge—Power Relationships: A Rancièrian Provocation for Music Education," *Philosophy of Music Education Review* 24, no. 1 (2016): 24–44.

3

MUSIC EDUCATION FOR THE COMMON GOOD? BETWEEN HUBRIS AND RESIGNATION

A Call for Temperance

Hanne Rinholm and Øivind Varkøy

Hubris or Resignation?

Music educators sometimes seem to perceive music, and art in general, as something that can wake us up and make us more conscious as well as create good formative conditions—build bridges between people, fight racism, and so on. In short, it is claimed, music and arts education can change individuals and societies for the better. Such a belief in education's transformative powers—in one way or the other—also serves as an underlying premise for this book collection and for the UNESCO report *Rethinking Education: Towards a Global Common Good?*, to which this collection is a response.[1] However, such a way of thinking, according to critical research, is sometimes characterized by a certain hubris. When studies claim to document the positive effects of music, the question of causality is of course crucial. How can we be certain that it really is the experience of music, and not other factors, that lead to the acclaimed positive effect?[2] Research indicating that art and culture, in general, generate positive effects has been criticized for methodological weaknesses and inadequacies and for ideological biases.[3] Further, studies that show the positive effects of art and music have been criticized for having an ideological agenda, where the positive effects of art and music have been overestimated and the negative dimensions underestimated.[4]

Historically, one of the most prominent critics of the idea that music and music education can make significant contributions to communities and societies is Theodor W. Adorno. In Germany, the *Jugendmusikbewegung* (German youth music movement) was a pedagogical reform movement that played a dominant role in German music education in the first half of the twentieth century. Its key educational concept, *Musische Erziehung* (artistic, aesthetic education), which was basically inspired by ancient Greek ideas about arts education and the importance of art for society, attempted to renew and transform German culture and society through the power of art and music. One of the ideals of *Musische Erziehung* was the *Musikant* (musical amateur), who enjoyed playing simple and easy music on favored instruments—the fiddle and the recorder—which were simple to master. Adorno's view of the term *Musikant* implies that it is more important that one makes music than *what* music one plays.[5] Situated within a holistic educational approach that placed great emphasis on music, the arts and physical education were believed to produce a creative and active citizen who was expected to fit into a new and better society. A simple life, natural lifestyle, active social life, and the energy of a national musical community under strong leadership were ingredients in this educational approach, which Hitler misused to support the nationalist ideology during the Third Reich.[6]

The protagonists of artistic, aesthetic education believed in singing and playing together as a means of overcoming social differences between people from different social backgrounds and classes. Adorno is critical of this kind of thinking.[7] He criticizes the *Jugendmusikbewegung* for its romantic and naïve view of music, including its strong belief in the positive social and societal impacts of music and musical activities. With reference to Marx, he argues that alienation is closely linked to economic conditions, which makes it impossible for the aesthetic "community will" alone to be able to overcome human alienation and lack of harmony.[8] In this context, he argues that the *Jugendmusikbewegung* seems to relate to a kind of ritual logic and points out its similarities to earlier religious and metaphysical beliefs concerning the effects of music proposed by Plato and the founders of the early Christian church, for instance. The *Jugendmusikbewegung*'s belief in the effects of music and music making through "aesthetic forces" merely represents a secularized version of this old school of thought, Adorno argues, where the religious ritualistic function of music has been transferred to a belief in the social effects of music and musical practice. Further, the risk identified by Adorno's very harsh critique of the period and culture, like that of the *Jugendmusikbewegung*, is that music can lead to an ideology that focuses on the "original" and "popular" in a manner that cultivates anti-intellectualism. Adorno, in fact, argues that the *Jugendmusikbewegung* has this in common with fascism.[9] We think that Adorno's critical discussion of hubris with respect to the transformative powers of music and music education is still relevant.

It is, however, vital that the critique of the overconfidence in music's transformative powers does not lead to resignation with respect to the significance of music and music education for society and the individual. Thus, in the following, we will seek to establish a position that is characterized by temperance: a sober and down-to-earth optimism in regards to what music and music education can bring about. Our position is expressed as a hope (more than a conviction) that music and music education may promote humanity for the benefit of humankind, society, and the individual. As in our earlier works, we will use the German term *Bildung*, which, in our opinion, is still of relevance and able to offer valuable insight in this context.[10]

The Tradition of *Bildung*

Bildung may be compared to the Delors report's concept of education as a "continuous process of forming whole human beings," later reformulated into the "four pillars of learning." *Bildung* arguably encompasses all four pillars—"learning to know," "learning to do," "learning to live together," and "learning to be"—since the development of the whole person is a pivotal idea in the concept of *Bildung*.[11] Being *gebildet*, in the common understanding of the term, means that a person is well educated and able to think critically; behave politely, wisely, and responsively; and treat others with respect (among other things).[12] *Bildung*, therefore, is precisely a concept of "humane" education that includes the idea of nurturing human potential. The ultimate goal of *Bildung*, its outcome, is both the individual and the common good.[13] However, we cannot bring forth *Bildung* by force. We can only prepare for it and hope for it to happen. *Bildung* is related to personal development, through both knowing and understanding one's own cultural, philosophical, and scientific heritage and through processes of meeting the unknown.

A broad current of opinion in the *Bildung* tradition sees *Bildung* as a means of cultivating humanity, democracy, tolerance, and world citizenship.[14] In this current, we find the Irish writer and philosopher Iris Murdoch and the American philosopher Martha Nussbaum. Although their works primarily concern the relationship between literature and human formation, their thinking is relevant to our reflection on music and *Bildung* in relation to humanity.

Moral Transformation

Murdoch's thinking on formation through literature is not about how many works from the classical literary canon a person knows, but rather about the role of literature in the profound *Bildung* of the human being. Murdoch's writings deal with the moral transformation of the individual through literature, which implicates a development toward realism and unselfishness. Since literature and art can show us different ways of living in the world, reading literature may contribute to an individual's moral development, which involves developing an awareness of these different life designs. Thereby, the individual has the possibility of becoming less egocentric. The term *unselfing* is central in this context.[15] Unselfing is a moral state of mind characterized by unselfishness and sensibility to other people and their views and needs.[16] It is a condition of presence and engagement in human relations. Reading experiences may contribute to unselfing if the text has literary qualities that evoke imagination.[17] Such a way of seeing moral development in relation to artistic expression—literature, in this context, and more specifically, fiction—represents a reversal of the distinction between aesthetics and ethics established by Immanuel Kant, among others, at the end of the eighteenth century.[18]

Literature and Ethics

Nussbaum also challenges the formalist and "pure" aesthetically oriented view of literature that emerged in the wake of Kant. She does so through her interlinking of art and morals and her politicized view of literature. Nussbaum argues for the significance of literature in society by maintaining that it contributes to the development of ethical reason and that it is vital to the public dialogue.[19] Literature conveys insight into the human condition and creates acknowledgement of important aspects of life. Literary imaginativeness helps us to understand other people's lives and challenges our ability to empathize with others.[20] Nussbaum highlights the importance of our emotions for *Bildung* processes. According to her, educating people in world citizenship requires more than the transfer of factual knowledge and the cultivation of rational thinking. It demands love and the development of what she calls "narrative imagination."[21] This narrative imagination, which may be developed through the intense pursuit of art and literature and which furthers the individual's ability to see the world from the perspective of others and stimulates critical reflection, represents the first step toward a democratic comportment.[22] An important question is then, of course, whether all literature will function in this way and whether all forms of reception of literature will bring about such outcomes. This question easily leads to the well-known canon discussion and the assumption that some literary works have a greater potential for creating insight and *Bildung* than others. Nussbaum does not reject the importance of canonized works but rather argues that noncanonized literature, for example political and working class literature, or literature written by women and authors from non-Western cultures, should also have a place.

Nussbaum suggests that factors that concern literature may, to a certain degree, also concern other art forms: "Music, dance, painting and sculpture, architecture—all have a role in shaping our understanding of the people around us."[23]

Not Literature but Music

What is it, then, that music offers, seen in relation to Murdoch and Nussbaum's views of literature's inherent possibilities? The philosophy of music education, from a historical perspective, is rich in ideas and arguments that concern the positive effects of music on the individual and society. We find this in the thinking of Plato, the church fathers, Friedrich Schiller, the German youth music movement, and the American music educator Bennett Reimer, among others.[24] As an expressionist, Reimer maintains that the structure of the emotions is reflected in music. Aesthetic experience, then, contributes to the clearing, organizing, deepening, concentrating, and refining of the individual's consciousness regarding its own and others' emotional life.[25] Reimer's thinking points to a hope, namely the hope that musical experiences may further our ability for awareness and empathy, abilities that can certainly contribute to participation in democratic dialogue and development toward world citizenship.[26] Is this hope connected to musical experiences thus a hope that can be linked to all music, regardless of genre and form of expression?

Quality

Undoubtedly, Murdoch and Nussbaum care about artistic quality. Here we move into a conceptual landscape that is marked by strong ideological tensions. The moment someone says or writes the words *artistic quality*, he or she is promptly labeled as a somewhat reactionary elitist, who insists on classical music's superiority in all areas, especially in relation to popular music.[27] It is necessary to make it clear that the question of quality is not connected with certain genres or certain forms of reception. Our argument definitively deals with the discussion of music's aesthetic as well as functional (or social) dimensions.[28] Aesthetic experiences will necessarily carry subjective and collective interests, values, and identities. In our view, it is precisely in this realm between music's aesthetic and social dimensions, where it is both one thing and the other, that *Bildung* processes happen.

Nevertheless, we want to maintain the necessity of discussing artistic or aesthetic quality in the context of music education, in relation to the aims of the specific educational activity. A key idea in both Murdoch and Nussbaum's thinking is that it is the quality of literature, with respect to what is appropriate, that matters. The evaluation of artistic quality, then, must be seen in relation to which processes of *Bildung* we want to achieve or in relation to the aim of the educational activity. This simply means being conscious of how different forms of music offer different experiences. Pointing out this banal fact, however, does not imply that we think that all music should be put into one common hierarchy of values. Nevertheless, it appears that music educators must be willing to enter into discussions concerning quality of both an aesthetic and ethical nature. This is about developing a nuanced and multiperspective way of thinking in music education in relation to the complex relationship between music and *Bildung*.[29]

If we are to orient ourselves to such a quality standard, the position we seek to establish must not be characterized by relativism. We do not believe that the type of music or the time and purpose of its use in music teaching is irrelevant. Neither are the attitudes and values conveyed in music education activities. All education is conducted in the spirit of certain values, whether we are aware of this or not. When we discuss the direction of education, as we do in this text, we will always and necessarily make value judgments.[30] The values with which we want to connect our position are down-to-earth and temperate, but at the same time optimistic. They are inspired by the Canadian moral philosopher Charles Taylor—who indeed also deals with both Murdoch and Nussbaum—and the Danish music educator Frede V. Nielsen.

What Makes Life Worth Living

Charles Taylor argues that not all values have equal status and distinguishes between what he calls strong and weak evaluations.[31] Strong evaluations concern matters that really make a difference in our lives. These are issues that are more important than "mere preferences," which may be described as weak evaluations. When we make strong evaluations, we express our values. Strong evaluations are related to the three axes of Taylor's moral framework: respect, what makes life worth living, and dignity.[32] Hence, acting morally means taking a stance on questions related to one or more of these issues. What makes life worth living is an existential question. For Taylor, moral conduct is less about doing the right thing and more about what makes it good to be a human being.[33]

There are actually strong links between Taylor's moral frameworks and the set of universal ethical principles that are proposed as the foundations for the humanistic approach to education presented in the UNESCO report, *Rethinking Education*. These humanistic values or ethical principles include "*respect for life and human dignity, equal rights and social justice, cultural and social diversity, and a sense of human solidarity and shared responsibility for our common future.*"[34] Only by building on such ethical foundations can education be transformative and contribute to a sustainable future for all, the report states.[35] The report thereby clearly expresses its ethical values as being about existential questions, about what makes life worth living for all, much like Taylor's framework. Taylor, for his part, arguably recommends sustainable moral values that not only serve the immediate needs of the individual or commercial interests but also promote common humanistic goods that are of value in the long term for both the individual and society.

However, Taylor mainly seems to be addressing the moral, rational, and autonomous human being. The aspects of our existence for which we do not have words and that we cannot control, and that are precisely the domain of art, as we argue, fall behind in his analysis of the modern self.[36] Here, there are shortcomings in Taylor's thinking. His concern is that the individual should take a stance on existential issues, but he is not able to make a point about what art has to do with these issues or what role art may play at all in the formation of the individual's identity.

Taylor himself seems to be aware of the shortcomings in his thinking when he compares his own position to that of Murdoch in the field of moral philosophy.[37] He describes how they have both moved among three positions. He himself has moved from focusing on what we ought to do, or doing the "right" thing, to being concerned with how it is good to live, or "the good life." He says, however, that Murdoch has gone even further than he has, since in her writings, she has transcended both of these positions by giving attention to what it is good to love. The first of these positions, where the "right" has priority over the "good," Taylor describes as "the narrow corral of morality." In the second position, where he places his own thinking, he has delivered himself from the narrow corral and moved on to "the wider pasture, to the broad fields of ethics." Beyond this field again are "the untracked forests of the unconditional," and this is where Murdoch is located with her later work, according to Taylor.[38] It is here that it is possible to find what it is good to love, what we dream of and long for, what moves us and inspires us.[39] These untracked forests represent a moral philosophical position, where the emotions are significant as a source of moral development and *Bildung* and lead to insights about the human condition. The untracked forests thus represent a position where music education for humanity must relate to both aesthetics and ethics, to both the human and the musical spheres.

A Double Ethical and Aesthetic Framework

Nielsen claims that if we enter into the rich potential of music, no less than "a multi-spectral universe of meaning" unfolds.[40] Music does not merely have exterior layers of meaning, such as acoustic and structural layers, it also has inner ones, which are emotional and spiritual, or existential, layers. Music has depths that concern our existence as human beings. It has an artistic dimension, which belongs to the wordless area of our perception and recognition (much like Murdoch's wild, untracked forests). Nielsen's concept of music as a multispectral universe of meaning is arguably a framework that displays different aesthetic values, analogous to Taylor's framework of strong and weak evaluations, which establishes a set of ethical values.[41] Some of these values—in both Nielsen's and Taylor's frameworks—go more deeply than others and have a more profound significance to us in that they concern issues that are crucial to us because they are about life, our existence, and our life together with others. In order to establish a philosophical position that promotes a humanist music education, it is necessary to anchor this position in both aesthetic and ethical values and theoretical perspectives. We can imagine how Nielsen's aesthetic framework may be overlain on the ethical framework of Taylor and of UNESCO's *Rethinking Education* to form a double aesthetic and ethical framework that allows for both the heights and depths of music and the human potential and that makes provisions for both music and existence in its completeness.[42]

By using the word *anchor* above, we are aware that this concerns the core of this essay, namely the conflict between hubris and resignation, the two extremes between which we intend to balance our position. A key feature of the hubris we have described in this text is the fact that the belief in the power of music is not adequately anchored or reasoned. The belief in the effects of music and music education seems to be taken for granted, without the reasons for this belief being sought or established. Another feature of this hubris is a failing balance between ethical and aesthetic perspectives. It is easy to be unmindful of the ethical perspective. The presumed ethical effects of music making should, it is suggested, just appear by themselves. Further, those who are affected by hubris choose to merely relate to the surface dimensions of music or to "mere preferences," both ethically and aesthetically. In this case, music and music education lose their multispectral nature. They become one-sided and lack depth. Consequently, such a music education will not have the necessary quality standards required for a *Bildung* to humanity.

With Taylor and *Rethinking Education*, it may be argued that the strong values are connected to the big issues that really matter in our lives. By adding Nielsen's focus on the deeper layers and meaning in music, the emotional and the existential, as "stronger" aesthetic values than those represented by the outer layers of meaning, we can glimpse some of the premises for a further educational discussion on the question of quality that deals with both ethical and aesthetic values. Again, this discussion should not be limited to a question of musical genres.

Considering the need for a nuanced and precise discussion of the relationship between music and *Bildung*, it is hard to imagine that all music should always have the same potential for *Bildung* for all people in all contexts. It is necessary to consider music's aesthetic, functional, and social dimensions. It is also necessary to reflect on the emotional and existential dimensions in different musical expressions. Last but not least, the fact that popular music often comes with lyrics is also an important aspect for discussion. The contrast is undoubtedly big between Leonard Cohen's lyrics for "The Future," on the one hand, and Bill Haley and the Comets' "Shake, Rattle and Roll," on the other hand, for instance.

Central in Nielsen's theory about music as a multispectral universe of meaning is its emphasis on *offer*. When someone has a musical experience, this experience and the effect of it is not something that can be prescribed or planned in advance but rather happens beyond our control.[43]

Not Belief but Hope

Art (and music) has shown itself to be incapable of providing sufficient protection against barbarianism, and maybe it is true that culture is merely nail polish on the claws of the barbarians, as the abovementioned Cohen once said.[44] A well-known objection in discussions concerning the claim that art and literature contribute to our moral development involves the numerous examples of evil among "cultivated" people. The ultimate argument is made through stories about how "prominent Nazi leaders managed concentration camps with one hand and read Goethe with the other; shut one ear to the sound of the captive's cries in pain and despair and listened to Bach and Beethoven with the other."[45] Ultimately, it may be argued that *how* we read and listen is also crucial, not just *what* we read and listen to. It is only when we let art and music shake, disquiet, and challenge us in relation to conventional "truths" and values that they can unfold their transformative potential. Only then can they "cultivate capacities of judgement and sensitivity that can and should be expressed in the choices a citizen makes."[46]

Our position is, as stated above, in no way characterized by relativism. We would emphasize the importance of being able to discuss both artistic and educational quality in the context of musical *Bildung*, when considering the tension between aesthetic and social dimensions. There will be no simple answers to the question of whether and how music can contribute to *Bildung* in humanity. However, we know two things for sure. First, we know that not all music offers the same thing to all people, at all times, and under all circumstances. Second, we still know that music has an effect on us, emotionally and existentially. However, we can only hope for the ability to convert and implement what music offers us in terms of a reflective and meaningful life. This hope is our down-to-earth, realistic, and balanced alternative to hubris as well as to resignation. It is a hope that is rooted in what the Danish psychologist Sven Brinkmann calls "standpoints" or "existential motives that are worth sticking to because they have value in themselves": the good, the dignity, the promise, the self, the truth, the responsibility, the love, the forgiveness, the freedom and the death.[47] We are talking about a hope. Hope is not the same as naïve optimism. Nor is it the same as belief in the form of hubris similar to a religious faith, which is "the assurance of things hoped for, the conviction of things not seen."[48] Hope in our context is not the conviction that something will end well, but the consciousness of something being meaningful.

HANNE RINHOLM (previously Fossum) is Associate Professor of Music at Oslo Metropolitan University, Norway.

ØIVIND VARKØY is Professor of Music Education at the Norwegian Academy of Music and Visiting Professor of Music at Oslo Metropolitan University, Norway.

Notes

1. UNESCO, *Rethinking Education: Towards a Global Common Good?* (Paris: UNESCO, 2015), http://unesdoc.unesco.org/images/0023/002325/232555e.pdf.

2. Petter Dyndahl, Siw Graabræk Nielsen, and Sidsel Karlsen, "Musikkfagets effekter og verdier" [The effect of and values in music education], originally published as an op-ed, Musikkultur.no, June 6, 2013, http://hdl.handle.net/11250/2614269.

3. Research concerning, for instance, learning in other school subjects, emotional and social development, general creativity, cognitive skills, social intelligence, group solidarity, learning motivation, self-esteem, and so on—as well as critical discussions of this research—has been done both in Europe and in the United States. See, for example, Hans Günther Bastian, *Musik(erziehung) und ihre Wirkung. Eine Langzeitstudie an Berliner Grundschulen* [Music (education) and its effects. A study of general education in Berlin] (Mainz: Schott, 2000); Michael L. Mark, "Nonmusical Outcomes of Music Education," in *The New Handbook of Research on Music Teaching and Learning*, ed. Richard Colwell and Carol Richardson (Oxford: Oxford University Press, 2002), 1053–1065; Merryl Goldberg and Carol Scott-Kassner, "Teaching Other Subjects through Music," in *The New Handbook of Research on Music Teaching and Learning*, ed. Colwell and Richardson, 1053–1065; Ellen Winner, Thalia R. Goldstein, and Stéphan Vincent-Lacrin, *Arts for Art's Sake? The Impact of Arts Education* (Paris: OECD, 2013), doi:10.1787/9789264180789-en.

4. Frank van Puffelen, "Abuses of Conventional Impact Studies in the Arts," *Cultural Policy* 2, no. 2 (1996); Knut Vareide and Lars Ueland Kobro, "Skaper kultur attraktive steder?" [Does culture make attractive places?] TF-notat [memorandum] 1/2012 (Bø: Telemarksforsking, 2012), 1–30, https://intra.tmforsk.no/publikasjoner/filer/1989.pdf.

5. Theodor W. Adorno, *Dissonanzen. Musik in der verwalteten Welt* [Dissonances: music in the administered world] (1956; Göttingen: Vandenboeck und Ruprecht, 2003), 69.

6. For a more comprehensive presentation and discussion of *Musische Erziehung*, see Alexandra Kertz-Welzel, "The Pied Piper of Hamelin: Adorno on Music Education," *Research Studies in Music Education* 25, no. 1 (2005): 1–12, as well as "The Singing Muse:

Three Centuries of Music Education in Germany," *Journal of Historical Research in Music Education* 26, no. 1 (2004): 23.

7. Adorno, *Dissonanzen.*

8. Ibid., 63.

9. Ibid., 83–84.

10. Øivind Varkøy, "The Concept of Bildung," *Philosophy of Music Education Review* 18, no. 1 (Spring 2010): 85–96; Øivind Varkøy, "Bildung: Between Cultural Heritage and the Unknown, Instrumentalism and Existence," in *The Routledge International Handbook of the Arts and Education*, ed. Mike Flemming, Liora Bresler, and John O'Toole (London: Routledge, 2015), 19–29.

11. UNESCO, *Learning: The Treasure Within* (Paris: UNESCO, 1996), 19, 20–21, http://unesdoc.unesco.org/images/0010/001095/109590eo.pdf (also referred to as the Delors report).

12. For a brief historical survey of the German idea of *Bildung*, and especially musical *Bildung*, see Jürgen Vogt, "Musikalische Bildung—ein lexikalischer Versuch" [Musical education—A lexical approach], *Zeitschrift fur Kritische Musikpädagogik (ZfKM)*, 2012, http://www.zfkm.org/12-vogt.pdf.

13. See Iris M. Yob, "Introduction: Education for the Common Good in a Diverse World," in this collection, for a discussion of the relation between "humane education" and "common good," with the latter being defined as the outcome of the former. We follow this distinction, even though our contribution questions the self-evidence of the idea that the one will lead to the other as a matter of course.

14. See Alexandra Kertz-Welzel, Leonard Tan, Martin Berger, and David Lines, "A Humanistic Approach to Music Education: (Critical) International Perspectives" in this collection, concerning *Bildung* and related concepts in a global perspective.

15. Anna-Lova Olsson, *Strävan mot Unselfing: En pedagogisk studie av bildningstanken hos Iris Murdoch.* [Striving for unselfing: an educational study of the Bildung-idea in Iris Murdoch's works] (Örebro, Sweden: Örebro Studies in Education, 2015), 50.

16. Concerning discussion about training openness and sensitivity in music education, see Blakeley Menghini, "Rethinking Education: The Four Pillars of Education in the Suzuki Studio," in this collection.

17. Iris Murdoch, *Existentialists and Mystics: Writings on Philosophy and Literature* (1959; London: Penguin, 1997); Murdoch, *Metaphysics as a Guide to Morals* (London: Vintage, 2003). See also David Carr, "Four Perspectives on the Value of Literature for Character Education," *Journal of Aesthetic Education* 48, no. 4 (2014): 1–16. See Betty Anne Younker, "Inquiry-Based Learning: A Value for Music in Education with Aims to Cultivate a Humane Society," as well as Kevin Shorner-Johnson, "Doing the Common Good Work: Rebalancing Individual 'Preparation For' with Collectivist Being," both in this collection, for discussions of music education and nurturing of imagination.

18. With his *Critique of Judgment* in 1790, Kant established aesthetics as a particular field of knowledge in addition to moral philosophy, which was dealt with in his *Critique of Practical Reason* from 1788, and his theory of cognition, which was addressed in the *Critique of Pure Reason* from 1781. See Immanuel Kant, *Critique of Judgment*, trans. Werner Pluhar (Indianapolis: Hackett, 1987). See also Paul Guyer, *Kant and the Experience of Freedom: Essays on Aesthetics and Morality* (Cambridge: Cambridge University Press, 1996).

19. See Bernt Gustavsson, "Bildning och nytta" [Bildning and usefulness], in *Om nytte og unytte* [On usefulness and uselessness], ed. Øivind Varkøy (Oslo: Abstrakt, 2012), 93–111.

20. See Deanne Bogdan, "Dissociation/Reintegration of Literary/Musical Sensibility," in this collection.

21. Martha Nussbaum, "The Narrative Imagination," in *Cultivating Humanity: A Classical Defense of Reform in Liberal Education* (1998; Cambridge, MA: Harvard University Press, 2003), 85–112.

22. See other essays in this collection that in different ways and contexts focus on others and the Other. See also Martha Nussbaum, "Non-relative Virtues: An Aristotelian Approach," in *Ethical Theory: Character and Virtue, Midwest Studies in Philosophy*, vol. 13, ed. Peter. A. French, Theodore. E. Uhling Jr., and Howard. K. Wettstein (Notre Dame, IN: University of Notre Dame Press, 1998), 32–53; and Martha Nussbaum, *Cultivating Humanity*.

23. Nussbaum, *Cultivating Humanity*, 86.

24. Bennett Reimer, *A Philosophy of Music Education* (New Jersey: Prentice-Hall, 1970); see also Varkøy, *Hvorfor musikk? En musikkpedagogisk idéhistorie* [Why music? A history of ideas on music education] (Oslo: Gyldendal Akademisk, 2015).

25. Øivind Varkøy, *Musikk, strategi og lykke: bidrag til en musikkpedagogisk grunnlagstenkning* [Music, strategy and happiness: Contributions to the fundamentals of music education] (Oslo: Cappelen akademisk, 2003), 32–33.

26. Peter Kemp, *Världsmedborgaren: Politisk och pedagogisk filosofi för det 21 århundradet* [World citizenship: Political and educational philosophy for the 21st century] (Göteborg: Daidalos, 2005).

27. See Emily Howe, André de Quadros, Andrew Clark, and Kinh T. Vu, "The Tuning of the Music Educator: A Pedagogy of the 'Common Good' for the Twenty-First Century," in this collection.

28. See Simon Frith, "Music and Identity," in *Questions of Cultural Identity*, ed. S. Hall and P. D. Gay (London: Sage, 1996), 108–127.

29. See Dag Østerberg and Rudolf Terland Bjørnerem, *Musikkfeltet. Innføring i musikksosiologi* [The field of music. Introduction to music sociology] (Oslo: Cappelen Damm Akademisk, 2017), 38.

30. See Gert Biesta, *Good Education in an Age of Measurement* (London: Paradigm, 2009), 12.

31. Charles Taylor, "What Is Human Agency?," in *Human Agency and Language* (Cambridge: Cambridge University Press, 1985), 15–44; Charles Taylor, *Sources of the Self: The Making of the Modern Identity* (Cambridge, MA: Harvard University Press, 1989), 3–52.

32. Taylor, *Sources of the Self*, 15.

33. Ibid., 3.

34. UNESCO, *Rethinking Education*, 38 (emphasis in the original).

35. Ibid.

36. Taylor, *Sources of the Self*.

37. Taylor, "Iris Murdoch and Moral Philosophy," in *Iris Murdoch and the Search for Human Goodness*, ed. Maria Antonaccio and William Schweiker (Chicago: University of Chicago Press, 1996), 3–28.

38. Ibid., 5.

39. Ibid., 15.

40. Frede V. Nielsen, *Almen musikdidaktik* [General music Didaktik], (København: Christian Ejlers', 1998), 136.

41. Taylor, *Sources of the Self*.

42. See Hanne Fossum, "From Relevance Rationality to Multi-Stratified Authenticity in Music Teacher Education: Ethical and Aesthetical Frameworks Revisited," *Philosophy of Music Education Review* 25, no. 1 (Spring 2017): 46–66; Hanne Fossum, "Musikkundervisning og verdighet" [Music education and dignity], *Musikkpedagogen* [The music educator] 4 (2015): 6–14.

43. See Otto Friedrich Bollnow, *Eksistensfilosofi og pedagogikk* [Existential philosophy and education] (Oslo: Fabritius, 1969).

44. Max Horkheimer and Theodor W. Adorno, *Dialectic of Enlightenment* (New York: Seabury, 1972).

45. Irene Engelstad, "Innledning" [Introduction], in Martha Nussbaum, *Litteraturens etikk: Følelser og forestillingsevne* [The ethics of literature: Emotions and imagination] (Oslo: Pax, 2016), 11 (our translation).

46. Nussbaum, "Narrative Imagination," 86.

47. Svend Brinkmann, *Ståsteder. 10 gamle ideer til en ny verden* [Standpoints: 10 old ideas to a new world] (Oslo: Forlaget, 2017), 39. Brinkmann's existential motives can be compared to similar motives found in UNESCO, *Rethinking Education*; Taylor, *Sources of the Self*; Charles Taylor, *The Ethics of Authenticity* (Cambridge, MA: Harvard University Press, 1991); Murdoch, *Existentialists and Mystics*; and Murdoch, *Metaphysics as a Guide to Morals*.

48. Hebrews 11:1 (English Standard Version Bible).

4

DOING THE COMMON GOOD WORK

Rebalancing Individual "Preparation for" with Collectivist Being

Kevin Shorner-Johnson

ONTEXTS OF VIOLENCE, MILITARISTIC POSTURING, AND UNSUSTAIN-ABLE CONSUMERISM make the presence of UNESCO's 2015 *Rethinking Education: Towards a Global Common Good?* an important contribution that seeks to interrupt deterministic global violence.[1] The report is the third in a series of UNESCO reports that imagine the reification of education as a global, humanistic good. While the report brings a more nuanced approach to assumptions about "progress," it continues to privilege a linear-progress view of time and leave problematic notions of individualistic future-oriented time unchallenged. In this chapter, I seek to analyze and critique the rhetoric of progress and destiny in the report and, more specifically, in the "four pillars of education." These pillars (learning to know, do, be, and live together) are a grounding device in a call for action and an example of problematic assumptions about time and agency. Because the UNESCO authors call for questioning how the four pillars can be strengthened and renewed, I end by imagining how music education might balance toward multitemporal social praxis.[2]

Progress and Destiny

I work at a college grounded in the heritage of Amish, Mennonite, and Brethren religious traditions. One narrative of Amish experience is that of resistance to an accelerated sense of time. From pacifist traditions, many Anabaptists conceive of progress and technological time as forms of violence.[3] If violence is broadly defined, the Faure,[4] Delors,[5] and *Rethinking Education* reports identify dehumanization, environmental destruction, limited pluralistic understanding, and unjust difference as violent evidence that educational change is necessary. At the center of this rhetoric, the UNESCO reports wrestle with the meaning of progress and destiny within the pursuit of greater good.

The 1972 Faure report mixes language of human conquerings, evolution, progress, possibility, destiny, and the greatness of man to speak of linear empowerment. The authors wrote, "Yet modern man has never ceased conquering new environmental conditions, as if his biological ability to adapt were growing. This is mere illusion. In reality, man is able to survive today in a polluted environment . . . because of knowledge handed down and enriched from generation to generation."[6] Authors sometimes used linear language to describe "backward countries" and uneducated peoples.[7] However, UNESCO political documents are made complex through the contributions of multiple voices. Iranian Minister Majid Rahnema added complexity to the linearity of the Faure report by advocating for language from Paulo Freire and Ivan Illich.[8] Both authors have much to say about how power is articulated within linear progress.

The 1996 Delors report came after sustained twentieth-century mechanization, efficiency, progress, and the collapse of power arrangements that sustained the Cold War. The report is marked by a more circumspect attitude about progress.[9] Delors authors questioned whether the good of "all-out economic growth" could be reconciled "with equity, respect for the human condition and respect for the natural assets . . . [that are handed on to] future generations."[10] Language about future generations introduces an ethical concept of care that envisions futures as constrained by present action, not as limitless sites of possibility.

The *Rethinking Education* report challenges privatized educational structures and encourages education to foster a transnational sense of "shared destiny."[11] When education's purpose is to maintain a privatized or nation-state level of resource consumption, the ethical impact of continual progress is never fully examined. The authors argue that utopian dreams are far from realized, and the pursuit of technological progress may have degraded pluralistic human connection and environmental care.[12]

Problems of Progress, Temporal Speed, and Relational Disruption

Notions of progress as continual improvement are broken by the persistence of dehumanized time, disconnection, and differential agency. As twentieth-century populaces moved toward industrialization, the nature of time was changed to increase uniformity, productivity, and efficiency. Krista Cowman and Louise A. Jackson suggested that "large-scale factories led to the apparent uniformity and discipline of 'clock' time, which was linear."[13] Time management became a means toward economic ends.

As worker time accumulated precise value within financial arrangements, speed and efficiency became more important. Barbara Adam and Chris Groves noted speed was an unquestionable good that provided evolutionary advantage.[14] As time accelerates in a digital age, feelings of empowerment may be reduced. Thomas Sutherland referred to teleological "network speed" as a violent, retreating "distant horizon" that reduces human agency and determinacy.[15]

Critical theorists and feminists have critiqued dominant conceptions of time as being devoid of complexity and a sense of caring ethics. Beliefs about educational efficiency transformed learning pathways into demarcated levels or grades, with each level having sets of objectives, expectations, and scripts. Catherine Compton-Lilly critiqued, "Essentially, failure in school is not merely about what students can and cannot do; it is about what skills and strategies they display or do not display at particular points in time."[16] Nel Noddings argued that fixations on principle and efficiency deprive education of relational and differentiated care. To make her point, Noddings contrasted a masculine ethic of principle with a feminine ethic of care. She imagined that "a different sort of world may be built on the natural caring familiar to women."[17]

Disconnection and Asynchronous Being

Studies of mother-child attachment and the "natural caring familiar to women" appear to indicate the power of responsive relationship, interactional synchrony, and the dangers of relational disruption. Within breast feeding and other rituals of interaction, mother and child work out foundational responsive relationships.[18] Responsive interactions build senses of security, healthy eating patterns, and habits of turn-taking, mutual engagement, responsiveness, and positive affect.[19]

However, a growing body of evidence points to the risks of mobile technology as a distractor and disruptor of responsive relationship. Rebecca Pollack Golen and Alison K. Ventura found that technological distractors interrupted 52 percent of mother-child time during bottle feeding.[20] Similarly, Jenny S. Radesky et al. found that forty out of fifty-five caregivers were distracted by devices at a fast-food restaurant. Qualitative observational data indicated that distracted interactions often began with slowed responsiveness to child behavior and escalated to scolding tones of voice, repeated instructions in a somewhat robotic manner, or physical responses such as kicking or pushing a child.[21]

The disruption of responsive relationship is highly problematic when viewed through the lens of empirical studies on empathetic imagination and moral development. In a review of research, Ian Ravenscroft notes the importance of imitative emotional modeling between caregiver and child as a foundation for empathetic experience and imagination.[22] Adam and Groves wrote that ethics are learned through relationship as children learn to nurture friendships and family relation.[23] Intersectional experiences of relationship, imitation, and imagination empower moral thinking by extending "our zone of action"; negotiating tensions between personal interest and common good.[24] Many voices in this book set up a contrast between intimate, hospitable, relevant, slowed, and relational time and quick, efficient, and powerful "network speed." [25]

Empty Futures and Lived Futures

As a means of examining how UNESCO's orientations toward time have ethical consequences, consider Adam and Groves's work on empty versus lived futures.[26] Graduation speakers and policy makers often describe futures as empty spaces of possibility awaiting colonization. This dominant view of time is constructed through forms of economic rationality, where the "sole purpose" of academic bodies is to "produce, perceive, and interpret the world."[27] The Faure report's 1972 language of destiny and progress is often structured by this language of possibility and human conquering.

While the landscape of empty futures is possibility, it may also be a site of competitive violence and a restriction of freedom. Individuals who march toward empty futures imagine they advance power and control over their own personal destiny. However, as each self colonizes the Other, the Other simultaneously constrains the self through similar patterns of production and consumption.[28] *Rethinking Education* references Amartya Sen to note that traditional notions of economic development often involve a loss of human freedom.[29] Sen's text notes that freedoms of agency, gender equity, health, and food security must be the means and goal of humane development.[30]

In contrast to the constrained freedom of empty futures, lived futures are co-constructed in present action through ethics of relational care.[31] Elizabeth Johnson advocated breaking linear ecological trauma for "modes of becoming with which we enjoin with nonhumans in a struggle for collective existence."[32] The *Rethinking Education* authors note that humane goals of enhancing "dignity, capacity, and welfare" within human and natural world relationships may be "the fundamental purpose of education in the twenty-first century."[33] To challenge patterns of production and consumption, we necessarily extend human[e] care of lived futures to nonhuman and human alike.

The Four Pillars

The Delors and the 2015 *Rethinking Education* reports stake out claims on the future through the anchoring device of the four pillars of education (learning to know, do, be, and live together). Each of the four pillars begins with the phrase *learning to*, which implies education is a form of work toward future capacity. Within *learning to do*, I acquire this thing called *competence*, which I later apply toward common good work. *Learning to be* has the strongest language regarding individual talent and "the attainment of common goals." According to the authors, talents lay "hidden like buried treasure" until they can be unlocked through "self-realization" education.[34] Individual work is done toward future ends.

Harbans S. Bhola identified that the pillars of education represent a firmly entrenched belief that education is preparation for a distant future. He stated, "Thus, the educational ideology of the [Delors] report reflects its overall political ideology and development theory: education as preparation for a future working life, not for social praxis in the present."[35] The *Rethinking Education* report continues to offer conflicting language about how education balances individual futures with the social present.[36] On one hand, authors discuss future-oriented transfer, enabling, and ultimate purposes: "Education is the deliberate process of acquiring knowledge and developing the competencies to apply that knowledge in relevant situations.

The development and use of knowledge are the ultimate purposes of education, guided by principles of the type of society to which we aspire."[37] The teacher is defined as "a guide who enables learners . . . to develop and advance . . . through the constantly expanding maze of knowledge."[38] A teacher as an enabler is qualitatively different from a teacher as an engager, an individual who works dialogically with students in the present.

On the other hand, aspects of *Rethinking Education* speak of participatory and shared action.[39] Language about democracy and participatory processes implies that human beings are educated through present doing. The authors describe "the participatory process" as a state in which "shared action is intrinsic, as well as instrumental, to the good itself, with benefits derived also in the course of shared action."[40]

In the same year that *Rethinking Education* was published, the United Nations Security Council resolution 2250 called for participatory youth engagement in shaping peace. A follow-up 2018 report to resolution 2250 challenged "waithood," claiming students should exercise critique and conflict resolution in the here and now.[41] Differences in rhetoric in the same year from the same general policy-making body (the UN) demonstrate that notions of time and agency are critical, complex, and contested.

Ethical Dimensions of Collective Multitemporality

Examinations of cultural and religious perspectives and scientific theories reveal a diversity of temporalities. Māori *whakawhanaungatanga*, South African *ubuntu*, and Confucian *ren* offer ways of being in time together that challenge dominant Western-colonized time.[42] Balinese overlapping calendars and cyclical Gamelan patterns are means of living the past into the present "just as the musician's grandmother lives on in him."[43] Likewise, an African framework of past-present time explores ancestor existence within present-moment thinking and being.[44] Hindu traditions identify overlapping temporalities as sites of spiritual union, transcendence, and generative action.[45] Recent scholarship in physics has opened understandings that space-time is far more complex than what has been theorized through Newtonian mechanics or experienced through human consciousness.[46]

While these examples identify pluralistic temporalities, Western educational space is often marked by individual goal-directed work. Estelle R. Jorgensen identified *curriculum as system* as the dominant educational model within the Western, industrialized twentieth century. Education in this sense is a "closed system" that supports a stage-like process of forward progression.[47] Educational orientations toward time matter because they frame the nature of work within classrooms. If students are preparing for individual futures, work is differentiated and focused on the accumulation of skill and knowledge. If teachers perceive collective futures to be constructed in the present, work is collaborative and applied to present-day problems.

Common good work necessarily requires a diversity of temporal orientations. UNESCO advances a linear view of time because policy making necessitates moving large groups toward attainable goals. However, this dominant view of time may privilege work over relationship, mind over embodied being, and human rationality over cyclical processes of the natural world.[48] Recognizing this "authenticity" gap, John Paul Lederach called for balancing linear peacemaking with nonlinear peacebuilding. Peacemaking is a linear process, driven by the empowered, toward defined notions of peace and greater good. On the other hand, peacebuilding is a messy, back-and-forth construction explained through metaphors of spider webs and artistic processes.[49] Recognizing the plurality of human existence, common good pursuits are only fully authentic when they embrace and balance diversities of temporal and social, individual ways of being.

Musical Praxis toward Common Good

Because the medium of sonic art has the capacity to move out of individual linear time and into liminal spaces of imagination, music education may be a means of reclaiming temporal sites of interactional synchrony, liminality, critique, and restoration. In this next section, I argue that when students engage in artistic praxis, they challenge and reinterpret the violence of colonized time. A humane artistic vision can address brokenness and bring about restorative action.

If the breakdown of responsive relationship leads toward a narrowing of ethical thinking and action, then explorations of synchrony and imitation are critical restorative acts. When music students tune instruments, match vocal color, or align rhythmic performance, they pursue collective journeys in synchrony.[50] Matching, imitating, and sharing states of being are the spaces of empathy or feeling into the Other.[51] Indeed, research appears to indicate that imitated participants are more likely to describe themselves as interdependent and altruistic.[52]

Communities that work with shared intentionality can alter the perceived flow of time, potentially entering liminal space. June Boyce-Tillman and Victor Turner relate liminal space as the experience of moving out of "everyday consciousness" and into another space/time dimension of imagination, paradoxical knowing, collective vulnerability, and statuslessness.[53] Within liminal space, participants renegotiate relationship, offer critique, cradle paradox, and feel into more humane ways of being.

Noting the importance of metaphors and models to encourage diverse imaginings, Jorgensen wrote, "imagination feeds on ambiguity, and we need to keep alive metaphoric thinking if we are to spark imaginative action."[54] Lederach encourages peace builders to "watch" the imaginative action of metaphors and embrace paradox to transform conflict into deeper forms of care.[55] Within metaphors of sound, musickers enact new ways of thinking and being, marrying critique with humane constructions of new possibilities.

This may be the essence of Émile Jaques-Dalcroze and Shinichi Suzuki's work in developing new temporalities for music education. Dalcroze's spirituality may have reached a liminal sense of ethicality by collapsing the past, present, and future.[56] Suzuki was informed by his Zen Buddhist tradition in seeking the transcendent "quality of a musician's soul" in tone.[57] The essence of expressive and humane awakening may be found in new embodiments of rhythmic weight and sonic resonance.[58]

To build a common good, a musical education must engage musickers in playing with realities. Walter Brueggeman saw the artist through Christian prophetic traditions as one who is "conjuring and proposing alternative futures."[59] Exploring sonic possibilities, we enter the deep time of liminal space, challenging linear chains of cause and effect, wandering imaginations to new positions, and examining what is and could be from every angle. This is the essence of a humane education for a common good.

Further, the arts allow individuals to play beyond human experiences of perceptual time. Rob Nixon notes that humans are often unable to sense the "slow violence" of human action and environmental harm across decades, if not centuries of time.[60] If humans act most ethically toward that which we see and feel, "what happens when we are unsighted, when what extends before us—in the space and time that we most deeply inhabit—remains invisible?"[61] The arts may be perfectly disposed to solve these perceptual challenges. Using one art form as exemplar, Nixon states, "imaginative writing can help make the unapparent appear . . . [offering] us a different kind of witnessing: of sights unseen."[62] Music, theater, fine art, dance, film, and literature have the potential to extend perceptual capacity, play with time, and generate humane questions from liminal space.

Implications and Conclusion

Rethinking Education attempts to address many existential and relational questions. However, it persists in privileging future-oriented individuality. A balance between future-oriented individuality and multitemporal collective being is necessary because it is the essence of a humane education. Multitemporal orientations are necessary because a common good may be as much a verb as a noun; students can only learn about common, humanistic goods by engaging in the present-moment work of common good. When students do multitemporal and multirelational work, our imaginative capacity as humane citizens enlarges toward the complexity of our challenges.

As I embrace the intent of the four pillars, I choose to remove the linear "learning to" phrase to emphasize that learning toward future capacity is only one of many ways of pursuing common goods. Drawing upon frameworks of peacebuilding, I ground preservice teacher field experiences in multitemporal mutuality, agency, and imagination.[63] We balance linear, objectives-informed instruction with humane notions of slowed mutuality and the "sacred space" of eye contact.[64] We empower students' musical voices and listening spaces, challenging artistic imaginations through metaphorical prompts ("play like nobility" or "move like a feather"). In knowing, doing, living, and being together, music education opens humane dimensions of imagination, sensation, and action. This multitemporal, paradoxical, and relational praxis is essential as a common good and as a pursuit of common goods. With a past heritage brought into the now, responsive listening and sounding in the present, and development and imagination toward futures, musicians hold and encounter complexities of past, present, and future at a magical nexus.

KEVIN SHORNER-JOHNSON is Associate Professor of Music Education at Elizabethtown College, Pennsylvania.

Notes

1. UNESCO, *Rethinking Education: Towards a Global Common Good?* (Paris: UNESCO, 2015), http://unesdoc.unesco.org/images/0023/002325/232555e.pdf.

2. Question posed in UNESCO, *Rethinking Education*, 83.

3. See Donald Kraybill, *The Riddle of Amish Culture* (Baltimore: Johns Hopkins University Press, 2001), 188–212.

4. UNESCO, *Learning to Be: The World of Education Today and Tomorrow* (Paris: UNESCO, 1972), http://unesdoc.unesco.org/images/0000/000018/001801e.pdf.

5. UNESCO, *Learning: The Treasure Within* (Paris, UNESCO, 1996), http://unesdoc.unesco.org/images/0010/001095/109590eo.pdf.

6. UNESCO, *Learning to Be*, 4.

7. Ibid., xxiii (my emphasis).

8. Maren Elfert, "UNESCO, the Faure Report, the Delors Report, and the Political Utopia of Lifelong Learning," *European Journal of Education* 50, no. 1 (2015): 90, doi:10.1111/ejed.12104.

9. Sobhi Tawil and Marie Cougoureux, "Revisiting 'Learning: The Treasure Within': Assessing the Influence of the 1996 Delors Report," *UNESCO Education Research and Foresight Occasional Papers* (2013), accessed February 19, 2016, http://unesdoc.unesco.org/images/0022/002200/220050e.pdf.

10. UNESCO, *Learning: The Treasure Within*, 13.

11. UNESCO, *Rethinking Education*, 55–77.

12. UNESCO, *Rethinking Education*, 9–12.

13. Krista Cowman and Louise A. Jackson, "Time," in *A Concise Companion to Feminist Theory*, ed. Mary Eagleton (Oxford: Blackwell, 2003), 38.

14. Barbara Adam and Chris Groves, *Future Matters: Action, Knowledge, Ethics* (Boston: Brill, 2007), 102.

15. Thomas Sutherland, "Getting Nowhere Fast: A Teleological Conception of Socio-Technical Acceleration," *Time and Society* 23, no. 1 (2014): 59.

16. Catherine Compton-Lilly, "Time in Education: Intertwined Dimensions and Theoretical Possibilities," *Time and Society* 25, no. 3 (2016): 583–584.

17. Nel Noddings, *Caring: A Relational Approach to Ethics and Moral Education* (Berkeley: University of California Press, 2013), 46.

18. Russell A. Isabella and Jay Belsky, "Interactional Synchrony and the Origins of Infant-Mother Attachment: A Replication Study," *Child Development* 62, no. 2 (1991): 373–384, doi:10.1111/j.1467-8624.1991.tb01538.x.

19. Cassandra Pasiak, "Mother-Child Synchrony: Implications for Young Children's Aggression and Social Competence," *Journal of Child and Family Studies* 24, no. 10 (2015): 3079–3092, doi:10.1007/s10826-015-0113-y.

20. Rebecca Pollack Golen and Alison K. Ventura, "What Are the Mothers Doing While Bottle-Feeding Their Infants? Exploring the Prevalence of Maternal Distraction during Bottle-Feeding Interactions," *Early Human Development* 91, no. 12 (2015): 787–791, doi:10.1016/j.earlhumdev.2015.09.006.

21. Jenny S. Radesky et al., "Patterns of Mobile Device Use by Caregivers and Children during Meals in Fast Food Restaurants," *Pediatrics* 133, no. 4 (2014): 843–849.

22. Ian Ravenscroft, "Fiction, Imagination, and Ethics," in *Emotions, Imagination, and Moral Reasoning*, ed. Robyn Langdon and Catriona Mackenzie (New York: Taylor and Francis, 2012), 80.

23. Adam and Groves, *Future Matters*, 151.

24. Ibid.

25. See for instance, Eleni Lapidaki, "Toward the Discovery of Contemporary Trust and Intimacy in Higher Music Education"; Jacob Axel Berglin and Thomas Murphy O'Hara, "Working with Transgender Students as a Humane Act: Hospitality in Research and Practice"; and Emily Howe, André de Quadros, Andrew Clark, Kinh T. Vu, "The Tuning of the Music Educator: A Pedagogy of the 'Common Good' for the Twenty-First Century," in this collection.

26. Adam and Groves, *Future Matters.*

27. Riyad A. Shahjahan, "Being 'Lazy' and Slowing Down: Toward Decolonizing Time, Our Body, and Pedagogy." *Educational Philosophy and Theory* 47, no. 5 (2015): 495, doi:10.1080 /00131857.2014.880645.

28. Martin Buber, *I and Thou* (New York: Simon and Schuster, 1970), 97.

29. UNESCO, *Rethinking Education,* 37.

30. Amartya Sen, *Development as Freedom* (New York: Random House, 1999).

31. Adam and Groves, *Future Matters.*

32. Elizabeth Johnson, "At the Limits of Species Being: Sensing the Anthropocene," *South Atlantic Quarterly* 116, no. 2 (April 2017): 287, doi:10.1215/00382876-3829401.

33. UNESCO, *Rethinking Education,* 38.

34. Ibid.

35. Harbans S. Bhola, "Adult Education Policy Projections in the Delors Report," *Prospects* 27, no. 2 (1997): 216, doi:10.1007/BF02737166.

36. UNESCO, *Rethinking Education,* 39.

37. Ibid., 79.

38. Ibid., 54.

39. Ibid., 78.

40. Ibid.

41. UN Security Council, Resolution 2250, Progress Study on Youth and Peace and Security (S/RES/2250), March 2, 2018, https://www.youth4peace.info/ProgressStudy.

42. Alexandra Kertz-Welzel, Leonard Tan, Martin Berger, and David Lines, "A Humanistic Approach to Music Education: (Critical) International Perspectives," in this collection.

43. Lisa Gold, *Music in Bali: Experiencing Music, Expressing Culture* (New York: Oxford University Press, 2005), 149.

44. John S. Mbiti, *African Religions and Philosophy* (New York: Praeger, 1969).

45. Harold Coward, "Time in Hinduism," *Journal of Hindu-Christian Studies* 12, no. 8 (1999): 26, doi:10.7825/2164-6279.1206.

46. Michael Silberstein, W. M. Stuckey, and Timothy McDevitt, *Beyond the Dynamical Universe: Unifying Block Universe Physics and Time as Experienced* (New York: Oxford University Press, 2018).

47. Estelle R. Jorgensen, "Philosophical Issues in Curriculum," in *The New Handbook of Research on Music Teaching and Learning,* ed. Richard Colwell and Carol Richardson (New York: Oxford University Press, 2002), 52.

48. Shahjahan, "Being 'Lazy' and Slowing Down," 495.

49. John Paul Lederach, *The Moral Imagination: The Art and Soul of Building Peace* (New York: Oxford University Press, 2005), 162.

50. Thomas A. Regelski, *A Brief Introduction to a Philosophy of Music and Music Education as Social Praxis* (New York: Routledge, 2016).

51. Ellen Dissanayake, *Art and Intimacy: How the Arts Began* (Seattle: University of Washington Press, 2000), 40.

52. Susan E. Cross, Erin E. Hardin, and Berna Gercek-Swing, "The What, How, Why, and Where of Self-Construal," *Personality and Social Psychology Review* 15, no. 2 (2011): 165, doi:10 .1177/1088868310373752.

53. June Boyce-Tillman, "The Transformative Qualities of a Liminal Space Created by Musicking," *Philosophy of Music Education Review* 17, no. 2 (2009): 189, doi:10.2979/PME .2009.17.2.184; Victor W. Turner, *The Ritual Process* (New York: Aldine, 1969), 97.

54. Estelle R. Jorgensen, *Pictures of Music Education* (Bloomington: Indiana University Press, 2011), 7.

55. Lederach, *Moral Imagination*, 72.

56. John Habron and Liesl van der Merwe, "A Conceptual Study of Spirituality in Selected Writings of Émile Jaques-Dalcroze," *International Journal of Music Education* 35, no. 2 (2015): 178–179, doi:10.1177/0255761415620532.

57. Karin S. Hendricks, "The Philosophy of Shinichi Suzuki: 'Music Education as Love Education,'" *Philosophy of Music Education Review* 19, no. 2 (2011): 143, doi:10.2979 /philmusieducrevi.19.2.136.

58. On Suzuki, also see Blakeley Menghini, "Rethinking Education: The Four Pillars of Education in the Suzuki Studio," in this collection.

59. Walter Brueggemann, *The Prophetic Imagination* (Philadelphia: Fortress, 1978), 45.

60. Rob Nixon, *Slow Violence and the Environmentalism of the Poor* (Cambridge, MA: Harvard University Press, 2011).

61. Ibid., 15.

62. Ibid.

63. Kevin Shorner-Johnson, "Peacebuilding as Vocation: The Journey of One Program towards Mutuality, Agency, and Imagination," in *Voices of Vocation: Stories of Purposeful Life Work in Teaching, Mentoring, and Leading*, ed. Tracy Wenger Sadd (Elizabethtown, PA: Elizabethtown College Press, 2017), 187–206.

64. Michael G. Long, *Peaceful Neighbor: Discovering the Countercultural Mister Rogers* (Louisville, KY: Westminster John Knox Press, 2015).

5

MUSIC, RESISTANCE, AND HUMANE VIBRATIONS

Ebru Tuncer Boon

The Song of Gezi Resistance: "Come, Come, Whoever You Are . . ."

In May 2013, Istanbul exploded in a new wave of sounds as forms of protest: evening choruses of pots and pans from balconies. It was a call. This rapidly growing sound communication, which involved millions of people, fueled and reflected waves of demonstrations in Turkey that came to be known as the Gezi Uprising. The initial purpose of the movement was to protest the government's urban development plan for Istanbul's Gezi Park, which is in the center of the city's main commercial and tourist district and is one of the last green spaces in the city. When authorities announced they intended to raze the park and put in its place a replica of a nineteenth-century Ottoman barracks containing a shopping mall, many residents of Istanbul were outraged, and sit-in protests began at the park, with the earliest protesters chaining themselves to trees.

Following a night of intense police activity against the protesters, the movement widened and took on greater urgency in Istanbul and across Turkey, with people proclaiming a wide range of issues, at the core of which were environmental concerns, freedom of the press, and freedom of expression and assembly. The Gezi protests have been compared to the Occupy movement in the West and to the protests of May 1968, when a student revolt that began in a suburb of Paris soon became by a general strike, eventually involving some ten million workers. Three and a half million of Turkey's eighty million people are estimated to have taken an active part in almost five thousand demonstrations across Turkey connected with the original Gezi Park protest. The events at Gezi Park began on May 28, 2013, and intensified until police took action on May 31. The sit-in at the park was then restored after police withdrew from Taksim Square on June 1, and the park quickly developed into an Occupy-like camp, with thousands of protesters in tents organizing a library, a medical center, food distribution centers, their own media and radio, and educational, artistic, and musical workshops. After the Gezi Park camp was cleared by police later that June, protesters began to meet in other parks all around Turkey and to organize public forums to discuss ways to move forward with the protests. The movement's communal aspects had already begun spreading. Social media played a key part in the protests. Widely documented through social media, the demonstrations also sparked a great number of cultural, creative, and musical phenomena. Artistic reactions flourished during Gezi, ranging from performance pieces to graffiti, a five-thousand-book park library, and ongoing street concerts. Gezi displayed a new generation of people who cared about the well-being of one another beyond the confines of nationality, race, or class. This generation expressed hope that they could sing together, make music together, and make of this old world a new world for the "common good of humanity."[1] An image of a whirling dervish wearing a gas mask while performing in Gezi Park became the most recognized symbol of the protesters and was stenciled on city walls, streets, and roads along with "Come Along," a reference to a poem by Rumi, one of the greatest Sufis of Anatolia, whose followers had founded the order of the whirling dervishes. The poem was written in the thirteenth century and remains powerful and moving in the context of the Occupy Gezi movement:

> Come, come, whoever you are. Wanderer, worshiper, lover of leaving. It doesn't matter. Ours is not a caravan of despair. Come, even if you have broken your vows a thousand times. Come, yet again, come, come.[2]

Music's spontaneous, humane, communal, and socializing power was very visible during the four months of the Gezi protests. People, no matter their age or artistic talent, as expressed in Rumi's poem, gathered around the trees to protect nature and formed music groups, bands, and choirs to send their messages. They approached the arts and music in new, creative, and personal ways. The protest's starting signal, the song of pots and pans from the city's windows and balconies, went on every night as soon as the clock struck nine. In between their protest chants, songs, and water cannon dousings, demonstrators camped out in one of the city's last green spaces, Gezi Park, attempting to save it from bulldozers.

Gezi was a lesson in democracy and a search for environmental justice through critical and creative protests; it was a learning process about how to break the wall of fear for a humanitarian concern and the possibility of creating a better world. Gezi changed the foundations of language and politics, as well as social perceptions of environmental issues in Turkey; it also changed the perceptions of making music and forms of performative practices. As Ashley R. Gromis and William G. Roy addressed in their work, social movements creatively use cultural products and themselves act as sources of cultural creativity. "Because of its temporal [emotional] synchronicity, its expression in lyrics,"[3] and its unlimited openness to expressive forms, music was an especially powerful tool of cultural expression during Gezi.

There is a widespread recognition that humanity faces multiple crises. UNESCO's 2015 report titled *Rethinking Education: Towards a Global Common Good?* stressed that "education must be about learning to live on a planet under pressure."[4] It must be about cultural literacy, multiple worldviews, alternative knowledge systems, learning throughout life through rapidly changing realities, and the challenge of working toward solutions on political, social, economic, and environmental issues. Putting the Gezi Park resistance and creative protests at the center, in this chapter I rethink music education with the guidance of the principles in the UNESCO report. I also inquire and present literature on how music is capable of creating unique social vibrations and resonances. In addition, I explore more specific questions: How can we connect music's communal and socializing power with individuals' creative autonomy for the "common good of humanity," and how can we bring some of Gezi's creative performances and musical practices to music education (as opposed to centralized and top-down policies and practices in music education)?

Trees have special importance in Turkish culture. Turkish tribes in central Asia were identified with branches of a tree whose trunk signifies the unity of humanity. In Altaic Turkic myths, this "Tree of Life" was said to connect earthly shamans through its branches, giving them the opportunity to reach other worlds.[5] In addition, the word *humane* is marked by sympathy and compassion for other human beings, animals, and nature.[6] In light of this understanding of *humane*, the Gezi movement was a sequence of events rooted in humane concerns. It was a bottom-up response to the government's plan to build a shopping mall on a small yet symbolic park in the cultural heart of Istanbul. The Gezi protesters took on the responsibility of protecting some six hundred trees, which symbolized the citizens' relationship with nature in the midst of a soaring metropolis.

As opposed to the government's Gezi Park plans, which were top-down, centralized, and authoritarian, the protesters had no centralized power to back up their actions and beliefs. They demanded to live in a just society that was harmonious with nature and ripe with cultural expression. Trees became symbols of unity for the common good of humanity, expressing the possibility of a society without centralized authority to determine who shares common spaces and what activities can be undertaken in such spaces.

The UNESCO document argues that there is a need for "a humanistic vision of education and development, based on respect for life and human dignity, equal rights, social justice, cultural diversity, international solidarity and shared responsibility for a sustainable future for the common good."[7] This view guided me in this essay in analyzing Gezi and rethinking music education creatively and critically. The report urges us to reconsider the notion of education as a common good of humanity, and for that reason, political, social, cultural, and environmental issues should be the concern of music education. Echoing these same sentiments, François Hautart writes, "There has to be a change of paradigms to permit a symbiosis between human beings and nature, access of all to goods and services and the participation of every individual and every collective group in the social and political organizing processes, each having their own cultural and ethical expression: in other words to realize the Common Good of Humanity. This will be a generally long-term process, dialectic and not linear, and the result of many social struggles."[8]

Schools and music classrooms do not exist in a vacuum; they are like living organisms. They reflect our local and global societies, their cultures and practices, as well as their problems. For instance, classrooms and musical communities are not free from what musically, culturally, technologically, and politically happens on the street, in the media, or in the world. Music teachers and their students bring their subjectivities, experiences, and struggles to the classroom. They are involved in music in a number of environments outside of the classroom that can transform the classroom into a place where multiple backgrounds and identities can be expressed.

For education to be a force for the "common good of humanity," it must be humane. One definition of humane education is an attempt to develop altruism and a sense of compassion in a world where all other pressures are in opposition to it.[9] Humane education looks holistically at the individual and at the interconnectedness and interdependence of all living beings.[10] Zoe Weil, the founder of the Institute for Humane Education, broadens this focus and defines humane education as a comprehensive field of study that draws connections between all forms of social justice. It examines what is happening on our planet, from human oppression to ecological degradation. It invites students to envision creative solutions and to take individual action so that together we can bring about a world in which integrity is the guiding principle in our choices and relationships.[11] Both these definitions of humane education are compatible with the aims of this collection, which are designed to steer scholars and teachers toward a more expansive view what education is.

Humanly Organized Sounds and Social Vibrations

Musicality is a fundamental part of being human. Steven Mithen posits that we cannot understand the origin and nature of humans without addressing why and how we are a musical species.[12] The fact that music is more than just patterned sound becomes obvious when we study and listen to music. In most cultures, music involves not just sound, but action.[13] For the common good of humanity, Gezi's music became a social interaction and a collection of actions and practices. Forming bands and choirs and engaging in collaboration and invention in musical performances created a sense of collectiveness and strengthened social bonds. Music is a sphere in which the cultural practices of peoples, nations, ethnic and social groups, and individuals manifest themselves. In the context of Gezi, that meant music became more than music: it united people toward the goal of protecting the green space. They soon realized that larger goals were at stake concerning the country's future and especially the intimate relations of state power, the construction sector, and ideology.[14]

Additional evidence suggests that music is capable of creating social vibrations. Music can function as an instigator. It can create conditions that excite people toward social action. This is what happened at Gezi Park in 2013. Some research shows that "the membership of a group influences how individuals experience both affective and cognitive aspects of empathy:

emotional responsiveness to, and participation in, musical activities is rewarding and activates brain areas that share common features with affective empathic processing circuitries."[15] When playing music together, "recording of brain wave activity points to activity patterns in the cortex. This reflects empathic processes in musicians observing their own musical performance in ensemble."[16] Some musical behaviors and functions such as dance, its use in rituals and ceremonies, and its connection with affect appear almost universal.[17] Therefore, music and associated synchronized behaviors can reinforce empathy and affective engagement and enhance the recognition and sharing of emotional states, all indicators of the importance of music as a social glue in human relations and support for the common good.

As was demonstrated in Gezi, music and dance brought individuals together and created a sense of social bonding with a special social context that unified them in body and in mind. Days and nights, the parks echoed with different rhythms. There were women singing in chorus and folk groups playing and dancing together or dancing groups with gas masks. Environmental degradation and rampant construction in an already over-constructed, overpopulated city, as well as the political Left's dissatisfaction with the ruling party, made protests almost inevitable. Music-like choruses of pots and pans and spontaneous performances fueled the Gezi spirit. As I see it, although the Gezi Park protests only partially succeeded, perhaps for the first time in Turkish history, environmental concerns rose to the forefront of social and political discourse.[18]

There is also evidence in history that political or religious leaders have understood the power of music to influence populations. A few historical examples are worth mentioning. Music was critical, for instance, in the organization of early slave uprisings. Using drums to spread messages in a rhythmic language undecipherable by whites, slaves could orchestrate revolts on land and on slave ships, as well.[19] Between the seventeenth and nineteenth centuries, when musical instruments, especially drums (which could be used for communication and revolt, as well as spiritual remembrances and affirmation), were forbidden, African Americans used their bodies as instruments. The coordinated interdependence of multiple percussive instrumental voices in a composite statement is found in the "Pattin' Juba," the hand-clapping and foot-stomps of African Americans throughout the South.[20]

"Lili Marleen," a Nazi love song, became popular during the Second World War throughout Europe and the Mediterranean. After the occupation of Belgrade in 1941, Radio Belgrade became the German forces' radio station under the name "Soldiers' Radio," with transmissions heard throughout Europe and the Mediterranean. The radio played the song frequently. Joseph Goebbels, Hitler's propaganda chief, reportedly hated the song for not being "military" enough. He wanted it changed into a stirring march. To loyal Nazis, the song seemed to be antiwar, even close to treason, and singer Lale Andersen, its performer, was believed to be sympathetic toward Jews. The song was banned, and both Andersen and the composer of the song, Norbert Schultze, were charged with "moral sabotage" of the nation's aims.

The start of the Gezi Park protests was also sudden and quite puzzling and also very emotional. The uprising created an enduring spirit of resistance among the millions who had never been involved in street activism before. The clanging of pots and pans on Istanbul's balconies during the Gezi events—forbidden, unsanctioned sounds—recalled these other sounds in history when authority was challenged.

Drumming, dancing, and synchronous singing can bring people to ritualistic trance-like states, "entrain neural activity, and elicit a unified, collective state of consciousness."[21] Joseph Jordania calls this state a "battle trance," in which there is reduced fear, reduced perception of risk, and a willingness to sacrifice for the whole, for the common good.[22] Besides the psychologically enhancing aspects of music and dance pertaining to each individual, "this communication stream forges coalitions and alliances within and between culturally like-minded groups, deters enemies, advertises group strength, and delineates territory."[23] Calls, codes, singing, and dancing allow for a rich array of styles, sound clusters, and messages to flourish across the world and create soundscapes with negative or positive collective meanings. These meanings then help to nourish emotional ties between groups, even disparate groups: "Music [sound] in a sense is a structure of emotions. It creates mood and in a way can communicate a feeling of common purpose, even among actors who have no previous historical connections with one another. It can be recorded and reproduced, and enter into memory, individually as well as collectively, to such an extent that it can be recalled or remembered at other times and places."[24] In such a fashion, music can recall not only situationally bound shared experiences but also a more general commitment to a common cause and to collective action.[25] During the Gezi uprising, through participation and social inter-action, protesters demonstrated that music and dance were at the center of this movement.

Music is one way to reflect and express our creative autonomy and cognitive and social capabilities. Jay Schulkin and Greata B. Raglan write that "music intersects with cultural boundaries, facilitating our 'social self' by linking our shared experiences and intentions."[26] Music is fundamental to our social roots.[27] Coordinated rituals allow us to resonate with others in chorus, for which shared intentional movements and actions are bound to one another. [28] Harvey states that music is able to maintain a harmony of souls during the emergence of a "society of selves."[29] Not only is music a shared experience, but it is also a space for expressing individuality. Every evening, a piano was brought to the center of Taksim Square. The people listened and were united in a way they never were before. Men and women in the three rival soccer jerseys of Istanbul's professional clubs put their enmity aside and tried to save the park.

Implications for Music Education

The Gezi experience inspired me to rethink music education and especially what such an experience may bring to music education. We need to con-nect music's communal and socializing power with individuals' creative autonomy. Music making and musical communities can exist practically anywhere: on a stage, in the street, or in a classroom with or without an audience. Music education practices can be creative processes built together with students by emphasizing openness to unpredictable musical outcomes or responses to social injustice and collaborative invention of new music; these practices should create a strong sense of community as a natural by-product. Community music making is not directed at the reproduction of fixed musical works, but focused on the musical activities of the group rather than on some finished musical product.[30] Wayne Bowman writes: "communities are not just places where we engage in musically education-al practices: they are also creations of those practices."[31] In other words, the community becomes a community through interaction, sharing, and practice; it is a phenomenon that organically emerges from shared com-mitments. Music education can foster personal autonomy in the direction of students' lives. Music classrooms, especially, can offer a democratic en-vironment where children and teachers can discuss and experience each other's perceptions of music and the world. They can pose critiques and understand how music is experienced and learned in different cultural environments and social spaces. When music education involves collective organization, student inventiveness and individuality, and the interpretation, evaluation, and expression of different musical realities, and most importantly cultural expressions in music making, then it can be a force for the "common good of humanity."

As strongly emphasized in the UNESCO report, "education and learning in today's changing world need to go beyond the process of acquiring, validating, and using knowledge. They must also address the fundamental issues of the creation and control of knowledge."[32] Thus, music educators should be committed to the democratization of society through art and music education and seek to reach their emancipatory goals by creating awareness of, revealing, and resisting hidden forms of power.[33] In this way, music education can make social change through the cultivation and nurturing of individuals who are active participants and critical thinkers inside and outside of the classroom.

Music might emanate from the body itself in terms of vibrations. Much literature in music focuses on this very idea—for example, Joscelyn Godwin's *Harmonies of Heaven and Earth: Mysticism in Music from Antiquity to the Avant-Garde*.[34] Godwin explores music's effects on matter, living things, and human behavior. She traces the history of the idea that, since ancient times, the whole cosmos, with its circling planets and stars, is in some way a musical or harmonious entity. Protesters formed small crowds at first. They were spontaneous gatherings, but then they later formed communities, millions standing up for the same purpose. They chose to join together by vibrating different frequencies and thus transformed to a new form of society, more aware of environmental issues, the value of arts and music, and the role of creative processes for the common good. The process of change is nothing else than the evolutionary pattern of life and creativity.

EBRU TUNCER BOON is Associate Professor in Music Education at Dokuz Eylül University, Turkey.

Notes

1. François Hautart, "From 'Common Goods' to the 'Common Good of Humanity'" (paper presented by Francine Mestrum at the From "Common Goods" to the "Common Good" of Humanity conference, Rosa Luxembourg Foundation, Rome April 28–29, 2011).

2. Alim Konukçu, *Aşk'a Gel* (İstanbul: Eğitim Kitabevi Yayınları, 2016).

3. Ashley R. Gromis and William G. Roy, "Music and Social Movements," in *The Wiley Blackwell Encyclopedia of Social and Political Movements*, ed. David A. Snow, Donatella della Porta, Bert Klandermans, and Doug McAdam (Hoboken, NJ: Wiley-Blackwell, 2013).

4. UNESCO, *Rethinking Education: Towards a Global Common Good?* (Paris: UNESCO, 2015), 3, http://unesdoc.unesco.org/images/0023/002325/232555e.pdf.

5. Lindsey Addawoo, "Turkish Protests: It Started with a Tree," June 5, 2013, https://globalnews.ca/news/616750/turkish-protests-it-started-with-a-tree-2/.

6. UNESCO, *Rethinking Education*, 20.

7. Ibid., 10.

8. Hautart, "From 'Common Goods,'" 35.

9. Kelly L. Thompson and Eleonora Gullone, "Promotion of Empathy and Prosocial Behavior in Children through Humane Education," *Australian Psychologist* (2003): 175–182.

10. Ibid.

11. Zoe Weil, *The Power and Promise of Humane Education* (Gabriola Island, Canada: New Society, 2004).

12. Steven Mithen, *The Singing Neanderthals: The Origin of Music, Language, Mind and Body* (London: Weidenfeld and Nicholson, 2015).

13. John Blacking, *Music, Culture, and Experience* (Chicago: University of Chicago Press, 1995), 241.

14. Revolutionary protest action usually expands this way: it originates with an isolated issue but then brings larger issues to light.

15. Alan R. Harvey, *Music, Evolution, and the Harmony of Souls* (Oxford: Oxford University Press, 2017).

16. Claudio Babiloni et al., "Brains 'in Concert': Frontal Oscillatory Alpha Rhythms and Empathy in Professional Musicians," *Neuroimage* 60 (2012): 111.

17. Bruno Nettl, "An Ethnomusicologist Contemplates Universals in Musical Sounds and Musical Cultures," in *The Origins of Music*, ed. N. Wallin, B. Merker, and S. Brown (Cambridge, MA; MIT Press, 2000), 463–472; Ian Cross, "Music, Mind, and Evolution," *Psychology of Music* 29 (2001): 6; Ellen Dissanayake, *Art and Intimacy: How the Arts Began* (Seattle: University of Washington, 2000).

18. The government's proposed Ottoman Barracks and shopping mall plan was ultimately scrapped, but a portion of the park was destroyed as the government began transforming the face of Taksim Square in central Istanbul.

19. Megan Sullivan, "African-American Music as Rebellion: From Slavesong to Hip-Hop," accessed March 2, 2017, http://eatmos.com/johnnyotis/juba.sullivan.pdf.

20. Bessie Jones and Bess B. Hawes, *Step It Down: Games, Plays, Songs, and Stories from the Afro-American Heritage* (Athens: University of Georgia Press, 1972), 37–40.

21. Harvey, *Music, Evolution, and the Harmony of Souls.*

22. Joseph Jordania, *Tigers, Lions and Humans: History of Rivalry, Conflict, Reverence and Love* (Tbilisi: Logos, 2014).

23. Harvey, *Music, Evolution, and the Harmony of Souls.*

24. Ron Ayerman and Andrew Jamison, *Music and Social Movements: Mobilizing Traditions in the Twentieth Century* (Cambridge: Cambridge University Press, 1998).

25. Ibid., 23.

26. Jay Schulkin and Greata B. Raglan, "The Evolution of Music and Human Social Capability," *Frontiers in Neuroscience* 8 (September 2014): 292.

27. Ian Cross, "The Evolutionary Basis of Meaning in Music: Some Neurological and Neuroscientific Implications," in *The Neurology of Music*, ed. Clifford Rose (London: Imperial College Press, 2010), 1–15.

28. Steven Brown, "Biomusicology, and Three Biological Paradoxes about Music," *Bulletin of Psychology and the Arts* 4 (2003): 15–28.

29. Harvey, *Music, Evolution, and the Harmony of Souls.*

30. Constantijn Koopman, "Community Music as Music Education: On the Educational Potential of Community Music," *International Journal of Music Education* 25, no. 2 (2007): 151–162.

31. Wayne Bowman, "The Community in Music," *International Journal of Community Music* 2, nos. 2–3 (2009): 109–128.

32. UNESCO, *Rethinking Education*, 79.

33. Joe Kincheloe, *Teachers as Researchers: Qualitative Inquiry as a Path to Empowerment* (New York: Falmer, 1991).

34. Joscelyn Godwin, *Harmonies of Heaven and Earth: Mysticism in Music from Antiquity to the Avant-Garde* (Rochester: Inner Traditions International, 1995).

PART II

PEDAGOGY AND TEACHER PREPARATION

6

INQUIRY-BASED LEARNING

A Value for Music Education with Aims to Cultivate a Humane Society

Betty Anne Younker

HISTORICALLY, A UNIVERSITY INCLUDED A COMMUNITY OF LEARNERS and teachers who had the autonomy to self-regulate and determine who qualified to enter the community. It was of the belief that learned people would constitute an educated society and thus enhance the quality of life at the individual and collective levels and approach challenging issues in an informed manner while striving for a common good. One core part of our learning process involves interpretation, which is central to the humanities. Through interpretation, we engage reflectively on what is articulated, reflecting on the past while examining the present and shaping the future. Throughout the process, we are mindful of the ethical presence that guides us as we make choices, a notion of "guardians to humanistic culture."[1] Embedded in the process is inculcating habits of mind to pursue honorable lives that are productive and constructive. This, in part, reflects the humanistic vision of education as outlined in UNESCO's *Rethinking Education: Towards a Global Common Good?*[2] In moving toward a common good, one gains understanding about how to be productive and constructive and comes to a shared value of living in communities of "respect and equal dignity."[3] As stated in the UNESCO document, learning to live together and learning to be inclusive, tolerant, and fair are essential educational endeavors in building communities for the common good.

This focus of education, however, has changed in response to specific events in history, including post-Enlightenment, the Industrial Revolution, and social upheavals after WWII. These and other events have contributed to many changes around the world, including those related to economic engines. While recognizing these catalysts of change, Antonio and Hanna Damasio suggested that the current environment has been constructed through changes of a larger magnitude and thus of "a more profound human consequence."[4] Specifically, they suggest that, most notably after WWII, what we produce and consume and how we communicate and "move about in the world" have changed. These changes, in turn, have had an impact on markets and economic sectors both in composition and function. They have been made possible through scientific, engineering, and informatics bodies of knowledge and technical skills that have become more desirable on campuses and are increasingly viewed as what really matters. As the growth of bodies of knowledge and technical skills continues, we are beginning to realize that a gap is emerging in our growth as human beings, a growth that is related to the kind of education that is required to balance ethical and moral considerations as new bodies of knowledge emerge. Such considerations are grounded in inquiry-based learning, which is critical for a common good to be cultivated and maintained. The importance of discussing, writing about, and contemplating ethical considerations of what has been created in response to new knowledge and how those creations are utilized in the world is becoming more noted. Time to analyze and critique what might become valuable and understanding reasons for a value are necessary because of how values shape our engagement with each other as we strive for inclusiveness, tolerance, and fairness. What is occurring across campuses, however, is a diminishing focus on the arts and humanities, and the community is coming to see economic advantage as the primary value of an education, especially one that is fueled by disciplines in science, technology, engineering, and mathematics. Governments are requiring increasing sets of metrics that "define" the success of an education, including how an education contributes to the economy. The value of process—including process as experienced in inquiry-based learning—has shifted to products that indicate measurable results and identifiable contributions to the economy.

Having described this current situation, Damasio and Damasio caution against this increased value of economic advantage with a decreased emphasis on the arts and humanities because of the imbalance of knowing and understanding and its impact on values, a common good, and thus citizenship.[5] The "socialization function of education" as reflected in two of the four pillars of learning found in the UNESCO document ("learning to be" and "to live together") is necessary for growth in citizenship within humane approaches to education, which are currently threatened.[6]

Another human disadvantage to the shifts in perception of the value of an education is the disconnect between cognitive processing and emotional processing. As noted by Damasio and Damasio and based on research in cognitive neuroscience, the inter-relationship between cognitive processing and emotional processing is critical in decision-making processes.[7] Emotion is an informant for cognitive activity, including cognitive creativity. Each comprises different sets of processes that occur at different speeds, but each is necessary as we reason and make decisions. With increasing quantities of information being made available in shorter time spans, cognitive processing has gathered speed. Emotional processing, slower than cognitive processing, is experiencing an increasing gap in terms of time to process. Time is necessary to make decisions that are morally and ethically based, which can inform citizenship. Input of emotion is critical because "emotions work as qualifiers for actions and for ideas."[8] Emotions qualify the ideas and the plans for the actions as well as the actual actions based on relevant content. Emotional processing involves classifying, qualifying, and reflecting on ideas as they are implemented and experienced. Input of social emotions serves as a grounding for moral development—including one's acceptance of social conventions and ethical rules—as has been revealed through research. Minkang Kim reminds us that, "neuroscientific studies indicate that in fully functional brains there is a strong link between emotion, action, and real-life moral decision-making."[9]

Damasio and Damasio suggest that inclusion of arts and humanities education is "one way of conducting the moral exercises on which citizenship is grounded."[10] Science, technology, engineering, and mathematics (the STEM disciplines) involve knowledge about things and ideas and represent the ambiguities of human life; it is through the arts and humanities that we *exercise* that knowledge and representation. We learn about the emotional consequences, we discuss and debate, reflect and formulate, appreciate and experience, examine conflict and instill cooperation, and learn about respect and tolerance. An education can make transparent the moral structure required for a healthy society. Such an education can nurture the human potential to imagine, which is necessary for innovation, renewal, and sustainability. Artistic experiences, including musical experiences, provide opportunities to utilize and strengthen emotional processing, to cultivate a core of who we are as human beings—the humanness of being human. Further strengthening can occur as we inquire, analyze, reflect, and evaluate the significance of such experiences as well as the cultural, political, and social ramifications of art in culture and its impact on us individually and as a community. An education in the arts and humanities has the potential to be a model of how this might be done through inquiry-based learning. Can other disciplines be models as well? Of course; the differentiation, however, is that inquiry-based learning in the arts and humanities is not about seeking truth and absolutes but rather direction for situated understandings and values. And the balance of both is supported by the UNESCO document—the need for "a holistic approach to education and learning" that is void of "dichotomies between cognitive, emotional, and ethical aspects."[11]

Purpose

The purpose of this chapter is twofold: first, to offer core principles of learning for music education that are constructed within the framework of inquiry-based learning and second, to examine cognitive and emotional processing, with an eye on the role of the arts in ethical and moral development. I will focus on the process of making transparent the intent as we engage with students and the hope of moving toward a more humane and civilized society through the next generation. This focus resonates with the UNESCO document in that inquiry-based learning can inform pedagogy that values diversity, inclusivity, and civility.[12]

Definition of Inquiry-Based Learning

At the root of inquiry-based learning is active learning, motivated by a sense of dissonance that is identified as a problem. The engagement begins by posing questions in response to the problem as felt, noted, or presented. The problem could be a specific part of a larger context or it could arise within a scenario that is being formulated. The key is that students are active learners from the onset of framing or identifying the problem. Throughout, the educator serves as a facilitator who assists as necessary in constructive ways. In music education environments, students are the problem "framers and identifiers," as they create original music within parameters identified by them; solve musical problems within given parameters that result in original music; identify musical challenges and negotiate and evaluate those solutions in performing and listening environments; interpret given music in ways that are meaningful to them in solo and group performance-based settings; and interpret that which is heard through critical ears while applying theoretical, historical, social, and political knowledge as it relates to the music.

Music does not "own" inquiry-based learning, nor do the arts and humanities; however, they differ from disciplines that seek truth and right answers in ongoing research. As with the arts and humanities, music focuses on interpretation and translation. This occurs as cultures examine and evaluate that which will be retained and could evolve, transition, and be transformed. The process involves seeking a construct on which to make decisions—to act on, engage, and build, and in turn provide direction for further issues within a framework that is inclusive of diverse voices across multiple arenas.

Specifically, What Is the Role of Inquiry-Based Learning?

The role of inquiry-based learning is to gain knowledge and seek understanding of issues as they are related to self, others, culture, society, and community, a process done at the individual and collective levels. Inquiry-based learning in music settings includes interpreting and translating created music abstractly and contextually and creating original music in individual or group settings. Over time, the interpretation and translation can change as the lens shifts from an abstracted to a context-based position—a cultural, historical, social, or political position. Both interpretation and translation can be restrictive and restricted, oppressing and freeing. Art (music) can embrace, divide, challenge, and disturb; it can be adaptive pending the "environmental niche."[13] In prescribed environments, art can either conform to the rules or be freed and is thus varied and unpredictable. The variability occurs for a variety of reasons including the variability of the systems that are engaged throughout the musical experience—our sensory, emotional, and cognitive systems—all of which contribute to our varied and unpredictable experiences.[14] Herein lies the messiness of experiences, the grayness of our musical growth, and thus our fund of experience, as well as the recursive nature of each experience. And yet, the experience as felt is more precise than we can articulate through words and thus is ineffable. The journey may be messy, but the experienced moment is clear and precise.

Music, as experienced, opens up spaces for critique, debate, and reflection—including issues that are ethically and morally based. As artifacts of culture are investigated, analyzed, interpreted, and contemplated within the various forms situated in time and place, choices are made about retaining, evolving, and transforming the values that have provided direction for ethical and moral concerns. In these spaces, relationships are cultivated with respect, tolerance, and fairness—critical to educational experiences.[15]

Within the musical world, ethical and moral considerations might include but not be limited to whose music is used where, when, and why: whose music is excluded or included within school-based music education settings; how music might be considered for an enhanced quality of life with questions arising about how quality is defined and by whom. These considerations need attention, as our music education programs continue to be dominated, for the most part, by the Western classical music tradition.[16] We need to examine inclusion versus exclusion as we respect and understand students' musical intent and potential, their culture and community, and as we strive for "meaningful and relevant learning."[17] As Joseph Shively notes, this level of inquiry goes far beyond teaching current and prospective music educators techniques, methods, and approaches to asking about what to teach, when, to whom, and how.[18] It is necessary that students are cultivated to be consistent inquirers as choices are made about content, methods and approaches, and pedagogy, to be responsive to populations of students for whom our music education-based environments are unfamiliar, and whose musical cultures are unfamiliar to us. It is necessary that students understand that to educate is to draw out from students what they know and are coming to know, musically, culturally, ethically, and morally—to understand living together and being, and to recognize their part in a possible growing of a common good.[19]

In such spaces, the engagement shapes minds and understandings that are at the core of being educated and responsible. In such spaces, our growth is recognized through "meaning, imagination, wonder, speculation, personal theorizing, self-realization, democratic deliberation, and social action."[20] Maxine Greene views imagination as "the possibility of looking at things as if they could be otherwise."[21] For her, imagination allows space to be "jarred" and to loosen habituation. The world of "what-ifs" requires critiques of standardization, calcification, and rule-abiding requirements. For her, education is about questioning the comfortable and tradition—it is through the arts that we increase our capacity "to look *through* the windows of the actual, to bring as-ifs into being in experience"—this is imagination at work and play.[22]

Inquiry-based learning in each discipline requires that we guide students in questioning the literature, theoretical frameworks, and research questions, the analysis and conclusions of research, and interpretations, implications, and recommendations, including their own. Inquiry-based learning continues to be as critical as it has been historically—some would argue even more critical—as we continue to strive for a humane and civilized society in a time of tribalism and divisiveness. There is a growing body of literature that supports the need "to think critically, communicate clearly, and solve complex problems."[23] The ability to solve complex problems in groups, to work collectively as well as individually, and to recognize the strengths and challenges one brings to the group dynamics is of great importance; the "what if" question needs to be exercised and practiced as well as "finding the right answer" to the problem. The former is about possibilities and seeking structures that are meaningful within contextually situated environments.

Core Principles That Reflect Inquiry-Based Learning in Democratic Environments

The following core principles resonate with the four pillars of learning first discussed in the 1996 Delors report,[24] brought again to our attention via *Rethinking Education: Towards a Global Common Good?*[25] They reflect a humanistic approach that is based on renewed ethical and moral foundations.

Acquisition of Knowledge: Examining, Reflecting, Transforming, and Questioning

Thinking critically is at the center of how teachers and learners embrace ambivalence, vulnerability, surprise, and joy as challenges are met with open-mindedness and reasoned thinking.[26] We deconstruct what we know as we encounter dissonances in our daily experiences. We realize that our "claimed" knowledge and understanding is open for negotiation and to possibilities and multiple "truths." This learning and relearning reflect the nonformulaic aspect of experiential learning on a daily basis. Questions (curiosities) arise when a dissonance is experienced that intersects with one's continuum of the day. We rely on our past experiences to understand

and situate a current experience, identified by Dewey as a "fund of experience."[27] Through this fund, we are able to examine "what is," reflect on and examine our understandings, and move forward with deeper knowledge that may reflect prior knowledge or reflect a transformation of our understanding. Herbart embraced this cognitive framework and suggested that learning occurs through utilizing a collection of experiences when making sense of new experiences. The teacher's role is to present new material within the known context and make transparent the connections within and across known and new. Herbart offered six steps of learning, which resemble processes experienced when thinking critically and which are experienced recursively—"preparation, presentation, comparison, abstraction, generalization, and application."[28] There is no prescribed order of steps or expected goals within each; instead, students experience them as required by the problem that is situated. Regarding this, one can find several schools of thought that have grown into schools of action, one of them being the Montessori system. Based on the work of Maria Montessori, a female physician who believed that all children could succeed given educative environments, the role of the student in his or her education is that of an inquirer—one who addresses the problem through a process of critical thinking.

A Democratic Vision for Education: Foundational for Inquiry-Based Learning

Educators who purport a democratic vision for education insist on critical capacity, curiosity, and autonomy of the learner.[29] Such values are the basis of education in the arts and humanities.[30] Within musical communities, these values are enacted as we examine (1) the history of music as studied—whose music, written by whom, in what contexts, and for what purpose; (2) what constitutes music education—whose music, interpretation, performances, and musical voices; and (3) criteria for identifying music making and musicians—which genres and styles, which parameters and qualifiers, whose context, whose "club"? Such inquiries interrogate and shape *a* vision and open spaces for visions that are individually based and yet might speak to a larger perception of a vision. The intent is not to seek out *the* genre, style, approach, method, or theory but rather to resemble musical lives and individual and collective encounters that cause us to pause, reflect, interpret, and implement. For Dewey, predetermined methodologies and approaches did not resemble life, nor did they resemble thoughtful and critical engagement in response to those dissonances that intersected with one's daily life. Within a humanistic vision of education for the common good, we learn and grow from negotiating our own values through engaging with and questioning others.[31]

Core of Learning: The Student's Capacity, Curiosity, and Intent

As Dewey reminded us, it is the educator's responsibility to identify the student's capacity, curiosity, and intent and to provide experiences to nurture the curiosity; this guides new and prospective interests and learning. To gain insights about who our students are and which musical values shaped their communities is to understand their musical lives. These are the immediate points for engagement. It is here that we engage in others' musical experiences and widen our musical worlds as problems are identified, framed, and solved for further reflection, each one situated musically, culturally, socially, and politically and each one individually meaningful with understanding being offered by all.[32]

For Rousseau, learning occurred when children pursued their own interests that are anticipated by educators. Experiences are guided, utilize the senses and feelings, and are beneficial and educative. Rousseau's thinking influenced the open education movement in the 1960s and 1970s—one example being an open-based school, Summerhill. The foundation of Rousseau's thinking, as reflected in "open" schools, was experiential learning that focused on observing, doing, and feeling. Formal lessons that consisted of prescribed content chosen by the teacher were not deemed appropriate.[33]

Embracing Diversities Reflects a Democratic Vision

Reflecting and inquiring about "what is" shapes and challenges our ethics and morals—dimensions of our communities and cultures. While sciences seek new information and solutions to determine what is true, the arts and humanities seek the essence, value, and constructive or destructive nature of the information and solutions. Claims to truth are questioned and thus viewed as changeable. There are many truths based on individual understandings that "arrive" through frameworks of diverse strengths, beliefs, and perspectives, which in turn enrich various dimensions of communities. As we question these various lenses of strengths, beliefs, and perspectives, we continue to shape the common good as we strive for a more inclusive and humane society with individuals contributing as they can and should. And it is in educative environments that such shaping is examined, hence the critical role played by the (music) teacher in promoting the common good.[34]

Plato, a disciple of Socrates, reflected on who should be educated and how, with the goal being that we educate for the diversities of human talent and that those educated should address society's needs. Aristotle thought students should be educated with a focus on their strengths. As educated, each should then contribute to the community. This makes transparent the relationship between being entitled (being educated) and the expected responsibilities to serve the common good (contributing to the community by utilizing one's potentials that have been strengthened through education).

When engaging with others of differing perspectives and beliefs, we are responsible to model and nurture fairness and respect. It is here that we negotiate purpose and intent and consider the possibilities of options and solutions, all with tolerance and respect for differing sets of opinions, all of which are heard and acknowledged.

Continuous Reflective Practice Is Core to Inquiry-Based Learning

There is a responsibility to think critically in our practice.[35] Paulo Freire referred to "educative practice," which *might* include maintaining the status quo; however, if a core value is promoting growth through critical reflection, then to maintain the value would require a thoughtful and reasoned argument as to "why."[36] Such critical reflection requires space for multiple interpretations and perspectives, each of which might be perceived through individual beliefs. The continuous reflection dissipates ideological thinking about the "correct," "allowed," and "accepted" music, tradition, interpretation, practice, and history. This is a responsibility in an inclusive musical world in which we learn from each other, increase our musical capacity, and strengthen our potential to engage with diverse musical practices.

Summary of Core Principles

This offering of core principles of pedagogy for music classrooms, as demonstrated in thinking of those who built a foundation of such pedagogy, embraces notions of situatedness, context, student-based learning from a curiosity perspective, and constructivist and experiential learning with inquiry driving the process. They are offered as guiding principles and are foundational to inquiry-based learning. This thinking has been with us for centuries, and today is being substantiated, to some degree, by cognitive science research that speculates about the role of arts-based inquiry in the education of moral and ethical reasoning.

The Role of the Principles in Examining and Cultivating Societies

Dewey stated that, "The most notable distinction between living and inanimate things is that the former maintain themselves by renewal," a statement reflected in a number of the core principles offered above.[37] Without consistent informed critical reflection, we become the antithesis of human. To be human is to reflect and, in response, to understand why we retain and transform. We, individually and collectively, are evolving organisms that continue to be created and re-created and to emerge. We witness this in cultures and societies as identifying features that have emerged over time. Educating, therefore, should reflect this human notion of "living." What makes us ethical is our "capacity to spiritualize the world."[38] This reflects one role of the principles of learning—to recognize the potential in each of us, to put into action the potentials we have as human beings, and to provide environments that nurture and provide space for growth. Our ability to think critically allows for acts of greatness and dignity. It also allows for indignity and destruction—and it is here that the need for moral education is imperative.

Dewey's term "educative experiences" is characterized by the promotion of growth.[39] Freire states that one characterization of that growth is cultivating ethical beings. In the cultivating, we recognize decency and compare, evaluate, intervene, decide, and continue to evaluate while constituting ourselves as "ethical beings."[40] Freire continues by stating that "the condition of becoming is the condition of being," and this condition is the ethical aspect of growth. "If we have any serious regard for what it means to be human, the teaching of content cannot be separated from the moral formation of the learners."[41] A second role of the principles of learning, therefore, is engaging students in thoughtful and critical processes while negotiating with self and others.

A third role is to engage children with their interests and allow the time and space necessary for their imagination and curiosity to flourish. Educating is less about content and more about educative engagement and growth. In a world of high stakes testing, where accountability is based on what students can remember and perhaps apply, we have lost the imaginative notion of learning and being—the process of following our curiosities.

Finally, a fourth role of the principles of learning is to find spaces where we understand that disagreement is part of the growth. Values and practices of those values differ across societies and cultures—some of which may be harmful and miseducative. As responsible human beings, we must consider the morality of practices and work toward those that are respectful of each individual. Thus, tolerance of differences is critical, and we have a responsibility to examine the differing practices through a moral and ethical lens.

It is here that we resonate with the UNESCO document—humanistic values that include "respect for life and human dignity, equal rights and social justice, cultural and social diversity, and a sense of human solidarity and shared responsibility for our common future."[42] It is here that we acknowledge and accept responsibility for being active agents who strive for a common good, which is identified and made stronger because of the diversities found globally. It is here that we negotiate the value of constructing and negotiating musical environments that are inclusive of musical beliefs, cultures, and identities. It is here that we recognize the human capacity to engage with music intelligently in many ways and our responsibility to nurture that capacity. It is here that we recognize students' voices, interests, curiosities, and sense of wonder as starting points for sharing and constructing musical engagement. And it is here that we strive for a humane society that embraces tolerance, respect, fairness, and openness to listen and hear and to acknowledge and respond through inquiry. In so doing, we embrace agency as a responsibility while working toward a more just and tolerant society. And for us in music education, we do this through the practice of inquiry. How does this resonate with what we are experiencing today in a political climate that appears to be defying all of the above?

The Intent of the Core Principles Made Transparent within Educative Environments

To directly make transparent the intent of actions is to actively reflect on one's action and articulate reasoned arguments about choices made (why, for whom, when, and to where). It is here that values are shaped and morals are guided. Our values will be challenged, perhaps rejected, which can lead to feeling threatened and being less open to debate and reflection. However, within the tensions and disagreements are the opportunities for growth.[43] Thus, we need to be extremely cognizant about our reactions (immediate and less thoughtful) and responses (delayed and more thoughtful) to those who disagree or object to our values—our morals and sense of ethics—that which has shaped communities, cultures, societies, and our educational institutions, disciplines, and curriculum. Critical to our understanding is the "why" of our intent that reflects our values. Also critical is the consensus that differences will occur, and constructive dialogue about those differences needs to continue. Barring any harm from one's values in action, there needs to be an understanding of disagreement.

Intent is made transparent through inculcating agency into our students' practice as they create and reflect within their discipline. As Paul Hanstedt, a teacher of writing, reminds us it is not just the construction of text (or music)—the "how" of the construction but also of agency, "about a student's ability to move into the world fully cognizant of what's at stake in every rhetorical interaction."[44] How are those interactions constructed and by whom? Who has the power? What are the power dynamics? Discussions guided by such questions can make explicit the relationships that contribute to dynamics, which in turn can be moral and ethical. The role of arts and humanities leading the community in preserving and shaping culture while viewing values through other cultures while comparing and contrasting is critical. The hope would be for a semblance of global citizenship to evolve in which responsibilities to understand and be informed, to respect and be tolerant are embraced—and thus to experience the cultivation of one's soul.

Summary

Dewey plus others did conceive of art as a vital component of moral education, in which we challenge, question, and debate. Thinking about and through music can contribute to the growth of moral and ethical reasoning and, in turn, humanize our communities. The role of inquiry-based learning in which processes involve seeking ethical and moral reasoning is more critical now than ever before. As emphatically stated by Damasio and Damasio, "To forget the arts and humanities in the new curricula is equivalent to socio-cultural suicide."[45]

To avoid sociocultural suicide as we rethink education, we have a critical and urgent need to reflect on a growing misappropriation of the intent of education. This intent is not based solely on acquisition of knowledge and skills for economic advantages but rather includes, and thus values, inquiry-based learning that focuses on constituting and cultivating societies in ethical and moral dimensions. Such learning guides us as we construct a humane society that seeks a common good. In this chapter, I have argued for the role of inquiry-based learning in music education and offered core principals of such an approach. This is the essence of the UNESCO report: the critical role education plays in cultivating a humane society, and for us it is educating through music.

BETTY ANNE YOUNKER is Dean and Professor of Music Education as part of the Don Wright Faculty of Music at the University of Western Ontario, Canada.

Notes

1. Homi. K. Bhabha, "The Humanities and the Future of the Universe" (lecture, Harvard University, accessed September 2019, http://media.fas.harvard.edu/FAS/humanities_center /2013/HumanitiesPanel-20130430.mp4).

2. UNESCO, *Rethinking Education: Towards a Global Common Good?* (Paris: UNESCO, 2015), http://unesdoc.unesco.org/images/0023/002325/232555e.pdf.

3. Ibid., 3.

4. Antonio Damasio and Hanna Damasio, "Brain, Art, and Education" (paper presented at the UNESCO Conference on Arts and Education, University of Southern California, 2006), 3, http://www.unesco.org/new/fileadmin/MULTIMEDIA/HQ/CLT/CLT/pdf /AntonioDamasio-SpeechRevised.pdf.

5. Ibid.

6. UNESCO, *Rethinking Education*, 40.

7. Ibid.

8. Ibid., 9.

9. Minkang Kim, "Cultivating Teachers' Morality and the Pedagogy of Emotional Rationality," *Australian Journal of Teacher Education* 38, no. 1 (2013): 12–26, doi:10.14221/ajte .2013v38n1.2.

10. Damasio and Damasio, "Brain, Art, and Education," 12.

11. UNESCO, *Rethinking Education*, 39.

12. Ibid.

13. A. Chatterjee, *The Aesthetic Brain* (New York: Oxford University Press, 2014), 179.

14. Ibid.

15. UNESCO, *Rethinking Education*.

16. Emily Good-Perkins, "Rethinking Vocal Education as a Means to Encourage Positive Identity Development in Adolescents," in this collection.

17. UNESCO, *Rethinking Education*, 3.

18. Joseph Shively, "Navigating Music Teacher Education toward Humane Ends," in this collection.

19. Ibid.

20. William H. Schubert, *Love, Justice, and Education: John Dewey and the Utopians* (Charlotte, NC: Information Age Publishing, 2009), 80.

21. Maxine Greene, *Releasing the Imagination: Essays on Education, the Arts, and Social Change* (San Francisco: Jossey-Bass, 1995), 16.

22. Ibid., 140 (emphasis in the original).

23. See, for instance, a 2013 study by the American Association of Colleges and Universities: Katherine K. O'Sullivan, "Marketing the Unmarketable: From Medievalist to International Business School Thesis Coordinator," in *Forging a Rewarding Career in the Humanities: Advice for Academics*, ed. K. P. Zepeda and E. Mayock (Boston: Sense Publishers, 2014), 75; see also UNESCO, *Rethinking Education*.

24. UNESCO, *Learning: The Treasure Within* (Paris, UNESCO, 1996), http://unesdoc.unesco.org/images/0010/001095/109590eo.pdf.

25. UNESCO, *Rethinking Education*.

26. Estelle R. Jorgensen, *Transforming Music Education* (Bloomington: Indiana University Press, 2003).

27. John Dewey, *Experience and Education* (New York: Collier, Macmillan, 1938).

28. Nel Noddings, *Philosophy of Education* (Boulder, CO: Westview Press, 1998).

29. Dewey, *Experience and Education*.

30. Randall Allsup, "Mutual Learning and Democratic Action in Music Education," *Journal of Research in Music Education* 51, no. 1 (2003): 24–37; Jorgensen, *Transforming Music Education*; Paul Woodford, *Democracy and Music Education* (Bloomington: Indiana University Press, 2005).

31. UNESCO, *Rethinking Education*, 3.

32. Paulo Freire, *Pedagogy of Freedom: Ethics, Democracy, and Civic Courage* (Lanham, Maryland: Rowan and Littlefield, 2000).

33. Ibid.

34. Shively, "Navigating Music Teacher Education."

35. Donald Schon, *Educating the Reflective Practitioner* (San Francisco: Jossey-Bass, 1987). Originally writing for those learning architecture, Schon's work has been readily adopted by those who write and think about learning in the arts.

36. Freire, *Pedagogy of Freedom*.

37. John Dewey, *Democracy and Education* (London: Macmillan, 1916), 1.

38. Freire, *Pedagogy of Freedom*, 53.

39. Dewey, *Experience and Education*.

40. Freire, *Pedagogy of Freedom*, 38.

41. Ibid., 39.

42. UNESCO, *Rethinking Education*, 38.

43. Dewey, *Experience and Education*.

44. Paul Hanstedt, "The Generalist: Or Why Breadth Matters, Even in the Academy," in *Forging a Rewarding Career in the Humanities: Advice for Academics*, ed. K. P. Zepeda and E. Mayock (Boston: Sense Publishers, 2014), 38.

45. Damasio and Damasio, *Brain, Art, and Education*, 15.

7

A HUMANE APPROACH TO THE STUDIO

Christine A. Brown

THE SEARCH FOR PEDAGOGY BUILT ON HUMANE THOUGHT and practice shaped my teaching for many years. This desire for improvement led to studies of psychology, piano pedagogy, philosophy, and education. After processes of trial, feedback, and self-reflection, I drew two conclusions. The first was that the interaction between student and teacher occupies a pivotal role in developing the student's self-concept and sense of empowerment. Second, teaching is most effective when a student feels accepted as a unique individual. As these conclusions were refined over time, they established a base for the values and intentions guiding my work.

Rethinking Education prompted me to consider what studio teachers might bring to this proposal.[1] A private studio can provide a safe harbor where a mentor's listening ear and encouraging words can help students find their personal voice. In an earlier era, Shinichi Suzuki embraced an ideal of students developing beautiful hearts through music study.[2] Today, when humane values are challenged at every turn, young musicians are called to develop beautiful hearts that listen deeply and respond courageously to their worlds.

Amazing things can happen when instructors affirm the humanness of their students. Music educators transform classrooms by enabling students to encourage each other as they share personal narratives. Possibilities for transformation in the private studio exist as well. A more humane global society will emerge to the extent that we seek out the person evolving within each and every student. As Carl Rogers mused, "How does it happen that the deeper we go into ourselves as particular and unique . . . the more we find the whole human species?"[3]

Iris M. Yob reminds us that humane instruction nurtures each individual and promotes the common good.[4] With this in mind, I review the writings of psychologists Abraham Maslow and Carl Rogers to assess their relevance to goals expressed in *Rethinking Education*. I describe humane studio practices based on the psychologists' main tenets and discuss their contribution to the common good. For this essay, I use the term *humane approach* to denote genuine expression of concern, respect for the uniqueness of each person, and listening with empathy. The terms *humane* and *humanistic* plus *studio* and *private studio* are used interchangeably.[5]

Abraham Maslow

Abraham Maslow helped pioneer Third Force psychology, the twentieth-century alternative to behaviorist thought and Freudian psychoanalysis.[6] He was among the first to analyze healthy rather than unhealthy human behaviors and is remembered for his hierarchy of motivational needs that prioritize physiological wellness, safety, belonging, self-esteem, and self-actualization.[7] He focused on self-actualization and interviewed high-achieving subjects to learn more about the phenomenon. Maslow viewed it as a "high level of maturation, health, and self-fulfillment" and a process of making healthy life choices.[8] The drive to self-actualize is within all of us, claimed Maslow, and he theorized that some people self-actualize but either do not realize it or have been too preoccupied with daily concerns.[9] He also investigated peak experiences, those intense moments of joy or realization described by self-actualizing people. His views emerged from subjects' reported moments of insight, awe, heightened sense of the present, or loss of ego awareness. At first Maslow attributed the subjects' peak experiences to successful management of basic needs in order to leave time for meaningful pursuits.[10] As he investigated varying responses among his subjects, however, he determined that some subjects moved beyond self-actualization to lead enriched inner lives of self-reflection and outer lives of selfless dedication to noble causes. These extraordinary people fused inner growth with social outreach and attained what Maslow called self-transcendence. The similarities Maslow found among these particular subjects prompted him to name self-transcendence the sixth motivational need on his hierarchy. He helped establish a "Fourth Force" or transpersonal psychology and continued researching transcendence until his death in 1970.[11]

Alongside Maslow's psychological theories, one finds an array of opinions on teaching. His educational viewpoints stem from his belief that if students are taught to create, they can self-actualize and engage with the world as autonomous yet concerned persons. He asserted that artistic creativity builds adaptable, flexible thinking that potentially results in peak experiences, particularly when making music.[12] He considered hands-on music activity particularly effective at preparing young minds for innovative thinking, and he recommended that teachers encourage improvisation as a creative route to self-discovery. For Maslow, the purpose of arts education was not to produce artists but to produce better people possessing the self-awareness, spontaneity, and insight needed to move society toward a productive future.[13]

Maslow envisioned teaching as person-training in matters of character and not just imparting knowledge.[14] His pedagogy was student-centered, and he discouraged authoritarian teaching approaches, preferring instead the concept of teachers as receptive and calm "Taoist" mentors who introduce topics for exploration.[15] He encouraged educators to be enthusiastic and, to that end, suggested rhapsodic communication or the use of descriptive and emotionally compelling language to evoke honest and uninhibited responses. He used rhapsodic communication so that students would discover their innermost values and learn the self-discipline needed to participate responsibly in society.[16]

Maslow's impact on humanistic psychology was evident in the writings of psychologists who succeeded him. Mihaly Csikszentmihalyi's studies of flow, the deep enjoyment experienced while performing a challenging and engaging task, resembled Maslow's reports on peak experiences but drew from more sophisticated research than Maslow had available.[17] Martin Seligman cofounded the field of positive psychology and declared it the "scientific study of optimal functioning," suggesting a lack of empirical rigor in Maslow and Rogers' research.[18] Overlaps between humanistic and positive psychological theories were eventually acknowledged, and Maslow and Rogers are now regarded as ahead of their time.[19]

Maslow's theory of self-esteem as an intrinsic need is still subject to debate among psychologists since self-esteem is not valued or acknowledged in collectivist cultures.[20] Maslow's motivational hierarchy is criticized in the public sphere as well. Author and columnist David Brooks describes Maslow's motivational needs, particularly self-actualization, as glorifying selfishness. He favors "quieting and transcending" the self through commitment to a higher cause, as opposed to Maslow's "liberating and actualizing the self."[21] In my view, Brooks identifies self-actualization as Maslow's motivational highpoint and overlooks his theory of self-transcendence.[22] The notion that Maslow advocates self-absorption does not explain the altruistic dedication displayed by his high-achieving subjects. Maslow's exhortation to think as global citizens and treat others with full acceptance reflects his hope that mature adults will join other nations in resolving their differences. His body of work offers a view of transcendence that integrates self with others, introspection with outreach.[23] In actuality, Brooks's quiet transcendence of self is not that far from Maslow's holistic vision.

Maslow and Educational Reform

Maslow's views reflect the humanistic ideals articulated in *Rethinking Education*. He argues that creating and improvising music invites humans to experiment, make daring changes, and grow resourceful as they do. As a result, students learn to manage unexpected circumstances and respond to needs of the moment.[24] They actively engage with the music they perform while learning to trust their ideas, resulting in greater confidence and ability to think critically.[25] Spontaneous creative activity strengthens innate capabilities, Maslow claims, and flexible thinking used during artistic activity often produces the unexpected and transformative results educational reformers seek.[26]

Maslow's dream of a peaceful global community underscores the ongoing need for learning within an adaptive and culturally diverse framework.[27] To that end, music educators continue to reduce cultural bias by finding and supporting efforts to rebuild indigenous cultural legacies throughout the world.[28] Cultural values are starting to reshape curriculum, as seen in David Lines's account of music learning in New Zealand. He describes a bicultural curriculum that includes community involvement and embraces Māori values of well-being, belonging, communication, contribution, and exploration.[29]

Finally, Maslow reminds us that humans require self-respect to thrive, and the creative resourcefulness developed through arts participation is more supportive of self-esteem than once believed.[30] Concerned educators and therapists are finding ways to change the lives of uprooted, imprisoned, at-risk, or special needs youth by providing them opportunities to make their own personal statements through such projects as songwriting.[31] Bringing arts to the disenfranchised reclaims creativity as a right for all, thus benefitting the individual and the common good.[32]

Carl Rogers

Humanistic psychologist Carl Rogers exerted a lasting influence on counseling and educational practices of his day. His client-centered therapeutic approach set a new standard for the profession, and aspects of his method have been applied to therapeutic practices ever since.[33] His description of necessary conditions for successful client-centered therapy began with the client seeking help and attending therapy appointments. During every session, Rogers displayed genuineness (congruence), empathy, and unconditional approval toward a client. Once the client perceived these expressions of acceptance and care, meaningful interaction and healing could occur.[34] Rogers claimed that if therapy proceeded in this manner, clients became less fearful, more openly communicative, and ready to assume responsibility for their lives and choices. He coined the term *fully functioning person* to describe anyone experiencing significant, lasting change resulting from therapy.[35]

Rogers applied his approach to educational settings by adapting congruence, approval, and empathy to student-centered instruction.[36] Rogers envisioned teachers as facilitators who supply resources rather than lecture. He urged that students be given as much choice as possible when selecting courses of study, small-group collaborations, self-evaluation, and student contracts in lieu of grades.[37] He believed exams were unproductive and considered true learning to be initiated by the learner. Self-directed learning was in his view the most beneficial route to enhancing student attitudes, behaviors, and levels of knowledge.[38]

Rogers's impact is seen in counseling techniques emerging after his death in 1987. Positive psychologists previously dismissing Rogers's approach now admit they address the same issues as Rogers in terms of personal growth and relief from suffering.[39] Other offshoots of positive psychology, such as life coaching, reportedly use aspects of his methods in their strategies.[40] Recently the technique of motivational interviewing has been recognized for its effective therapeutic results with clients. Adapting Rogers's practice of empathic listening, motivational interviewers restate (reflect) clients' verbalized desires for personal change rather than offering them a plan of action. The research findings support Rogers's belief that clients are most successful when they see the process of change as initiated on their own. As a result, motivational interviewing is now widely used in helping professions such as rehabilitation, public health, social work, and corrections.[41]

Rogers's influence can still be found in current educational settings including the "flipped classroom" wherein students view online lectures at their convenience so class time can be reserved for student projects.[42] In student-centered K-12 settings such as Montessori schools, students work independently and in small groups while being overseen by facilitative instructors.[43] Rogers's emphasis on student-directed learning resonates throughout education communities and continues to inform today's practices.[44]

Rogers and Educational Reform

Rogers's educational philosophy echoes many of the humanistic values reiterated in *Rethinking Education,* particularly those pertaining to relationships and empathic communication. His person-centered values exemplify respect for human dignity and have been proven to enhance student-centered methods in private and group settings.[45] His work with encounter groups offers useful strategies for building trust between local communities and humanistic educators.[46] Emily Howe underscores these relationships, for instance, in her appeal to listen and learn alongside the community we serve.[47] Suzuki and Montessori programs rely heavily on parental involvement and small-group activities and thus provide additional examples of humanistic practice in community settings.[48]

Rogers's therapeutic practice of empathic listening dignifies the person speaking by affirming her right to be heard. Viewer responses to video recordings of Rogers conducting therapy sessions indicate that clients often use a therapist's display of empathy to instigate their own healing process.[49] Empathy can affect group dynamics as well. Ebru Tuncer-Boon's narrative of empathic response to protest music illustrates the power of mutuality among people sharing a common cause.[50] In each of these cases empathy ennobles human relationships and for this reason Rogers declares the truest act of love as listening deeply to whoever needs it.[51]

Studio Practices from a Humane Perspective

The shared purpose, creative expression, and empathic listening mentioned above remind us that humane teaching can alter a studio dynamic and enhance crucial relationships for the developing musician.[52] To illustrate Maslow and Rogers's contributions to this setting, I use select themes from their works and apply them to one-to-one instruction. Discussion of research and traditions regarding the studio follows.[53]

Maslow envisions teaching as mentoring and describes processes of receiving, guiding, and inspiring students. The mentor approaches lessons with a receptive and peaceful attitude. She knows the power of building the student's sense of personal agency and therefore avoids constant interference or micromanagement.[54] These attitudes reflect Maslow's ideal of guiding students without excessive regimentation or in Lao-Tzu's words, "leading them by the nose."[55]

The mentor guides by gradually leading the student to form his own strategies and monitor his own progress while practicing. She engages the student by watching, listening, and responding to the student from the perspective of her experience.[56] She might also employ rhapsodic communication when a student needs an imaginative illustration or inspiring thought. Maslow's first use of this technique was serendipitous. His aim was not to create a peak experience but rather to help an interviewed subject recall and describe one. Since clinical wording was ineffective, Maslow resorted to more expressive verbiage that intensified as he spoke. The wording evoked an emotionally charged memory that enabled the subject to describe the peak experience with ease.[57] Such moments affect student and teacher when meaningful discussion and fortuitous timing intersect. They might evolve when discussing a work's deeper meaning or as Maslow describes, listening for the "beauty and wonder of life" embedded in its artistry.[58] Inspiration cannot be planned, but it can be encouraged when instructor and student communicate about an art form rich with meanings unique to each person.[59]

Rogers's approach addresses the studio using the teaching style of facilitator and featuring practices of empathic listening, collaborating, and approving. The facilitator eases the learning process by responding to the student's needs and encouraging him to make choices and assume responsibility through such actions as maintaining a self-reflection diary.[60] In this manner, a humane facilitator upholds studio instruction as an ongoing collaborative project of artistic and personal growth built on unconditional approval, student choice, and mutual respect.[61]

The facilitator also listens to the student with an attitude of empathy. During conversation, he intently hears a student comment, restates it then encourages the student to correct him if the comment was misunderstood. The student offers feedback as needed, and the process continues until both parties know they understand each other.[62] The facilitator gains further insight by observing the student's face, posture, nonverbal expressions (mouth noises, for example) and motions for signs of tension, anxiety, or other need. As the facilitator actively addresses student needs, his reassurances preserve the student's self-confidence.[63]

Researchers are gaining access to the studio and have studied teaching styles ranging from authoritarian to collaborative and terse to relaxed.[64] Most pervasive is the traditional master-apprentice model that draws criticism for its teacher-centered design, potentially harmful practices, and limited scope of repertoire.[65] The traditional studio experience does not, however, have to be humiliating or rigidly authoritarian. Estelle Jorgensen addresses these issues by acknowledging inherent dangers of the model while affirming its role in the extensive preparation of music students.[66] She argues for alternative scenarios to be considered such as the sharing of power between instructor and student, or the instructor's role being redefined as responding to needs and interests of the student.[67] Both options allow room for the student to develop his imagination and determined effort over time, while gaining the knowledge and skills offered by an expert.[68]

Adding music from an array of eras and cultures would surely enrich student experience and enhance music programs. The practical question is how to include and teach non-Western music equitably without reducing the training needed for those pursuing degrees involving traditional classic repertoire. For smaller program budgets and programs constrained by state legislatures, answers do not come easily. Perhaps individualized degrees or double majors in ethnomusicology and education could be offered so that students pursuing a non-Western musical tradition would have academic options. Other alternatives could include bringing non-Western music into studio or ensemble settings and inviting master performers from various cultures to perform and give master classes.

Numerous authors challenge the dominance of Western classical pedagogy in public schools and urge teachers to maintain open spaces for student-directed creativity rather than predetermined traditional programs.[69] If I still taught in public schools, I would strive for my classroom to be anchored in student-generated music. Fertile territories exist when students create works derived from the culture of their backgrounds, and the more they discover their own heritage and share it with their colleagues, the greater good they enjoy from what and how they teach each other.[70]

Humane Teaching and the Common Good

The psychologists discussed here belong to a different era yet relate to today's reform efforts because the reasons behind their concerns still exist, and many of their solutions still hold promise. Maslow espouses creative processes as intrinsically beneficial and a common good to be enjoyed by all. He envisions students as future citizens of the world who share responsibility and treat others fairly, thus embracing ethics of justice and civility.[71] Maslow's self-actualized person is holistic and not a prisoner to "us versus them" thinking. His is the vision of educated, flexible, problem-solving, and caring adults.[72]

Rogers views students as self-directed humans who carefully listen and respond to others. They facilitate dialogue between groups and behave in the best interests and ultimately the common good of all.[73] Students seeking careers in music education, ethnomusicology, psychology, or administration would benefit by contemplating and practicing the ideals brought forward by these authors. Their legacies of acceptance, care, approval, collaboration, service, and resilient belief in the best of humanity could produce a unifying and heartening effect on local, regional, and international relations.

Maslow and Rogers confirm that humanistic teachers empathize with students and meet them by developing respectful and positive relationships.[74] Their affirmation of each person's worth inspires us to strive for human rights and equality as a global way of life. As educators, artists, and members of our world community, we are called to imagine humane possibilities for our next steps. We must work for the day when all people respect each other and share in the global common good. It is never easy to turn inspiration into action, and that is why we rely on the insights of others before us. We need the zeal of Abraham Maslow to inspire our efforts as we help students learn to live as world citizens.[75] And we need the compassion of Carl Rogers to infuse our teaching with care and understanding. Their messages remain clear, and their advice directs us toward meaningful interactions with each other and with the world.

CHRISTINE A. BROWN is Adjunct Lecturer of Piano and Music Theory at Indiana University Southeast, New Albany, Indiana.

Notes

1. UNESCO, *Rethinking Education: Towards a Global Common Good?* (Paris: UNESCO, 2015); Estelle R. Jorgensen, "Rethinking Music Education towards Humane Ends" (blog), January 19, 2016, https://www.estellejorgensen.com/blog/rethinking-music-education-towards-humane-ends.

2. Shinichi Suzuki, *Nurtured By Love* (New York: Exposition, 1969), 118. Also see Blakeley Menghini, "Rethinking Education: The Four Pillars of Education in the Suzuki Studio" in this collection.

3. Carl Rogers, as quoted in Abraham Maslow, *The Farther Reaches of Human Nature* (New York: Viking, 1971), 187.

4. Iris M. Yob, "Introduction: Education for the Common Good in a Diverse World," in this collection.

5. Christine A. Brown, "A Humane Approach to Private Piano Instruction: An Analysis and Application of the Ideas of Abraham Maslow, Carl Rogers, and Jerome Bruner" (DME dissertation, Indiana University, 2002), 7.

6. Abraham Maslow, *Toward a Psychology of Being*, 2nd ed. (New York: Van Nostrand Reinhold, 1968), iii.

7. Abraham Maslow, *The Farther Reaches of Human Nature* (New York: Viking, 1971), 41–53; Maslow, *Toward a Psychology*, 135–145. See also Krista Riggs, "Foundations for Flow: A Philosophical Model for Studio Instruction," *Philosophy of Music Education Review* 14, no. 2 (Fall 2006): 177–178.

8. Maslow, *Toward a Psychology*, 71, 153, 197.

9. Ibid., 173, 176, and 190; Maslow, *Farther Reaches*, 43–50; Edward L. Deci with Richard Flaste, *Why We Do What We Do: Understanding Self-Motivation* (New York: Penguin, 1995), 21–26.

10. Maslow, *Toward a Psychology*, 79–81, 100–102, 124–125, 167–169. See also Rollo May, *The Courage to Create* (New York: Bantam, 1976), 5; and John Whaley, John Sloboda, and Alf Gabrielsson, "Peak Experiences in Music," from *The Oxford Handbook of Music Psychology*, 2nd ed. (New York: Oxford University Press, 2016), 452–461.

11. Maslow, *Farther Reaches*, 269–279, 343–350; Maslow, *Toward a Psychology*, 180–189. Also Mark E. Koltko-Rivera, "Rediscovering the Later Version of Maslow's Hierarchy of Needs: Self-Transcendence and Opportunities for Theory, Research and Unification," *Review of General Psychology* 10 (2006), 302–317, doi:10.1037/1089-2680.10.4.302.

12. Abraham Maslow, "Music Education and Peak Experience," *Music Educators Journal* 54, no. 6 (February 1968): 167–171, http://www.jstor.org/stable/3391274; Thomas Schafer, Mario Smukalla, and Sarah-Ann Oelker, "How Music Changes Our Lives: A Qualitative Study of the Long-Term Effects of Intense Musical Experiences," *Psychology of Music* 42, no. 4 (2014): 525–544, doi:10.1177/0305735613482024.

13. Maslow, *Farther Reaches*, 57–60, 180–195; UNESCO, *Rethinking Education*, 44.

14. Maslow, *Farther Reaches*, 99.

15. Maslow, *Toward a Psychology*, 198–201; Lao Tzu, *Tao Teh Ching*, ed. Paul K. T. Sih, trans. John C. H. Wu (New York: St. John's University Press, 1961), 17: "In dealing with others, know how to be gentle and kind. In speaking, know how to keep your words."

16. Maslow, *Farther Reaches*, 48–50, 174, 195.

17. Mihaly Csikszentmihalyi, *Flow: The Psychology of Optimal Experience* (New York: HarperCollins, 1990), 70–75.

18. Hilde Eileen Nafstad, "Historical, Philosophical, and Epistemological Perspectives," in *Positive Psychology in Practice*, 2nd ed., ed. Stephen Joseph (Hoboken, NJ: John Wiley, 2015), 11; Harris Friedman, "Humanistic and Positive Psychology: The Methodological and Epistemological Divide," *Humanistic Psychologist*, 36, no. 2 (2008): 113–126, doi:10.1080 /08873260802111036; Martin Seligman and Mihaly Csikszentmihalyi, "Positive Psychology: An Introduction," *American Psychologist* 55 (2000): 5–14; Christopher Peterson, *A Primer in Positive Psychology* (New York: Oxford University Press, 2006), vii, 5–8; Nafstad, "Historical, Philosophical, and Epistemological Perspectives," 21.

19. Stephen Joseph, "The Future of Positive Psychology in Practice," in *Positive Psychology in Practice*, 2nd ed., ed. Stephen Joseph (Hoboken, NJ: John Wiley, 2015), 826; Brent Dean Robbins, "Building Bridges between Humanistic and Positive Psychology," in *Positive Psychology in Practice*, 2nd ed., ed. Stephen Joseph (Hoboken, NJ: John Wiley, 2015), 31–45.

20. John C. Christopher, Dennis C. Wendt, Jeanne Marecek, and David M. Goodman, "Critical Cultural Awareness: Contributions to a Globalizing Psychology," *American Psychologist*, 69, no. 7 (2014): 651–652, doi:10.1037/a0036851; Christopher Mruk and Travis Skelly, "Is Self-Esteem Absolute, Relative, or Functional? Implications for Cross-Cultural and Humanistic Psychology," *Humanistic Psychologist* 45, no. 4 (2017): 328–330, doi:10.1037/humo000075.

21. David Brooks, "When Life Asks for Everything," September 19, 2017, https://www.nytimes.com/2017/09/19/opinion/when-life-asks-for-everything.html.

22. Mark E. Koltko-Rivera, "Rediscovering the Later Version of Maslow's Hierarchy of Needs: Self-Transcendence and Opportunities for Theory, Research and Unification," *Review of General Psychology* 10 (2006): 302–317.

23. Maslow, *Toward a Psychology*, 180–189.

24. Maslow, *Farther Reaches*, 58, 61–70; Riggs, "Foundations for Flow," 177.

25. Maslow, *Farther Reaches*, 58, 61–79; Maslow, "Music Education and Peak Experience," 75; Maslow, *Toward a Psychology*, 210.

26. Maslow, *Farther Reaches*, 100–101; UNESCO, *Rethinking Education*, 38.

27. UNESCO, *Rethinking Education*, 13, 15, 28–29, 32, 41.

28. Danielle Sirek, "Our Culture Is Who We Are! 'Rescuing' Grenadian Identity through Musicking and Music Education," *International Journal of Music Education* 36, no. 1 (2018): 47–57, doi:10.177/0255761417703 783; Catherine Grant, "Learning and Teaching Traditional Music in Cambodia: Challenges and Incentives," *International Journal of Music Education* 35, no. 1 (2017): 5–16.

29. Alexandra Kertz-Welzel, Leonard Tan, Martin Berger, and David Lines, "A Humanistic Approach to Music Education: (Critical) International Perspectives," in this collection.

30. UNESCO, *Rethinking Education*, 38. Also Maslow, "Music Education and Peak Experience," 75; Maslow, *Toward a Psychology*, 210.

31. Renee Crawford, "Creating Unity through Celebrating Diversity: A Case Study That Explores the Impact of Music Education on Refugee Background Students," *International Journal of Music Education* 35, no. 3 (2017): 343–356, doi:10.1177/0255761416659511. See also Viggo Kruger and Bryonjulf Stige, "Musical Agency: A Perspective from Community Music Therapy," in *A Cultural Psychology of Musical Experience*, ed. Sven Hroar Klempe (Charlotte, NC: Information Age Publishing, 2016): 235–251; and Emily Howe, André de Quadros, Andrew Clark, and Kinh T. Vu, "The Tuning of the Music Educator: A Pedagogy of the 'Common Good' for the Twenty-First Century," in this collection.

32. UNESCO, *Rethinking Education*, 77, 78, 82.

33. Kimberly M. Jayne and Dee C. Ray, "Therapist-Provided Conditions in Child-Centered Play Therapy," *Journal of Humanistic Counseling* 54, no. 2 (July 2015): 86–103; Hannah B. Bayne and Danica G. Hays, "Examining Conditions for Empathy in Counseling: An Exploratory Model," *Journal of Humanistic Counseling* 56, no. 1 (April 2017): 32–52.

34. Carl Rogers, *On Becoming a Person: A Therapist's View of Psychotherapy* (Boston: Houghton Mifflin, 1961), 47–49, 286–295.

35. Ibid., 65–66, 183–184, 191–192.

36. Ibid., 281–285.

37. Carl Rogers, *Freedom to Learn for the 80s* (New York: Macmillan, 1983), 135–145, 147–159.

38. Rogers, *On Becoming a Person*, 275–278.

39. Nafstad, "Historical, Philosophical, and Epistemological Perspectives," 21–23.

40. Margarita Tarragona, "Positive Psychology and Life Coaching," in *Positive Psychology in Practice*, 2nd ed., ed. Stephen Joseph (Hoboken, NJ: John Wiley, 2015), 249, 252.

41. William R. Miller and Theresa B. Moyers, "Motivational Interviewing and the Clinical Sciences," *Journal of Counseling and Clinical Psychology* 85, no. 8 (2017): 757–766, doi:10.1037/ccp0000179.

42. C. Brame, "Flipping the Classroom," Vanderbilt University Center for Teaching, accessed June 9, 2017, http://cft.vanderbilt.edu/guides-sub-pages/flipping-the-classroom/.

43. Rekha S. Rajan, "Music Education in Montessori Schools: An Exploratory Study of School Directors' Perceptions in the United States," *International Journal of Music Education* 35, no. 2 (2017): 228, doi:10.1177/0255761416659508.

44. Joseph, "The Future of Positive Psychology," 825–826; Rogers, *Freedom to Learn*, 307.

45. Carl Rogers, *A Way of Being* (Boston: Houghton Mifflin, 1980), 181–188.

46. UNESCO, *Rethinking Education*, 26, 35.

47. Howe et al., "The Tuning of the Music Educator."

48. Menghini, "Rethinking Education"; Merlin Thompson, "Authenticity, Shinichi Suzuki, and 'Beautiful Tone with Living Soul,' Please," *Philosophy of Music Education Review* 24, no. 2 (2016): 170–190.

49. UNESCO, *Rethinking Education*, 38–39. Arthur C. Bohart and Gayle Byock, "Experiencing Carl Rogers from the Client's Point of View: A Vicarious Ethnographic Investigation, I. Extraction and Perception of Meaning," *Humanistic Psychologist* 33, no. 3 (2005): 190.

50. Ebru Tuncer Boon, "Music, Resistance, and Human Vibrations," in this collection.

51. Rogers, *On Becoming a Person*, 284.

52. Estelle R. Jorgensen, *The Art of Teaching Music* (Bloomington: Indiana University Press, 2008), 207–216.

53. Estelle R. Jorgensen, *Pictures in Music Education* (Bloomington: Indiana University Press, 2011), 57–60.

54. Susan O'Neill and Gary E. McPherson, "Motivation," in *The Science and Psychology of Music Performance: Creative Strategies for Teaching and Learning*, ed. Richard Parncutt and Gary E. McPherson (New York: Oxford University Press, 2002), 34.

55. Maslow, *Farther Reaches*, 68, 189; Lao Tzu, *Tao Teh Ching*, 131.

56. Jorgensen, *Art of Teaching Music*, 207–211.

57. W. Barnett Pearce, *Communication and the Human Condition* (Carbondale, IL: Board of Trustees, Southern Illinois University Press, 1989), 98.

58. Maslow, *Farther Reaches*, 190–191; Stewart Gordon, *Etudes for Piano Teachers: Reflections on the Teacher's Art* (New York: Oxford University Press, 1995), 14.

59. Richard Winter, "Language, Empathy, Archetype: Action-Metaphors of the Transcendental in Musical Experience," *Philosophy of Music Education Review* 21, no. 2 (Fall 2013): 117.

60. Jorgensen, *Pictures in Music Education*, 59–60, 218.

61. Nel Noddings, *Caring: A Feminine Approach to Ethics and Moral Education* (Berkeley: University of California Press, 1984), 30–31.

62. Kyle Arnold, "Behind the Mirror: Reflective Listening and Its Tain in the Work of Carl Rogers," *The Humanistic Psychologist* 42 (2014): 367, doi:10.1080/08873267.2014.913247.

63. Antonia Ivaldi, "Students' and Teachers' Orientation to Learning and Performing in Music Conservatoire Lesson Interactions," *Psychology of Music* 44, no. 2 (2016): 201, 215, doi:10.1177/0305735614562226; Robert Murray Diefendorf, *Release the Butterfly: A Manifesto for Change in the Studio* (Princeton, NJ: Butterfly Press, 2003), 124–127.

64. Leon Rene de Bruin, "Shaping Interpersonal Learning in the Jazz Improvisation Lesson: Observing a Dynamic Systems Approach," *International Journal of Music Education* 36, no. 2(2018): 160–181, doi:10.1177/0255761417712318; also Kim Burwell, "'She Did Miracles for Me': An Investigation of Dissonant Studio Practices in Higher Education," *Psychology of Music* 44, no. 3 (2016): 466–480, doi:10.1177/0305735615576263.

65. Randall Everett Allsup, "Music Teacher Quality and the Problem of Routine Expertise," *Philosophy of Music Education Review* 23, no. 1 (Spring 2015): 12–16; Riggs, "Foundations for Flow" 179, 181; Juliet Hess, "Remixing the Classroom: Toward an Open Philosophy of Music Education by Randall Everett Allsup, *Philosophy of Music Education Review* 25, no. 1 (Spring 2017), 102; William Westney, *The Perfect Wrong Note: Learning to Trust Your Musical Self* (Pompton Plains, NJ: Amadeus Press, 2003), 176–182.

66. Jorgensen, *Pictures in Music Education*, 57, 58, 67, 68.

67. Estelle R. Jorgensen and Iris M. Yob, "Metaphors for a Change: A Conversation about Images of Music Education and Social Change," *Journal of Aesthetic Education* 53, no. 2 (Summer 2019): 19–39.

68. Jorgensen, *Pictures in Music Education*, 59, 61, 62.

69. Randall Everett Allsup, *Remixing the Classroom: Toward an Open Philosophy of Music Education* (Bloomington: Indiana University Press, 2016), 13, 25, 43, 51–52; also Juliet Hess, "Troubling Whiteness: Music Education and the 'Messiness' of Equity Work," *International Society for Music Education* 36, no. 2 (2017): 128–144.

70. Hess, "Troubling Whiteness," 128–144.

71. Maslow, *Farther Reaches*, 83–84; UNESCO, *Rethinking Education*, 36, 75, 77, 80.

72. UNESCO, *Rethinking Education*, 32, 33, 38, 39.

73. UNESCO, *Rethinking Education*, 15, 77.

74. Brown, *Humane Approach*, 93.

75. Maslow, *Farther Reaches*, 184.

8

THE TUNING OF THE MUSIC EDUCATOR

A Pedagogy of the "Common Good" for the Twenty-First Century

Emily Howe, André de Quadros,
Andrew Clark, and Kinh T. Vu

Introduction

Emily Howe

English physician, astrologer, and occult philosopher Robert Fludd's 1618 treatise *De Musica Mundana* features a striking illustration of our solar system stretched out across the body of a single-stringed instrument and being tuned by the disembodied hand of a god. Titled "Divine Monochord," the image is meant to illustrate Fludd's theory that acoustic proportions mirror and perhaps even dictate cosmological ones.[1] On one hand, such concerns seem far removed from those discussed in this volume; nonetheless, the image of a divine hand tuning the world strikes me as an apt depiction of how the enterprise of music education has functioned, wittingly or unwittingly and for better or for worse, from the modern era and into the present. For whether deployed to expedite European objectives during the colonial era or in service of international development initiatives in the present, countless music educational projects have sought to develop, to convert, or to civilize local populations through exposure to "great" art.[2] And the music educator hears everything that she has made and, behold, it is very good.

But what is *good*, really? What musical practices are lost through the exercise of what is often a Eurocentric, hegemonic form of music pedagogy?[3]

How many stories, how many songs, how many sounds have been victims of what Rachel Beckles Willson has characterized as a sort of musical missionization?[4] As products of a music education system that has historically reinforced racist, sexist, classist, and ableist social hierarchies through repertoire selection, ensemble composition, and musical objectives, is it possible for music educators in the twenty-first century to challenge oppressive and inequitable societal structures through our practice? Perhaps the charge for music educators in the twenty-first century is to flip the script, or rather to invert the image. To strive to tune the world is neither humane nor sustainable. Instead, music educators in the twenty-first century must allow themselves to be tuned *by* the world: they must listen to, learn from, and respond to the people and communities they serve.[5]

In this chapter, André de Quadros, Andrew Clark, and Kinh T. Vu present portraits narrating and theorizing projects they have led with incarcerated university students in a Massachusetts prison, with musicians who experience disability and chronic illness at a summer music camp hosted by the Woodlands Foundation, and with a Cambodian community organizer in collaboration with Boston University music education students, respectively. Though the settings and learning objectives are quite different, the projects are guided by similar questions: What is the purpose of music education? Is it to create great art? To create socially relevant art? To create meaningful experiences for participants? And what is the role of the music educator? Is it to be a technician? A missionary? A curator? What kind of training is adequate and appropriate to prepare educators to lead such projects? Reflecting on the training they received while preparing for careers in music education and then recounting the joys and challenges they have faced when venturing beyond conventional music education practice, the authors argue for the importance of enacting a more inclusive approach to recruiting and training future music educators. It is here, in this place of inclusive, vulnerable, empathic music making, that we believe a humane education for the common good might be found.

In invoking the language of common good, I gesture toward the 2015 UNESCO report that has inspired this volume and consider how the profession of music education might orient itself toward the goals delineated therein.[6] Central to the report is the notion that both knowledge and education should be considered of and for the *common good*, which the authors define as that which "humans share intrinsically in common and that they communicate to each other."[7] Based on this definition, there can be little question that knowledge can be theorized as of the common good. Conceptualizing the pedagogical enterprise as of the common good, however, is more problematic. Noting that certain forms of education and certain modes of knowledge acquisition have long been prioritized and valued over others, the report's authors argue that twenty-first century education should be premised on the recognition of the inherent value of diverse forms of knowledge and be rooted in holistic approaches that reflect and refract the fundamental humanness of the process of knowledge creation, transmission, and acquisition.

And yet, while the UNESCO report offers a rose-tinted vision of a future where formal, informal, digital, and mobile learning spaces coexist and offer customizable learning experiences for increasingly empowered lifelong learners, it offers precious few indications of how community members, students, educators, administrators, and policy makers on the ground might reach consensus about what the common good is. Moreover, the report's authors are so committed to a bottom-up vision of education that they effectively deny the top-down, systemic workings of neoliberalism, Euro-American hegemony, ableism, misogyny, and heteronormativity on individuals and communities around the world as they make choices about what kind of education is good for them. For every community affirming local identity and, as the report's authors discuss, prioritizing local development ontologies in response to globalist development imperatives, there is another community choosing to assimilate.[8] And which choice is better? And who has the power to decide which choice is better?

In the end, the report offers few practical ways forward, in part because it also denies the systems that produce and dictate the livelihoods of educators. And though the report does not specifically address the field of music education, reflecting on our own field prompts us to consider the educational systems through which we are produced. What should be our response to the long-term and systemic erasure of whole bodies of musical knowledge and carriers of musical traditions from university music education curricula? Is music education, as most of us have come to know it, incompatible with the report's idealistic vision? What is the common good for our field, and how might we live into the common good as a collective? Finally, how might a theory of music education for the common good contribute to broader discussions about education for the common good?

This is where the notion of "tuning" may be productive as both metaphor and pedagogical methodology. For while we music educators are taught to tune ensembles, to train ears, and to cultivate listening, we rarely consider a retuning of our own aural epistemologies. What might happen if we listen to our students truly, wholly, deeply? What creative experiences might we discover if we forsake our own biases about what constitutes "good" music and learn to appreciate and even to teach the music our students value? How might we empower our students by allowing our ears and minds to be tuned by them? Returning to the UNESCO document with our ears tuned to the productive potential of listening, we can begin to hear how a sonic orientation toward pedagogy might clarify both what the common good is and how we might work toward it through our practice.

Attention to the diversity of global musical cultures and sound worlds prompts us to acknowledge that the "common" in the common good can never be homogenous. As the UNESCO report reminds us, the common good is never monolithic and is always context specific; what is natural in one setting might be anathema to another.[9] Similarly, despite what one might learn in a typical university music education program, there is more than one form of musical knowledge and more than one form of musical transmission. A music pedagogy of the common good, then, cannot be premised on an educator's attempts to simply reproduce hegemonic notions of whatever she believes to be good music, transmitted in the correct way. Instead, educators must seek to understand students' diverse knowledge bases, values, and goals and to collaboratively generate meaningful and authentic musical experiences. The role of the music educator must shift from that of knower, teacher, transmitter toward that of listener, learner, and facilitator whose responsibility is to generate the conditions for students to interrogate, to discover, and to create.[10]

On a related point, theorizing music education as common good provokes consideration of the degree to which music education is "common"—that is to say, how accessible music education is in varied contexts.[11] While discussions about access to music education frequently center on public school music programs, there are vast populations beyond school-age children who have long been underserved or outright neglected by the profession of music education.[12] Moreover, when music educators attempt to address this problem by offering music programs in prisons, nursing homes, homeless shelters, and the like, they often proceed by transplanting standard music educational norms, values, and goals into these contexts. In our opinion, such programs insufficiently address the problem of access. For the values that are prioritized in conventional music education programs—technical proficiency, music literacy, and the performance of "great works," among other things—may be meaningless in other contexts. Does it make sense to strive for musical perfection with a chorus of adults who have never sung before? Perhaps, but not necessarily. Making music education truly accessible, then, means not only that music educators need to be present in diverse communities; it means that they have an obligation to make themselves and their pedagogy relevant to these communities.

Finally, theorizing music education as common good prompts us to acknowledge the pitfalls in two seemingly opposed philosophies encapsulated in the word *good*. On one hand, the philosophy that treats music as commodity ("good") has led in many cases to the fetishization of technical proficiency over creative or emotive expression. On the other hand, the philosophy that treats certain types of music as inherently beneficent ("good") has led to discourses attributing positive characteristics to particular kinds of music (often "high art," often Euro-American) and not to others. A music education of the common good must work to elide this value hierarchy. Music educators must affirm the value of all musical expression and cultivate musical experiences that are meaningful in their particular context.

This is where the notion of humane music education seems particularly relevant. As Iris M. Yob notes in the introduction to this volume, a humane approach to education must attend not only to the common and to the community but also to the individuals who comprise the communities with which we work. Listening for both communal and individual musical values, goals, and repertoires and reflecting these practices back to our students through our teaching, we can perhaps live into the promise of a humane music education for the common good.

Consideration of the potentials and limitations of the enterprise of humane music education for the common good animates each of the three projects chronicled in this chapter. To that end, it is no coincidence that each of these projects has emerged in what might be deemed an unconventional educational setting, for it is in these settings that we have been most acutely confronted with the need to examine our own biases, to listen carefully and critically to people and music in the community, and to strive to understand and respond to knowledge and means of knowledge production that differ from those with which we are most familiar. As these portraits attest, our work in these settings has also prompted us to reconsider our musical and pedagogical practices in more conventional contexts: de Quadros notes that our process-oriented prison teaching has caused him to rethink product-oriented and narrow music teacher education curricula; Andrew Clark discusses how his work at the Woodlands has inspired him to reimagine the Harvard University choral program; and Kinh T. Vu describes how engagement with the concerns and priorities of Chantrea, his Cambodian activist interlocutor, inspired him and his Boston University students to interrogate the ethics of transnational collaboration. In other words, it is in those contexts where we feel the least prepared by our own musical and pedagogical training that we have been forced to listen, learn, and allow the world to tune us.

Ultimately, each portrait reflects our shared conviction that music education in the twenty-first century must be characterized by radical attunedness to the needs and desires of the communities with which we work. Such work demands that educators be not only sound musicians and reflective pedagogues but also philosophically committed to listening with and learning alongside their students in a lifelong process of self-inquiry rooted in contemporary social justice paradigms. It is only by being in tune with the community that the field of music education will help to advance music's promise as a common good. And so, in a spirit of exploration, we invite you to join us. Be tuned with us.

Facilitating an Interdisciplinary Music Course in Two American Prisons

André de Quadros

According to 2008 Pew Research Center statistics, in less than three decades, US prisons have expanded from housing three hundred thousand prisoners to more than two million.[13] A report by the Bureau of Justice in 2011 indicates that nearly seven million adults were under correctional supervision, including presentence and parole, in the United States.[14] To put this in perspective, based on a conservative extrapolation of National Center for Education Statistics reported in 2011, there were approximately 2.5 million music students in US high schools in 2004.[15] Even if school music enrollment has changed since 2004, the comparison between the number of high school music students and the number of people currently behind bars in US prisons is striking; in the United States, there are more people incarcerated in prisons than there are students in high school music programs, but few incarcerated people have access to music education, leaving a vast population of potential students neglected. Nevertheless, numerous accounts of prison music education exist, stretching back to the 1930s, and most of them speak of prisoners' high levels of motivation and overwhelming desire to participate.[16] We would argue that all people who desire access to music should have the opportunity to engage with it. And so, as educators, we must ask ourselves: in the twenty-first century, what kind of music education is appropriate in a prison setting? What kind of music education might be meaningful for a group of incarcerated adults?

With a combination of innocence, ignorance, and good intentions, Emily Howe, our colleague Jamie Hillman, and I began teaching in two Massachusetts prisons—men's and women's facilities—in 2012 as faculty members in Boston University's Prison Education Program.[17] As choral conductors and music educators, much of our training is in shaping vocal production and teaching music literacy—in short, teaching for skills and knowledge. While these objectives may well be satisfying for participants in many contexts, we quickly determined that they were essentially irrelevant in our prison classroom. This is not to suggest that our students would not be capable of achieving such goals were we to set them; on the contrary, our incarcerated students are some of the most competent and committed we have worked with in any context. However, for largely practical reasons, including our students' diversity of age, musical experience, and musical interests, we came to understand that the musical objectives we had been trained to strive toward and the musical values we had been trained to reproduce could not yield a creative and empowering experience for our students. We needed to focus on nurturing life values linked to lifelong learning, resonating with the recommendation in the UNESCO document that the focus of education should be less about skill acquisition.[18]

Thus, rather than simply transmitting our musical knowledge to our students, we sought to engage with the diverse group of people in the class, to understand each student's particular gifts, and to strive to integrate these gifts into a collaborative artistic experience. This radical rethinking of the curriculum is called for in the UNESCO document, specifically rejecting cultural hegemonic and reproductive practices.[19] Accordingly, we chose to sublimate the musico-normative objectives that have been ingrained in us as music educators—specifically, the goal of producing musical products crafted largely in accordance with Eurocentric aesthetic preferences. These goals serve to produce literate, disciplined musical subjects capable of virtuosic technical displays. Instead, we took on the pedagogical challenge to create conditions for all of our students to bring themselves fully to the experience of musicking in an inclusive environment regardless of prior experience or ability level.[20]

In response to a context in which an asymmetrical power dynamic of the classroom or the musical ensemble would resemble too much the authoritarian environment of the prison, we developed an approach we called "Empowering Song" in which the goals allow for a humane repurposing of music education to accommodate healing, consolation, love, personal expression, and community mobilization. In circles and in small groups, we used processes, tasks, and exercises that gave participants an authentic mediation of their realities and lived experiences through music, processes central to human musicking for more than sixty thousand years but frequently neglected by contemporary practice. We explored interdisciplinary connections with poetry, dramatic and visual arts, storytelling, and self-reflection and provided spaces for deep and subversive personal expression. This process-based approach, unencumbered by conventional emphases on the acquisition of skills and knowledge allowed us to "transform the educational landscape" not only for the students but for numerous colleagues who have used the Empowering Song approach in other settings.[21]

How, then, does this approach make sense of the guiding question of this book; that is, how can music education, by adopting a humane approach across its many contexts and for its various learners, contribute to the common good? Two brief illustrations may serve to illuminate this important question. The first concerns a classroom task, in which we invited our students to use music to express and reimagine existing patterns of behavior and interaction. Mark, an incarcerated man in his thirties with a teenage daughter, explained to us that his daughter and he had developed a contentious and adversarial way of conversing over the telephone.[22] As a result of the class prompt, Mark called his daughter and sang to her and, then, instead of talking to her, he just hung up. The following day, he called her, and the conversation was different, even tender.

The second illustration stems from a session in 2015, when a small group of singers from a New York organization visited our program in the men's prison. A letter written to me by Sharon, one of the guest singers, after this experience is quoted in a condensed version:

> It was a life-changing experience. . . . I had never been inside a prison wall and was not prepared for how that would feel. . . . And when we all met, shook hands . . . , I was touched. . . . The next day, we had a chance to meet a former member of the program who was released. Another life changing experience,

one about forgiveness. Fifteen years ago I lost a good friend in a brutal murder.... I developed opinions about ... our prison system ... and couldn't even think about forgiveness in a new way. ... I want my friends ... to have the experience ... seeing the excellent work that goes on. ... And I want them to have the experience of learning to forgive, to let go, and to sing with their whole heart.

After this event, and as a result of it, the organization in which this singer works, is planning an Empowering Song–based program in two New York prisons to start in the near future, thus adding to "common good" models and practice.

Were the fetishization of music, as referred to in the introduction of this chapter, to be taken to its natural conclusion in an incarcerated setting, the success or otherwise of music education initiatives in prison would mostly be judged on the quality of the product, with, possibly, a patronizing and salvationist narrative that would run something like, "Look at what they can do even though they are in prison; isn't music saving them from a life of violence ... ?" Regrettably, music normativity is so deeply embedded in the psyche of the music educator that the "sounding good" values of the conservatory and the school would have succeeded in transmitting skills and knowledge in the prison program. It is my contention, however, that had we simply transplanted the goals and values of the conservatory into the prison environment, we would have missed the opportunity to engage with participants' needs for power and expression. As prison music educators, we have learned much from being open to these students' talents and passions, and we are convinced that our students' learning experiences have also been enriched by the opportunity to learn from one another.

Our artistic and educational explorations from the past several years propel us to present two observations relevant to this book. Our first observation is that the academy largely does not prepare music educators to engage in musical or pedagogical processes outside of conventional primary and secondary school settings; and our second is simply that we, our educator colleagues, and our on-campus students at Boston University have benefitted in ways we could not possibly have anticipated from teaching and learning in this unconventional context. It is these observations that we emphasize. In her introduction to this volume, Iris M. Yob calls us to consider whose interests we serve in our music education practice. As a faculty member in a music education department, I can attest that the focus of music teacher education is almost exclusively on school music, leaving out not only the large number of incarcerated people but also substantial sectors of the dispossessed and marginalized American population. What is arguably more serious is that the focus on school music is perceived by many to prepare teachers adequately for alternative populations and settings. The Empowering Song approach is just one attempt at a solution, but educating teachers to break away from normative practice is essential if they are to work effectively in such settings. The common good is served in unexpected examples of humanity, with Mark's daughter receiving a father's love through song, and with Sharon learning to forgive. Such humane examples are transcendent and affirming results of a humane approach to music education, and the common good will ultimately be served by institutions forsaking the past and focusing on transformational, humanistic elements in music education rather than on the normative.

Disability Aesthetics as a Resource of Artistic and Pedagogical Ingenuity

Andrew Clark

In the preceding portrait, de Quadros pointed to a musico-normativity "embedded in the psyche of the music educator." The construct of normativity continues to be a primary focal point in the interdisciplinary field of disability studies.[23] When considering conventional music education practices through the lens of critical disability theory, we discover both common problematic ableist proclivities, as well as edifying possibilities for reclaiming music's generative role in shaping communities, advancing justice, and contributing to the common good.[24] Here, in response to the call for "multiple learning pathways" in the UNESCO report *Rethinking Education*, I reflect on diverse forms of knowledge encountered through teaching at a program for musicians experiencing disabilities.[25] I then illustrate how my work with musicians in this context continues to provide a rich, reflexive resource for reimagining concepts of music education for the choral program at Harvard University, where I serve as Director of Choral Activities.

Disability aesthetics explores ideals of beauty, meaning, and pleasure through the lens of non-normativity.[26] The late historian and disability advocate Paul Longmore summarizes this paradigm: "Some people with physical disabilities have been affirming the validity of values drawn from their own experience. Those values are markedly different from, and even opposed to, nondisabled majority values. They declare that they prize not self-sufficiency but self-determination, not independence but interdependence, not functional separateness but personal connection, not physical autonomy but human community. This values formation takes disability as the starting point. It uses disability experience as the source of values and norms."[27] Viewing the world from the vantage point of disability has long been a source of inspiration for artists, writers, composers, and others, "a liberating way of shattering conventions and of establishing radically new canons of beauty."[28] Thus it can be for music educators, as well.[29]

For nearly twenty years, I have had the privilege of exploring disability aesthetics with my colleagues and students as a faculty member at the Notes from the Heart music camp run by The Woodlands Foundation, a nonprofit organization near Pittsburgh dedicated to enriching the lives of children and adults with disabilities and chronic illness. The Woodlands' fifty-two-acre site enables participants to experience social, cultural, and recreational activities throughout the year. In 2000, the organization developed the Notes from the Heart music camp, now two weeklong summer programs, one each for children and for adults.

At Notes from the Heart, participants immerse themselves in universally designed[30] activities with daily instrumental, vocal, and music appreciation classes, as well as workshops and performances presented by local artists and ensembles. The week culminates in a concert of high production value curated in part by the participants themselves. This process-oriented work, guided by a commitment to equality and fairness, affirms the four foundational principles of *Rethinking Education:* respect for diversity, respect for human dignity, equal rights, and shared responsibility.[31] In the classroom and in performance, the participants are respected as musicians and given opportunities to showcase their gifts and musical interests and to collectively explore disability as an affirmed and nuanced identity.

Having participated in Notes from the Heart since its inception, I continue to be both enriched and challenged by the experience each year. Though I enjoy the bountiful benefits of my work at Harvard University, the weeks at the Woodlands often provoke a personal existential crisis of vocation. Shaped by a vibrant, creative, and affirming musicking, the experience provides an extraordinary space for reflection, transformation, and pedagogical ingenuity, purpose, and joy, continually prompting a difficult critique of my professional values and notions of musical worth and expertise. Each year, the work at Notes from the Heart cultivates virtues antithetical to my experience in conventional contexts, engendering sincerity, openness, inclusion, and compassion rather than the cynicism, defensiveness, elitism, and competitiveness often found at Harvard and other institutions.

Though one should aim to resist the ableist tropes of both essentializing disability experience and holding up disabled people as "master teachers," critical disability theory encourages us to see the world from the experience and vantage point of disability and to consider this perspective as a resource for broadening our ideas of musical experience and value. Ethnomusicologist Michael Bakan's extensive work in this area offers some fruitful direction in applying aspects of disability studies to community music and music education ventures. He proposes an "ethnographic model of disability," informed by his experience with the ARTISM ensemble in Florida:[32] "My core argument is that musical projects like these hold the capacity to contribute productively and meaningfully to the causes of disability self-advocacy and quality of life, modeling new horizons of possibility for the cultivation of neurodiverse environments of cultural co-creation and self-determination while transforming public perceptions of disability from the customary tropes of deficit, disorder, despair, hopelessness, and awareness to alternate visions of wholeness, ability, diversity, possibility, and acceptance."[33] My experience at the Woodlands has significantly informed my approach in leading the choral program at Harvard. In 2014, a performance and symposium entitled "Beyond the Concert Hall" convened musicians, researchers, and disability advocates in an exploration of the intersections of music and disability, neuroscience, and public health. In both concert and colloquium settings, Harvard's undergraduate mixed chorus, the Collegium Musicum, partnered with Joyful Noise, an ensemble from New Jersey of adults with physical and neurological challenges and acquired brain injuries.

In the months leading up to this event, singers from both the Harvard and Joyful Noise ensembles met to share and develop ideas toward a collective mission for the symposium. Throughout the project, singers from both groups wrestled with critical ethical questions, including how the social model and construct of disability, which defines disability as "culturally stigmatized bodily difference," might problematize standard approaches to community outreach and the efficacy of various interventions associated with the deficit-based medical model of disability, including music therapy.[34]

Eager to build upon this work, my colleague Jennifer Zuk and I developed a seminar entitled Music and Disability in the spring of 2015, the

Harvard Music Department's first course designed with Engaged Scholarship learning principles.[35] Through fieldwork, readings, discussions, and presentations, the course explores the emerging Music and Disability Studies literature and reflects on music's role in shaping communities and advancing social justice. Students design and implement inclusive and democratic community music projects while learning from local service organizations and experienced professionals in the field.

In the fall of 2016, the Harvard choruses applied aspects of the Woodlands' participant-curated concert model in a program entitled "One Music." Just as Notes from the Heart encourages participants to suggest themes, texts, songs, and staging, the Harvard singers selected and performed an eclectic array of works, including their own compositions, and worked collaboratively in creating a dramatic trajectory for a program that celebrated the diversity of their musical lives and the common bonds of their shared humanity.

Frequently, Notes from the Heart participants seek to alter perceptions of disability while advancing visions of possibility and acceptance through their performances. When given the platform of a concert, it is common for Woodlands' musicians to explicitly reject regimes of normalization, demand the right of self-representation, and challenge audiences with intersectional disability justice issues related to poverty, sexuality, and race. Emboldened by this example, the Harvard choruses have also aspired to advance social justice through performance in recent years. Concert projects have illuminated painful racist legacies of Harvard's own history, shared the stories of senseless hate crimes (Craig Hella Johnson's *Considering Matthew Shepard*), the enduring trauma of the Armenian genocide (Tigran Mansurian's *Requiem*), and the harrowing evils of scapegoating (Michael Tippett's *A Child of Our Time*), all relevant to contemporary societal challenges raised in *Rethinking Education*. Canonic masterworks have been recontextualized (such as advancing social justice causes as "period performance" in raising funds at a presentation of *Messiah* for a new homeless shelter, just as Handel did in his lifetime) and tours are planned with greater intention to promote cultural understanding and human rights.

Values and perspectives drawn from non-normative musicking contexts provide a rich resource for reclaiming music education for the common good. Around the world, compelling exemplars in community settings, particularly among the marginalized, insist on a music education practice rooted in respect for diversity, human dignity, social justice, and solidarity.

The Good(?) of a Community Partnership in
Secondary General Music Methods

Kinh T. Vu

In this section, I investigate "common good" as it is applied to curricular internationalization of a secondary general music methods class. This unit caused students to question the degree to which support (and possibly empathy) might be offered to a Cambodian woman, Chantrea, who is at risk of losing her house due to forced eviction.[36] On one level, this project had the potential to be and/or to do good, because students experienced how a song-writing project might be applied to secondary general music instruction, while Chantrea received audio and video recordings, photos, and stories to share with friends in her community. After having completed the course, however, I question the assumption that what might be good for the class (that is, expanding ideas about general music pedagogy) is conceivably good or even appropriate for our partner in Cambodia.

Internationalizing the curriculum is an important aspect of broadening students' worldviews by acting to "facilitate a knowledge base, skills and attitudes among students that prepare them for work and leadership in the context of global interdependence."[37] According to the Longview Foundation, "Students in the United States, especially those in low-income and minority communities, leave high school without the knowledge and skills to engage in the world effectively and responsibly."[38] While there is a diversity of views and experiences represented in the class, the extent to which students read others' worlds, rather than just words, is limited.[39] As a way to facilitate a widened gaze as well as action in the world, I designed the spring 2017 iteration of the course to incorporate a song-writing project in which students planned, composed, improvised, and produced original music for Chantrea and her neighbors.

Specific to music education, I recognize how internationalization can be realized in universities or study abroad settings. For example, Kathy Robinson created a model of choir teacher summer professional development in South Africa, while Akosua Addo implemented on-campus internationalizing strategies in elementary general music methods.[40] Jeremy Cohen, founder of ThisWorldMusic, "partner[ed] with educational institutions and arts organizations to offer hands-on cultural learning experiences" with musicians and dancers in Ghana and Cuba as a way to "create cultural bridges between people and communities."[41] At The First International

Music Education Conference of the Israel Philharmonic Orchestra in 2017, Yuval Dvir reported on two music universities that sought to diversify their curricula via an "ongoing international educational collaboration."[42] While these projects may not necessarily be exemplars, it seems that there is room for exploration when it comes to internationalization of music education curricula.

Approaches such as these to internationalizing music teacher education curricula are not standard; however, any effort might indicate that a "counterhegemonic educational process that occurs in an international context of knowledge and practice" is necessary to question standard-issue general music practices and simultaneously imagine non-normative curricula that will expand the range of music-making possibilities available to all learners.[43] It is not within the scope of this chapter to explore the gamut of curricular choices available to music teachers; however, the songwriting project designed in consultation with community partner Chantrea, a colleague from a Virginia university, and my students demonstrates an alternative possibility for general music instruction at middle and secondary levels.

Inspired by a fifth-grade classroom teacher in the Boston metro area who creates original songs with his students during a poetry-writing unit, I asked my preservice teachers to compose songs, each with instrumental and vocal tracks that share stories of home and the power of women. In the following sample, students wrote about a powerful woman including as their last four lines text from Maya Angelou's poem "Phenomenal Woman." This theme is not unique to Chantrea, yet links her personhood to the strength of women around the world:

> Our mothers and our sisters,
> Standin' hand-in hand, it's alright, it's alright.
> Ours aunts and our grandmothers,
> Standin' side-by-side, they build us up, they build us up.
> I [am] a woman
> Phenomenally.
> Phenomenal woman.
> That's me.[44]

Despite the heartfelt musical process and products, the class wrestled with the goodness of their work, calling into question how their gesture of solidarity might be an act of appropriation. Students' concerns centered on the uses of English language, Western European harmony, and instrumentation (such as ukuleles, violas, and flutes). More important than these logistical concerns was how the class risked appropriating Chantrea's story for their own purposes of developing a music education toolkit and ceding the ground with an aspect of what Beckles Willson described as settler colonialism.[45] Additionally, I experience(d) unease centered on how a social contract between my class and the partner was conceived. Had I truly fostered the common good of the curriculum to the advantage of learners and our partner, the project would have embraced diversity within the class, engaged our global partner in the intimate details of the project, and dedicated more time to seriously understanding the topic of land rights in a far-off land "equally to everyone's advantage."[46]

Mindful of these issues, I argue that critical pedagogical practices nevertheless lived within the song project. Students named important issues salient to Chantrea's community, reflected on how land grabs might affect Chantrea and even themselves, and acted by making music for the benefit of a world community partner.[47] The emergent goodness that is common to us all, class and partner, may be manifested only in the way the song project connected students to each other, to Chantrea, and to the problem of structural and personal violence in Cambodia.[48] As Betty Anne Younker suggests in her chapter, an arts education has power to "nurture human potential to imagine."[49] While this curricular strand neither fully addressed the serious political issues nor alleviated the suffering encountered by Chantrea and her neighbors, the music that emerged from the class was more than songs; it was a "heartwork" that imagined a promising way forward in preservice teacher education.

Conclusion

The UNESCO report offers a compelling philosophical rationale and vision for a radical rethinking of the goals and outcomes of education for the common good, but it leaves educators with few practical means of bringing this vision to life. We have argued that a sonic approach to the document enables us to *hear* a way forward: a way premised on listening, mutual learning, and creative expression. We believe that the discipline of music education, with its focus on the sonic, is perhaps uniquely suited to the task of reimagining humane education for the common good in the twenty-first century. We also believe that living into the promise of humane music education for the common good will require a radical shift in the way music educators are trained and music is taught; a shift toward understanding and celebrating diverse forms of knowledge production and preparing music educators to engage deeply and reflectively with music that is meaningful to students in their particular pedagogical context.

What might a teacher training program look like where the focus is not on producing educators capable of reproducing the normative values of the academy in diverse contexts but on producing educators capable of discerning and responding to the needs of the diverse communities in which they will work? What kind of music might emerge from a music education curriculum focused on cultivating the common good rather than on cultivating "good" music? In this chapter, we hope to have provided some insights into these questions by sharing our personal experiences leading programs that stretch beyond the contexts in which we have been trained to teach. These experiences have challenged us as educators, at times causing us to question our own values, priorities, and biases. But ultimately, these experiences have been deeply gratifying and transformative for us and for our students, and we believe they have led us at least closer to a common good.

We close with a brief music educator's meditation: may we always listen and learn as thoughtfully and carefully as we lecture and teach. May we continually interrogate and reimagine our best practices, for best practices may not be best in all contexts and for all time. May we always seek and serve the common good. And may we never stop being tuned.

EMILY HOWE is a PhD candidate in ethnomusicology at Boston University, Massachusetts.

ANDRÉ DE QUADROS is Professor of Music and Chair of Music Education at Boston University, Massachusetts. He is author of *Choral Music in Global Perspective*.

ANDREW CLARK is Director of Choral Activities and Senior Lecturer on Music at Harvard University, Massachusetts.

KINH T. VU is Assistant Professor of Music at Boston University, Massachusetts.

Notes

1. Robert Fludd, *De Musica Mundana* (1618), published in Fludd, *Ultriusque Cosmi Maioris Scilicet et Minoris Metaphysica, Physica atque Technical Historia: in Duo Volumina Secundum Cosmi Differentiam Diuisa* (Oppenheim: Theodore de Bry 1617–1624).

2. See Geoffrey Baker, *Imposing Harmony: Music and Society in Colonial Cuzco* (Durham, NC: Duke University Press, 2008); and Kofi Agawu, "Tonality as a Colonizing Force in Africa," in *Audible Empire: Music, Global Politics, Culture*, ed. Ronald Radano and Tejumola Olaniyan (Durham, NC: Duke University Press, 2016), for two striking accounts of music as a tool for the exercise of colonial power in Peru and in various African countries, respectively. For an ethnography and critique of the El Sistema program in Venezuela, see Geoffrey Baker, *El Sistema: Orchestrating Venezuela's Youth* (Oxford: Oxford University Press, 2014). For an ethnographic account of recent initiatives by European music educators to teach music in Palestine, see Rachel Beckles Willson, *Orientalism and Musical Mission: Palestine and the West* (New York: Cambridge University Press, 2013).

3. For a critique of Eurocentrism in music education, see Emily Good-Perkins, "Rethinking Vocal Education as a Means to Encourage Positive Identity Development in Adolescents," in this collection.

4. Beckles Willson, *Orientalism and Musical Mission*.

5. This metaphor of "tuning" resonates with the discussion of hospitality presented in Jacob Axel Berglin and Thomas Murphy O'Hara, "Working with Transgender Students as a Humane Act: Hospitality in Research and in Practice," in this collection.

6. UNESCO, *Rethinking Education: Towards a Global Common Good?* (Paris: UNESCO, 2015), http://unesdoc.unesco.org/images/0023/002325/232555e.pdf.

7. The UNESCO report takes its definition of the "common good" from Séverine Deneulin and Nicholas Townsend, "Public Goods, Global Public Goods, and the Common Good," *International Journal of Social Economics* 34, no. 1–2 (2007): 19–36.

8. The report's authors discuss *sumak kawsay* as an Andean concept of good living that has been adopted into the constitutions of Ecuador and Bolivia as an alternative to teleological notions of development promulgated by the global North. UNESCO, *Rethinking Education*, 31.

9. UNESCO, *Rethinking Education*, 77.

10. See Paulo Freire, *Pedagogy of the Oppressed* (New York: Continuum International, 2012), for a critique of what he calls the "banking model" of education. Freire and other critical pedagogues call for a move away from forms of education premised on the notion that the student is a container to be filled with information by the teacher.

11. In a related discussion, McConnell and Laird frame issues of access to music in terms of "musical hunger." See Johnnie-Margaret McConnell and Susan Laird, "Nourishing the Musically Hungry: Leaning from Undergraduate Amateur Musicking," in this collection.

12. For an analysis of this "core narrative" of music education, see Sandra Stauffer, "Another Perspective: Re-Placing Music Education," *Music Educators Journal* 102, no. 4 (June 2016): 71–76.

13. PEW Center on the States, *One in 100: Behind Bars in America 2008* (Washington, DC: PEW Center, 2008), 5.

14. "One in 34 Adults under Correctional Supervision in 2011," Bureau of Justice Statistics, accessed August 18, 2017, http://www.bjs.gov/content/pub/press/cpus11ppus11pr.cfm.

15. Ken Elpus and Carlos Abril, "High School Music Ensemble Students in the United States: A Demographic Profile," *Journal of Research in Music Education* 59, no. 2, (2011): 128–45. Elpus and Abril reported 621,895 high school seniors in band, orchestra, or choir in 2004.

16. For an introduction to and overview of music and music teaching in prisons, see "Criminal Justice and Music," ed. Mary Cohen, special issue, *International Journal of Community Music* 3, no. 1 (2010).

17. Trey Pratt joined the team of musical leaders much later. The other two coauthors, Clark and Vu, are regular collaborators in the prison music.

18. UNESCO, *Rethinking Education*, 37.

19. Ibid., 41.

20. Ibid., 42.

21. Ibid., 47.

22. Throughout this chapter, we have used pseudonyms for our interlocutors in an effort to preserve their privacy.

23. Leonard J. Davis, *Enforcing Normalcy: Disability, Deafness and the Body* (New York: Verso, 1995).

24. Thomas Hehir, "Eliminating Ableism in Education," *Harvard Educational Review* 72, no. 1 (2002): 1–32; Kay Kaufman Shelemay, "Musical Communities: Rethinking the Collective in Music," *Journal of the American Musicological Society* 64, no. 2 (2011): 349–390.

25. UNESCO, *Rethinking Education*, 64.

26. Pioneering work in this field was developed by the late Tobin Siebers in his monograph *Disability Aesthetics* (Ann Arbor, MI: University of Michigan Press, 2010).

27. Paul Longmore, *Why I Burned My Book and Other Essays on Disability* (Philadelphia: Temple University Press, 2003).

28. Joseph Straus, "On the Disability Aesthetics of Music," *Journal of the American Musicological Society* 69, no. 2 (2016): 532.

29. For an account of one such project, see Luca Tiszai, "Friendship, Solidarity, and Mutuality Discovered in Music," in this collection.

30. Universal Design for Learning (UDL) is an educational framework based on research in the learning sciences, including cognitive neuroscience, that guides the development of flexible learning environments that can accommodate individual learning differences.

31. UNESCO, *Rethinking Education*.

32. The ARTISM (Autism: Responding Together in Sound and Movement) Ensemble is a music program for children on the autism spectrum and their families at Florida State University.

33. Michael Bakan, "Toward an Ethnographic Model of Disability in the Ethnomusicology of Autism," in *The Oxford Handbook of Music and Disability Studies*, ed. Blake Howe, Stephanie Jensen-Moulton, Neil William Lerner, and Joseph Nathan Straus (Oxford: Oxford University Press, 2016).

34. Straus, "Disability Aesthetics of Music," 9.

35. Informed by experiential and service-learning pedagogical theory, the Mindich Engaged Scholarship program at Harvard University integrates academics, public service, and community engagement, linking coursework to real-world questions, problems, and opportunities.

36. Chantrea is a community activist living in a slum district in Phnom Penh, Cambodia. The situation that haunts her community is the flooding of a large lake with sand in 2009 that consequently (and forcibly) displaced thousands of residents in order to make room for malls and upscale housing.

37. Dilys Schoorman, "What Really Do We Mean by 'Internationalization'?," *Contemporary Education* 71, no. 4 (Jan. 1, 2000): 5, http://search.proquest.com/docview /1291789803?pq-origsite=gscholar.

38. Betsy Devlin-Foltz and Stevenson McIlvaine, "Teacher Preparation for the Global Age: The Imperative for Change," Longview Foundation, last modified February 2008, http://www .longviewfdn.org/programs/internationalizing-teacher-prep/.

39. Freire, *Pedagogy of the Oppressed.*

40. Kathy Robinson, "Professional Development in the Diamond Fields of South Africa: Musical and Personal Transformations," in *Cultural Diversity in Music Education*, ed. Patricia Shehan Campbell (Bowen Hills: Australian Academic Press, 2005); Akosua Obuo Addo, "Toward Internationalizing General Music Teacher Education in a U.S. Context," *Journal of Research in International Education* 8, no. 3 (2009).

41. "ThisWorldMusic," accessed August 23, 2017, https://thisworldmusic.com/organization-overview/.

42. Yuval Dvir, "Internationalization in Music Education in an Era of Globalization: The Kestenberg Collaboration Case Study," accessed August 26, 2017, https://events.eventact.com/ProgramView2/Agenda/Lecture?id=139919&code=2456958.

43. Schoorman, "What Really Do We Mean," 5; Ann C. Clements, *Alternative Approaches in Music Education: Case Studies from the Field* (Lanham, MD: Rowman and Littlefield, 2010).

44. Maya Angelou, "Phenomenal Woman," in *The Complete Collected Poems of Maya Angelou,* (New York: Random House, 1994), 130.

45. For a description of settler colonialism, see Beckles Willson, *Orientalism and Musical Mission*, 23.

46. Claire Andre and Manuel Velasquez, "The Common Good," *Issues in Ethics* 5, no. 1 (1992), https://legacy.scu.edu/ethics/publications/iie/v5n1/common.html, para. 3.

47. Joan Wink, *Critical Pedagogy: Notes from the Real World*, 4th ed. (Boston: Pearson, 2011), 9.

48. Johan Galtung, "Violence, Peace, and Peace Research," *Journal of Peace Research* 6, no. 3 (1969): 170.

49. Betty Anne Younker, "Inquiry-Based Learning: A Value for Music Education with Aims to Cultivate a Humane Society," in this collection.

9

NAVIGATING MUSIC TEACHER EDUCATION TOWARD HUMANE ENDS

Joseph Shively

THE UNESCO DOCUMENT THAT INSPIRED THIS COLLECTION OF essays reflects on the four pillars of learning first discussed in the 1996 Delors report and reintroduced in *Rethinking Education: Towards a Global Common Good?*[1] Beyond the pillars "learning to know" and "learning to do," "learning to be" and "learning to live together" are fundamental to rethinking music education toward humane ends.[2] *Rethinking Education* reexamines these four pillars and acknowledges they are "under threat in the context of current societal challenges, particularly the pillars of learning to be and learning to live together, which best reflect the socialization function of education. The strengthening of ethical principles and values in the process of learning is essential to protecting these pillars of a humanistic vision of education."[3] That is, the writers of the UNESCO documents argue that the pillars of learning to be and learning to live together are fundamental to education, regardless of what students are asked to know and do.

Teacher education plays an important role in promoting humane ends.[4] *Rethinking Education*, recognizing the importance of teachers, speaks to teacher education and the necessity to prepare teachers "to facilitate learning, to understand diversity, to be inclusive, and to develop competencies for living together," while using "a wide range of pedagogical and didactic strategies."[5] To this end, current practice in music teacher education might move beyond focusing on pedagogies and methods that privilege learning to know and do. It raises questions about how we might intentionally foster dispositions in music educators that lead to a more humane approach to music education, one that places learning to be and learning to live together at the center of the music teacher education curriculum. While the focus here is on music teacher education, the reader might also consider how this effort in music teacher education might influence the practice of those music educators once they move from preservice to in-service. Music educators will need to support their students' efforts to learn to be and live together.[6]

I turned to writers who have addressed broad issues that might inform efforts toward a more humane approach to music education. Writers such as Gloria Ladson-Billings, Maxine Greene, Nel Noddings, Parker Palmer, and Max van Manen ask important questions that reflect the intersection of education with what it means to be in today's world. These thinkers, each in his or her way, have also been calling for refocusing education on learning to be and learning to live together. Further, their ideas connect to the potential for more humane music education.

Because of postmodern influences on the UNESCO report, the implications of constructivism run throughout this document. Constructivism, as a basis for learning and teaching, values meaning making through authentic experiences reflecting multiple perspectives.[7] While I am a proponent of taking a constructivist stance, the ideas in the UNESCO documents exceed the range of any single pedagogical approach. Perhaps more than a constructivist stance, the ideas discussed in these publications are about taking a caring and loving stance—for students first and subject second. Careful consideration of stance is particularly critical during an era where many are challenging traditional practices in music education and recommending significant changes to what is learned and how it is learned. Music educators might benefit from a mind-set that guides what it means to teach toward a humane end that is resonant with the learners in their specific teaching settings. Current reform efforts call on us to acknowledge that "none of that will transform education if we fail to cherish—and challenge—the human heart that is the source of good teaching."[8] The development of a heart that is central to a teaching self should be a primary goal for all music teacher educators.

Music Teacher Education: More Than Methods

Taking a loving and caring stance asks a great deal of the music teacher and, therefore, of that teacher's education. Music education methods courses have long held a central place in the music teacher education curriculum, emphasizing the development of specific teaching techniques. However, *"good teaching cannot be reduced to technique; good teaching comes from the identity and integrity of the teacher."*[9] There are important questions for music teacher educators to consider: How might music teacher education foster the identity and integrity of the music educator? What are the struggles with identity in music teacher education, and how might we foster integrity? Considering this from the beginning of a music teacher education program is critical because, for many music educators, method or area is their teacher identity. It is not unusual to hear music teachers describe themselves as Orff or Kodály teachers or choir or band directors. Establishing a broader sense of identity and integrity as a music educator rather than as the teacher of a method or a director limited to a role as a specific ensemble might expand the possibilities for a more open, humane approach that places the needs of the students at the center of teacher decision-making. If this is a goal of music teacher education, it should be established at the outset of the curriculum.

Students enter music teacher education programs with highly developed beliefs about what it means to be a music teacher based on prior experience with their teachers. The "apprenticeship of observation" that they have served and continue to serve is a powerful one.[10] What they think they know about teaching from their time spent in classrooms as students can also limit their identity to that of their teachers. The initial coursework in music education should focus on establishing space for examining prior experience and traversing to future experience in a manner that maintains a broader view. I have approached this by attempting to unpack prior experiences, but I think it has too often centered on moving quickly to establishing a pedagogically specific stance in preparation for methods courses. Time should be taken and space should be made early in and throughout the music education curriculum to consider how prior experiences have already shaped identity and integrity. Intentional time and space will help our music education majors begin constructing a sense of who they truly are and how that shapes who they hope to be as music educators. We cannot begin to explore how they will teach until they have intentionally expressed who they are and hope to be as teachers. Further, we must do the same for ourselves and share this with those we are guiding toward a career in music education.

It is a matter not only of how we initially engage music education majors but also of how we guide them throughout their undergraduate education

into their careers. Non-methods experiences, whether in stand-alone courses or within other courses, should frame methods courses because using
methods courses as the central curriculum in music teacher education limits the development of teacher identity. These experiences should include
opportunities to use foundational, curricular, philosophical, psychological, and sociological lenses for exploring the profession. We cannot teach it
all and what constitutes professional knowledge in our field continues to
grow and change, so we should shift toward establishing a critical practice
to support meaningful and continual professional growth. I might go as far
as to recommend placing methods within broader music education courses
in an effort to break down the limiting nature of methods courses.

Connectedness

Approaches to learning and teaching, regardless of their pedagogical
grounding, are dependent on establishing connectedness in the classroom.
"The connections made by good teachers are held not in their methods but
in their heart—meaning "heart" in its ancient sense as the place where intellect and emotion and spirit and will converge in the human self."[11]

Connectedness in music education, whether in preservice or pre K–12
music education, is both reflective of the school classroom and of music
itself. Music education majors need opportunities to connect to one another, sharing stories of who they are and who they aspire to become. We,
as music teacher educators, need to share our stories as well.

Naturally occurring communities in music education, be they large
ensembles or performer and audience in a song-writing class, can serve as
points of connection to students' past and present experiences, providing
touch points for how our students are both in the moment and looking
toward the future—who they are learning to be by how they are learning
to live together. This should extend to how we think about learning in all
musical contexts. In this, we might strive to move past musical independence toward musical interdependence—the need to "learn to live together"
musically.

Caring

The care any educator demonstrates supports the processes of learning to be
and learning to live together. However, assumptions are often made about
the caring nature of teachers. "It is sometimes said that 'all teachers care.' It

is because they care that people go into teaching. However, this is not universally true; we all have known teachers who are cruel and uncaring and these people should not be in teaching at all."[12] Noddings recognizes that even teachers seen as caring prioritize students meeting goals over establishing care for their students as people. This is in juxtaposition to the vision that educators already possess innate goodness that has "called them" to teach or to the belief that teaching with a caring stance is something we add after solidifying teaching skills, if at all. This latter path is contrary to what will foster a stance that has the greatest potential to advance a humane music education practice, because establishing the importance of a caring teacher stance from the beginning may greatly alter how music education majors experience their development.

Theories about learning and teaching become meaningful when we have established a framework for caring. "The living other is more important than any theory, This is a central idea in an ethic of care."[13] In this, we see how to approach the learners in our classrooms. While it may seem antithetical to say this, we need to shift the mind-set from learner centered to learning centered.[14] "Learner centered" is too tied to a limiting definition of constructivism, as it reflects a pedagogical approach that can put too much emphasis on the learner as the source of all decision-making and what and how to learn, while "learning centered" allows for greater flexibility in how to best approach learning-teaching experiences. This reflects the idea of taking a teaching stance rather than adhering to a method.

Humane approaches to music teacher education are predicated on caring for our students above all else. One way of demonstrating this care is to constantly ask if we are best preparing them for their teaching positions. For example, I think we should ask ourselves to what extent we saddle our students with the responsibility for effecting change within the broader profession. This is not an antireform position, but rather a reminder to prepare our students for the jobs they will have along with the jobs we want them to have. It is one thing to question traditional school offerings such as band, choir, or orchestra, but it is an entirely different matter to approach their preparation to teach music as if schools and communities will not have expectations about the inclusion of traditional ensembles. Further, preparing our students to teach these ensembles with a caring stance may lead to change in how these ensembles are taught. From there, the expansion of music teacher education curricula to include a wider range of musical practices might best be considered.

Developing a Pedagogical Frame

The need for music education majors to learn what to teach and how to teach will always be crucial within the music teacher education curriculum. However, we should examine what influences music teacher educators in their pedagogical decision-making. Our efforts to guide music education majors from student to teacher should not be methods based. Even if introductory courses revolve around larger questions, we should carefully consider both the questions themselves and whether we present the process as preparing one for methods experiences. I know for myself that I have perhaps attempted to move too quickly past an opening experience of considering what makes a good music educator in an effort to shift the discussion away from the personal qualities that my students tend to value disproportionally. Creating a fertile context for the consideration of pedagogical or methodological differences and how these differences may or may not reflect a more caring stance is critical throughout the music teacher education program.

We all have strong beliefs about what future music educators should know and be able to do when they graduate. However, we should consider the extent to which we are simultaneously championing their need to be responsive to the students they teach while being prescriptive about the path they take to the profession, potentially ignoring their needs. This can be demonstrated in our pedagogical approach and in whether music education majors are provided the opportunity to experience and apply a broad range of pedagogical approaches.

Pedagogy, itself, is a term that is so common in our educational vocabulary that perhaps we used it without critical examination. Max van Manen and Noddings offer useful ways of thinking more deeply about it. In exploring pedagogical tact, van Manen reminds us, "Pedagogy is primarily neither a science or technology." Further, he declares, "Pedagogical tact needs to possess an inspirational quality together with a narrative structure that invites critical reflection and possibilities for insight and that leads to a personal appropriation of a moral intuition." He concludes, "It is possible to learn all the technique of instruction but to remain pedagogically unfit as a teacher."[15] He reminds us that pedagogical knowledge is insufficient, supporting the case for refocusing music teacher education programs.

In addressing pedagogical treasure, Noddings also challenges us to move beyond our pedagogical stance. In valuing behaviorist approaches in addition to constructivist perspectives, she recognizes the necessity for teaching certain skills via lessons with learning objectives. She counters, "Committed constructivists sometimes reject such lessons and, especially, anything that calls for *drill*; 'drill and kill' is to be avoided."[16] However, Noddings reflects further on the wealth of literature that supports the use of practice, particularly in support of more complex endeavors. This is useful because there is confusion about the nature of "drill" in the education of musical performers. As she recognizes, meaningful practice is critical to development. However, some critiques of performance-based music education attack musical practices such as playing scales as being atomistic. It is not the scales themselves that are problematic, but rather how our students apply their ability to play and understand scales. Thinking more carefully about what is taught and how it is being taught recognizes student needs.

A guiding disposition for music teacher educators' pedagogical consideration should be responsiveness to their students.[17] While the focus of Gloria Ladson-Billings's work has been on African American students, the principles of culturally relevant, responsive pedagogy inform how we might best engage each of our students, as they come to us with cultural connections both obvious and not so obvious. Culturally relevant teaching provides a pedagogical stance that serves as the basis for a caring teaching practice and offers flexibility in approaching a range of teaching situations. Teachers with culturally relevant practices have high self-esteem and high regard for others; see themselves as part of the community; see teaching as giving back to the community and encourage their students to do the same; see teaching as an art and themselves as artists; believe all students can succeed; help students make connections to their community, national, and global identities; and see teaching as "digging knowledge out" of students.[18] These are characteristics of teachers who place their students' needs first.

Responsiveness to the culture of the musical experiences our students bring to music teacher education programs is critical. Beyond the broader cultural considerations of educators, we should also consider learners' musical cultures, be they the music they most value or the musical experiences they have had both inside and outside of school. Care should be taken to not dismiss their music education cultural touch points when they don't align with our views. In rejecting the music our students value, we build barriers to a fertile learning environment and harm the learners, destroying the potential to foster dispositions toward humane approaches.

Reform and Educating toward Humane Ends

Music education reform efforts focused on what might be best for the children we teach, not on our ability to rationalize the approach we favor, be it traditional or progressive, are most likely to resonate with music educators. I have been in the classrooms of music educators who incorporate a range of pedagogical approaches while expressing love and care for their students through word and action. In some settings, this might be through a songwriting course that is student-centered in its orientation, and for others it might be in an ensemble community with a teacher-conductor seeking to provide an experience where those students perform at the very highest level. We do not know what is best for any specific group of students until we actually know those students and how they are learning to be and to live together.

Living together is not always living in agreement. This is even the case in questions that arise about music teacher education. How does our approach as teachers bring legitimacy to the consideration of multiple perspectives? How do we foster this in music education? Do we honestly consider multiple perspectives about music and music learning in our music education courses? While a proponent of constructivist approaches, I have to ask myself if this means I am closed to teaching approaches that conflict with what I believe about music learning and teaching. Do we value multiple perspectives as long as I accept the correct one? As many of us moved to some form of constructivist or student-centered learning, have we replaced one dominating pedagogical paradigm for another? Even this form of "methodolatry" in our methods courses and other music education courses creates an environment where we do not consider multiple perspectives about learning and teaching music.[19]

We can model reform that puts the needs of the learner in the forefront by breaking with tradition and creating music teacher programs that emphasize critical professional preparation. Again, this is not to say that methods are unimportant. To the contrary, music teachers need what they learn in these courses. However, the questions come in how these methods are deployed in classroom settings. The term *deployment* suggests methods packaged for consumption. We must ask to what extent methods grounded in constructivist approaches have objectivist roots—multiple perspectives as long as constructivism is the right one. "If we stopped lobbing pedagogical points at each other and spoke about *who we are* as teachers, a remarkable thing might happen: identity and integrity might grow within us and among us, instead of hardening as they do when we defend our fixed positions in the foxholes of the pedagogy wars."[20]

In music education, the points we lob are about both method and content, and many of these conversations are about relevance. When we hear the term *relevant* in a conversation about what we teach and how we teach it, we need to ask whether the unspoken intention is to make the case that something has been identified as not relevant. If modern band is relevant, then is traditional band not relevant? This is not to say that the conversations about what we teach and how we teach it are unimportant. Rather, these conversations might be more meaningful and, frankly, more productive if we approached them from positions that reflected recognition of who we are as music educators. "While I understand reform efforts are intended to challenge the status quo in music education, we should distinguish examining and questioning the status quo from attacking it. Even if the intent is not to attack, we must recognize the natural human response to having what one loves and has dedicated one's life to called into question. That response is likely to lead to a defensive posture, which is, at best, unproductive."[21] That which is in the best interest of the child should take precedence—certainly, a single approach is potentially problematic, as all students do not need the same pedagogy. It is fascinating that a constructive pedagogy built on multiple perspectives allows for only one way to learn and teach. Music education is imperfect, and by this I do not mean the parts of music education with which I disagree are imperfect and those that I might champion are superior. Acknowledging the flaws in our world is critical to establishing a genuine environment in which music education majors might come face-to-face with "our shadows and limits, our wounds and fears."[22]

Regardless of the music teacher education curriculum we seek to implement, we must consider the perspective of future music educators in our courses, keeping in mind our students come to us with what are, in their minds, clear goals about what they need to be able to do to enter the profession. "All teachers need to remember that exposing students to a well-thought-out curriculum is not the same thing as educating them, if educating them means, as I think it does, helping them learn how to integrate the contents of the curriculum into their minds, hearts, and everyday lives."[23] Music teacher educators can model this from the beginning of course work by establishing connections among all in the classroom with the musical experiences of their lives and with a broader sense of what it means to be in the world.

The Potential of Music to Foster Humane Ends: An Example

We should not shy away from the capacity of music to mediate the processes of learning to be and learning to live together. Through rehearsing and conducting Aldophus Hailstork's *American Guernica* with our university wind symphony, I considered how we might foster a sense of good in a traditional band setting. This work explores the 1963 bombing of the 16th Street Baptist Church in Birmingham, Alabama, in which four young women were murdered. Our study of this composition included learning about the event and considering how Hailstork encourages us to think about this heinous act. I believe this musical experience touched us all bringing us closer to a world where we all might live together. Through our immersion into an artistic meditation on such an inhumane act, I believe we found together that music, even in a tradition-bound performance setting such as the concert band, has the potential to illuminate what it means to learn to be and to learn to live together.

On the first day of rehearsal, I projected the pictures of the victims, Addie Mae Collins, Carol Robertson, Cynthia Wesley, all age 14, and Denise McNair, age 11, onto a screen in our rehearsal space. Every moment of rehearsing and performing this work placed us in a sonic space for us to reflect on the horror and outrage, as well as the grief and faith that surrounded this heinous attack.[24] I offer this example of how, in a traditional ensemble, our understanding of self and one another might be revealed. "Creating conditions under which students can conduct an inner search does not mean dictating answers to inner-life questions, which by definition do not have answers in any conventional sense. It means helping students learn how to ask questions that are worth asking because they are worth living, questions one can fruitfully hold at the center of one's life."[25] The search was taken together, with me as conductor along with an ensemble of university musicians, to live together and to be with those young women, giving them a voice at a time when their voices are desperately needed.

Conclusion

We might seek to bring music teacher education to the fullness of life, immersing our students in transformative experiences that will sustain them through their degree programs and beyond. Both the emphasis on and sheer quantity of methods courses in music teacher education curricula should be reconsidered. It is not that methods are unimportant, but rather that they might serve best as tools for shaping music educators as they place "learning to be" and "learning to live together" at the center of their professional and personal identities. Further, methods should not be structured to reinforce music teacher identities that are grounded in a method, hence my call to consider placing methods content in broader music education courses.

Keeping preservice music educators connected to the joy of the musical experience is also critical, particularly as communities learning to live together. "Teachers concerned about illumination and possibility know well that there is some profound sense in which a curriculum in the making is very much a part of a community in the making."[26] Music education provides a powerful medium for examining what it means to be human, and in this understanding of our humanity, for good and for bad, we advance ourselves. This calls us also to continue to expand the range of musical experiences that future music educators have during their preparation and that they are ready to teach. I think this would lead early-career music educators to be more open to new possibilities. This is not a call to shift away from traditional experiences, but rather to rethink them and to add new experiences, such as modern band or song writing.

Fostering humanity through music education is not dependent on one approach or another. It depends on the ethos of the learning environment. For one, it might be helpful if music teacher educators were not so certain about the right way to teach. Introductory experiences in music education, whether dedicated courses, components of other music education courses, or stand-alone experiences, are rich environments for establishing these dispositions. We need to challenge preservice music educators to examine their backgrounds, as they have a great deal to do with why they have come to music education as a major. However, there needs to be depth to this experience. Do not mistake my hope for a belief that this is a simple process. However, it does grow from a desire to continue to grow as a profession—a desire that emanates from a love of those I teach and the medium in which we work—music. Music education courses need to be spaces for future music educators to consider who they are and who they are becoming and what it means for their future. We might do well to start their journey by reaching out to our students and engaging their imaginations about the future of music within education. This is a future that connects back to their past, connects to their present, and looks forward with their teacher and colleagues navigating an ever-changing sense of self. Maxine Greene reminds us, "There are, of course, thousands of silenced voices still; there are thousands of beings striving for visibility; there are thousands of interpretations still to be made, thousands of questions to be posed."[27] If we respond to her call as we engage future music teachers in our courses, our efforts to learn to be and to learn to live together will help us navigate toward being more humane music educators.

JOSEPH SHIVELY is Associate Professor of Music and Interim Associate Dean of the College of Arts and Sciences at Oakland University, Michigan.

Notes

1. UNESCO, *Learning: The Treasure Within* (Paris: UNESCO, 1996), https://unesdoc.unesco.org/ark:/48223/pf0000109590, commonly referred to as the Delors report; UNESCO, *Rethinking Education: Towards a Global Common Good?* (Paris: UNESCO, 2015), https://unesdoc.unesco.org/ark:/48223/pf0000232555.

2. UNESCO, *Rethinking Education*, 39.

3. Ibid., 40.

4. Ibid., 78. One limitation of the UNESCO document can be seen in the discussion of knowledge as a good to be acquired, perhaps reflecting a more objectivist epistemological base. Because I take a constructivist stance, I focus on the diversity of humane ends rather than a common good. The idea of a common good can be incompatible with valuing multiple perspectives unless the "diverse cultural interpretations of what constitutes a common good" (ibid.) are considered along with the idea that diversity will most likely result in a range of interpretations or perspectives. Seeking to foster a common good has the potential to establish a dominant knowledge. However, an approach to music education that connects to a sense of diverse meaning making is more humane, allowing for a range of perspectives on what we seek in music education and music teacher education.

5. Ibid., 55.

6. Blakeley Menghini, "Rethinking Education: The Four Pillars of Education in the Suzuki Studio," in this collection, addresses this need (for example).

7. I have written about constructivism in several settings, with an emphasis on implications for performance-based music education. See, for example, Joseph Shively, "Constructivism in Music Education," *Arts Education Policy Review* 116, no. 3 (2015): 128–136, for a detailed discussion.

8. Parker Palmer, *The Courage to Teach: Exploring the Inner Landscape of a Teacher's Life*, 2nd ed. (San Francisco: John Wiley and Sons, 2007), 3.

9. Ibid., 10 (emphasis in the original).

10. Daniel Lortie, *Schoolteacher: A Sociological Study* (Chicago: University of Chicago Press, 1975).

11. Palmer, *Courage to Teach*, 11.

12. Nel Noddings, "Caring in Education," Infed.org, last modified 2005, http://infed.org /biblio/noddings_caring_in_education.htm.

13. Nel Noddings, *The Challenge to Care in Schools: An Alternative Approach to Education*, 2nd ed. (New York: Teachers College, 2005), xix.

14. Charles D. Morrison, "From 'Sage on the Stage' to 'Guide on the Side': A Good Start," *International Journal for the Scholarship of Teaching and Learning* 8, no. 1 (2014), http:// digitalcommons.georgiasouthern.edu/ij-sotl/vol8/iss1/4.

15. Max van Manen, *The Tact of Teaching: The Meaning of Pedagogical Tactfulness* (Albany: State University of New York Press, 1991), 9.

16. Nel Noddings, *Education and Democracy in the 21st Century* (New York: Teacher's College Press, 2013), 148.

17. While some have questioned the use of phrases such as *my students*, I find this phrase, when used with humane intent, to reflect the love and care we hope to model for future music educators.

18. Gloria Ladson-Billings, *The Dreamkeepers: Successful Teachers of African American Children* (San Francisco: Jossey-Bass, 2009).

19. Thomas Regelski, "On 'Methodolatry' and Music Teaching as Critical and Reflective Practice," *Philosophy of Music Education Review* 10, no. 2 (Fall 2002): 102–123.

20. Palmer, *Courage to Teach*, 11–12.

21. Joseph Shively, "Constructivism in Music Education," *Arts Education Policy Review* 116, no. 3 (2015): 128–136.

22. Palmer, *Courage to Teach*, 13.

23. Marshall W. Gregory, "Curriculum, Pedagogy, and Teacherly Ethos," *Pedagogy* (2001): 69–89, https://digitalcommons.butler.edu/facsch_papers/202.

24. I was struck that in the introduction to *Healing the Heart of Democracy: The Courage to Create a Politics Worthy of the Human Spirit* (San Francisco: Jossey-Bass, 2011), Parker Palmer dedicated his book to these four young women and Christina Taylor Green, who died in the attempted assassination of Congresswoman Gabrielle Giffords. He wrote, "When we forget that politics is about weaving a fabric of compassion and justice on which everyone can depend, the first to suffer are the most vulnerable among us" (4).

25. Palmer, *Healing the Heart of Democracy*, 124–125.

26. Maxine Greene, "Teaching as Possibility: A Light in Dark Times," *Journal of Pedagogy, Pluralism and Practice* 1, no. 1 (1997): 9.

27. Ibid.

PART III

EDUCATING OTHERS FOR THE COMMON GOOD

10

FRIENDSHIP, SOLIDARITY, AND MUTUALITY DISCOVERED IN MUSIC

Luca Tiszai

THIS CHAPTER REFLECTS ON A SPECIAL EVENT, A flash-mob project with the participation of the Nádizumzum Orchestra, a folk band with musicians with severe disabilities, four professional musicians who are members of the orchestra of the Hungarian State Opera, and around a hundred students of the Zoltán Kodály Hungarian Choir School. This project provides an example of the ideas expressed in the UNESCO document *Rethinking Education*, which defines the fundamental purpose of education as "sustaining and enhancing the dignity, capacity and welfare of the human person, in relation to others and to nature."[1] While education, even music education, is frequently associated with achieving cognitive or artistic goals, this document approaches education and learning from a holistic perspective that "overcomes the traditional dichotomies between cognitive, emotional and ethical aspects."[2] The aim of this chapter is to provide an example of implementing these values in successful musical projects in which musicians with severe disabilities, professional musicians, and adolescent music students collaborate. In the last eleven years, I experienced the power of musical communities: the experience of joy and togetherness decreased the sense of otherness. Treating the Other as not Other is not a unilateral action of tolerance, but a starting point of a mutual enriching journey.[3] Musical performances of people with a wide range of different abilities serve as a model of how musical communities promote inclusion and contribute to the common good of the human family.

The inspiration for this project came from the theoretical framework of community music therapy, a new subdiscipline of music therapy that displays the power of music in developing social consciousness and in building new pathways for social inclusion. Furthermore, this approach expands the traditional concept of "therapy" associated with treatment to offer a wider understanding that includes care and service, health promotion, and social change.[4] This concept is highly congruent with the aims of the UNESCO document reinforcing the importance of the socialization function of education as "learning to be and to live together."[5] In the case of inclusive performances not only did the Nádizumzum members play with more engagement, but the professional musicians played with more creativity and passion as well. Inclusion is a mutual learning process that is fruitful not only for people with disabilities but for all participants.

This holistic view of education is deeply rooted in the history of progressive education. In the educational concepts of Rudolf Steiner, Maria Montessori, or the "Education through Art" model described by Herbert Read, art education is considered as the core of the development of a wholesome human being.[6] In the second half of the twentieth century, the achievement-oriented and competitive approach of art education has been gradually changed. The new, holistic view of art education is conscious of the complex and extensive effects of arts on the whole personality. For example, Zoltán Kodály, the reformer of Hungarian music education, emphasized that the overall goal of music education is to help children reach their full potential, because "a person without music is incomplete."[7] In the twentieth century, a wide range of educational programs has developed with clearly articulated social and educational goals. The Venezuelan El-Sistema project provides "free classical music education that promotes human opportunity and development for impoverished children."[8] The Recycled Orchestra of Cateura is a Paraguayan orchestra of children who play musical instruments made of garbage from South America's largest landfills. Their motto is, "The world sends us garbage, we send back music."[9] These projects have many commonalities with Even Ruud's description of community music therapy: "new groups have gained access to the symbolic significance of musical participation in today's society with the accompanying social recognition."[10] As Andrew Clark notes in this collection regarding a similar project, Notes from the Heart, taking the viewpoint of someone with a disability can be a source of inspiration for humor, creativity, and artistic creation.[11]

Community Music Therapy—Solidarity in Action

Community and solidarity are important common key words in different progressive educational movements, as well as in the community music therapy approach. According to Brynjulf Stige and Leif Edvard Aaro, "Community Music Therapy encourages musical participation and social inclusion, equitable access to resources, and collaborative efforts for health and wellbeing in contemporary societies. It could be characterized as solidarity in practice."[12] The UNESCO document also emphasizes that to develop "respect for life and human dignity, equal rights and social justice, cultural and social diversity and a sense of human solidarity and shared responsibility for our common future" should be the "foundation and purpose of education."[13]

Stige and Aaro highlighted the most important features of community music therapy in the acronym PREPARE (which stands for participatory, resource-oriented, ecological, performative, activist, reflective, and ethics-driven). In short, they define the main goal of community music therapy as preparing marginalized groups or individuals for participation and preparing communities to accept and respect these previously excluded members. Similarly, the UNESCO document proclaims a humanistic and global view of education as "going behind narrow utilitarianism and economism to integrate the multiple dimensions of human existence"[14] and "inspired by the value of solidarity grounded in our common humanity."[15]

Individuals with Severe Disabilities

People with severe disabilities are defined as "individuals of all ages who require extensive ongoing support in more than one major life activity in order to participate in integrated community settings and to enjoy a quality of life that is available to citizens with fewer or no disabilities."[16] Most of these individuals are limited in their ability to communicate verbally. The worldwide social exclusion of individuals with severe disabilities is well documented.[17] In order to effect social change, it is essential to promote new approaches and establish new projects for positive encounters with this marginalized group.

Challenges of the Encounter

Coming into contact with individuals with atypical physical features is a challenging experience, because deformities of the body or the face trigger many subconscious mechanisms of rejection. The problem of exclusion of individuals with visible physical impairments is present throughout continents and cultures.[18] Moreover, people with severe disabilities are frequently unable to adapt their behavior to the unspoken predetermined roles of the given society; thus, they are usually associated with unpredictable or even dangerous behavior.[19] As a result, these encounters evoke fear, insecurity, guilt, and shame in someone not prepared for these unusual behaviors and lead to social isolation of people with severe disabilities. In short, people with severe disabilities are usually considered as Other, located in the margins of all human societies, deprived of equal opportunities and access to resources. Social isolation, as violation of social justice, has long-lasting and devastating social, political, economic, and cultural consequences for the whole society. Thus, overcoming the isolation by nurturing the Other is the way to nurturing our common humanity.[20]

The main goal of this community music therapy project was to establish a field of mutuality and equality, where individuals with severe disabilities and adolescent music students experience enrichment based on their common shared passion for music. Instead of preparing a social or disability-awareness program, they work together in common musical performances.

Nádizumzum Orchestra and the Consonante Method

The Nádizumzum Orchestra was founded in Szent Erzsébet nursing home for adults with severe disabilities in Ipolytölgyes, Hungary, in 2007. Nádizumzum is a Hungarian folk instrument made of cane, similar to the kazoo. The orchestra's increasing repertoire consists of 150 Hungarian folk songs, and it has presented more than sixty concerts throughout Hungary. The Consonante Method provides access to musical participation for individuals with limited intellectual, motor, and verbal skills.[21] The three pillars of the method, which has been developed in practice, are the application of custom-built instruments to suit individual motor patterns, the use of inborn natural musical behaviors and vitality affects, and simplified accompaniment with base sound and perfect fifth.

People with severe disabilities are rarely able to follow verbal instructions or play even a simple melody with a musical instrument, but they respond to music with rhythmically synchronized movements matching the contour of the music. The theory of music therapy uses the term *communicative musicality* to describe this innate natural basis of future musicianship. Daniel Stern, a psychologist and infant researcher, established the term *theory of vitality affects* to describe the parallels between music and preverbal communication. Vitality affects are multimodal and dynamic processes "experienced as dynamic shifts or patterned changes within ourselves."[22] These dynamic changes are characterized by changing tonal and temporal qualities or, in other words, cross-modal matching of the behavioral contour, "dynamic micro-momentary shifts in intensity over time."[23] In musical terms, diminuendo or accelerando serve as examples of these dynamic changes. Vitality affects play a crucial role in the feeling of connectedness or affective attunement, "allowing us, rather automatically and without awareness, to change to the other, to feel what has been perceived in the other."[24] The matching elements of movement and music, or the "fundamental dynamic pentad," consist of movement, time, force, space, and intention/directionality.[25] Thus, the early nonverbal mother-infant interaction can be considered as a musical improvisation.[26] Nonverbal people and individuals with limited understanding of language are often highly sensitive to the musical features of communication. The Consonante Method uses this sensitivity to musical forms of vitality affects to play music.

Music education also uses the power of vitality affects, although it does not have a name for it. For example, a choir or a symphonic orchestra responds with sound to the movements of the conductor, establishing a mutual, nonverbal, cross-modal communication. Movement-based approaches to music education, for example, Dalcroze Eurhythmics and the Hungarian Kokas method, are based on the conscious use of this cross-modal exchange: the innate ability to express movements with sounds and sounds with movements.[27] Both these methods are based on the observation that kinesthetic, physical experience involving the whole body provides a firm basis for musical understanding. Similar to Dalcroze, Klára Kokas (1929–2010), Hungarian music educator and professor of psychology and pedagogy, discovered that children take pleasure in expressing classical music with freely improvised body movements. Zsuzsa Pásztor studied the video recordings of Kokas's sessions in the early 1980s. Pásztor wrote that even toddlers are able to move in sync with the music, with these improvised dances expressing timing, harmony, form, structure, timbre, and their emotional experience. She explained that the process of responding to sound with spontaneous bodily movement is phylogenetically much older than intellectual concepts.[28] The translation of auditory signals to familiar bodily experiences and movement patterns allows small children and even nonverbal adults to perceive and respond to complex musical patterns that they would not be able to approach intellectually or express verbally.

The design for the Nádizumzum Orchestra was to use this innate musicality to perform music. The motor repertoire of individuals with severe disability is highly limited. Being encouraged by the avant-garde approach of using musical instruments in nontraditional ways, we decided to build specific, individualized musical instruments to suit the motor patterns of these future musicians. The next step was a careful analysis of frequently repeated movement patterns in response to music and the potential transformation of these musical gestures to sound-producing movements. To identify suitable instruments is usually a lengthy process, because in addition to requiring a natural movement that makes an instrument sound, the instrument must be captivating so that its musician is willing to repeat such movements for an hour-long concert.[29] In order to sound consonant, we used a bagpipe-bass, an accompaniment of the melody with base sound and perfect fifth. The inspiration came from the Hungarian zither, a typical Hungarian folk instrument. In this instrument, the melody is played on a few strings and the other strings, called the accompanying or "guest" strings, provide a constant sound or drone. The instruments of the musicians were tuned to function as these guest strings. Thus, as long as we play folk songs in the given key, it was not possible to play out of tune on these modified instruments. The unity of the orchestra was based on shared vitality affects and group synchronization, which seems to be an innate tendency of human beings when they act together.[30]

The Flash Mob Project

Hungarian education regulations changed in 2011. According to the new rules, a requirement of the secondary-school completion certificate is for students to perform fifty hours of community service,. We have established community music therapy projects as community social service that can fulfill this public service requirement. Participants in a social action are responsible to act for the benefit of a selected group of people. In the case of individuals with severe disabilities, this can be difficult because of the subconscious reactions on the part of the benefit providers as discussed earlier. To counteract these reactions, working on common shared musical goals can be a natural situation for both the Nádizumzum members and the music students. However, a helping attitude can lead to unequal relationships by putting individuals with severe disabilities in a subordinated role. On the contrary, common performance decreases the sense of strangeness or otherness and hierarchical standing by strengthening equality, mutuality, and group cohesion.[31] Furthermore, as Gary Ansdell explains, "being musical with the other is to be responsible, to be answerable to their voice."[32]

Zoltán Kodály Hungarian Choir School (ZKHCS) is an elementary, middle, and music school in Budapest, Hungary, founded in 1988 by Ferenc Sapszon Jr. The educational approach of the school is based on the principles of Zoltán Kodály. This school is devoted to music, especially choral singing. All of the students have daily singing lessons, choir rehearsals, individual vocal training, and optional instrumental lessons. According to the spirit of Kodály, the goal of music education is not only to be a good musician, but to develop open-minded and open-hearted, socially engaged people. Thus, the teachers of this school were highly committed to the collaboration of their students and the Nádizumzum Orchestra.

The first common performance of Nádzumzum musicians and students of the school was Kodály's Kállai Kettős (Kallo Double Dance) in 2014.[33] In 2015, Márta Dragonics, the representative of the Ars Sacra Foundation, supported a flash-mob project with the participants of ZKHCS students, the Nádizumzum Orchestra, and professional musicians of the Hungarian State Opera. The aim of this film was to advertise a week-long Hungarian art festival.[34]

These projects are built on the common shared passion for music through a preparation for common musical performances. During these events, the students and the Nádizumzum musicians built mutual friendships and some of the students regularly performed with the Nádizumzum Orchestra, while others started to do voluntary work in summer camps for children with autism. In order to provide a model for further successful projects, I use the acronym PREPARE to highlight the key factors and experiences of community music therapy.

PREPARE—Reflection on Practice

Participatory means that musical relationships are naturally equal and mutually reciprocal, thus, upending hierarchical relationships.[35] Musical performance is based on interdependent relationships and changing roles of the musicians and provides opportunities to try out different social roles:

leader, follower, soloist, while learning responsibility, independence, and the skills to be a sensitive listener and reliable accompanist. To some extent, marginalized members of the community are deprived of the possibility to take responsibility for their own lives or work for the community. This life experience could encourage immature, childish, or even antisocial behavior, causing a vicious cycle between socially inappropriate actions and social exclusion. Socially acceptable behavior is a condition and also a result of being a member of a regularly rehearsing orchestra, thus preparing these musicians for social inclusion.

In addition, musical performance provides a positive model of inclusion both for co-performers and for the audience. They learn to treat individuals with severe disabilities as equal members of the community. This situation teaches musicians or music students to adapt their abilities and talents to the group, focusing their attention on the musical abilities and talents of the fellow musicians. Musicians with disabilities can be highly responsive musically, developing interesting musical conversations with trained musicians who are aware of these small changes. For example, the members of the Nádizumzum like to improvise new rhythm patterns or change the stress in the accompaniment. They usually reinforce the communicative intention of these acts with a smile or most often a gaze. If fellow musicians respond to their initiatives, they smile and start an even more complex musical communication. They also respond to the improvisation of trained musicians, for example repeating the rhythm of a unique ornament. And the audience gains a positive image about inclusive community, in which musicians with and without disability are joyfully playing together.

Resource-oriented thinking focuses on strengths and potentials, such as the innate musicality of the Nádizumzum members. The resource-oriented thinking appears at the personal level and also as an overall positive and constructive attitude that considers challenges rather than problems. As the example of the Recycled Orchestra shows, these challenges can be social, environmental, and financial. In the case of individuals with severe disabilities, it is easy to focus on weakness or impossibilities. The challenge of these projects is to help participants experience the benefits of these encounters.

Ecological in this context means that community music therapy is applied in the context of musical activities, "promoting health within and between various layers of the socio-cultural community and/or physical environment."[36] Music can be a promoter of individual empowerment. As Even Ruud emphasized, "the music, the person, and the situation work together in a relational or mutual relation where changes in any of these components will change the meaning produced."[37] In a wider perspective, the goal of community music therapy is to build up mutually empowering relationships between individuals from different cultural or social statuses, as well as between vulnerable groups and the whole society. The aim of the ecological perspective is to reframe the given social context by giving voice to minority groups or building inclusive projects supporting the development of inclusion and positive self-image.

The word *performative* refers to public performances. Being part of a successful performing group with public concerts disrupts the vicious circle between disability and social isolation. In other words, a quality musical performance by someone with a disability has a strong positive impact on public opinion. The literature of community music therapy describes performative and participatory concerts. In the practice of the Nádizumzum, most of their performative concerts are inclusive because none of the core members are able to sing at an artistic level. Thus, in order to impress the audience, they ask someone with a good singing voice to make the texts of the songs intelligible. As well-known and popular folk songs are a part of their repertoire, they give participatory concerts that involve the audience. They offer workshops where people, even without good voices or previous musical training, can be a part of the orchestra due to the always consonant musical instruments. This is a reverse form of inclusion, where Nádizumzum as a musical community provides participation even for musically "excluded" or "marginalized" people due to the musical instruments that keep the group in tune. The visible vulnerability of the Nádizumzum musicians seems to allow people to take an active part in common musical creation regardless of their less visibly labeled or real "musical weaknesses."

Social media are increasingly important in participation and sharing, thus providing new ways of gaining public awareness. A short, professional video with artistic quality may strongly promote social inclusion. For example, Hungary is My Homeland [Magyaroszág az én hazám] is a popular video from 2015 in which János Kóti, a nine-year-old boy with severe disabilities, sings a Hungarian folk song with the accompaniment of the Budapest Unique Symphonic Orchestra and emblematic figures of Hungarian rock and classical music.[38]

Community music therapy is both an *activist* and a *reflexive* approach, because it acknowledges inequalities within the society, advocates for social justice, fights against discrimination, injustice, and unequal access to resources, and creates situations of equality and mutual respect. Community music therapy works to establish novel projects as vehicles of social change and to implement already successful projects in different sociocultural contexts. Sensitive and constantly attentive reflection on practice, awareness of interactions among different social and cultural systems, and personal and interpersonal experiences should be crucial parts of music education in changing cultural contexts.

Finally, *ethics driven* means that the theory and practice of community music therapy incorporates social justice and human rights within a life of dignity and promotes solidarity, freedom, respect, and equality. In community music therapy projects, "there is an implicit attitude that their work is in some way contributing to a wider social change agenda, whether this is consciously intended or not."[39]

Closing Thoughts: Not a Torture but a Joy

The last message of this orchestra for general music education is the culture of joy. Kodály emphasized that music should be a natural and joyful part of everyday education from early childhood. "Teach music and singing at school in such a way that it is not a torture but a joy for the pupil; instill a thirst for finer music in him, a thirst which will last for a lifetime."[40] In the case of Nádizumzum rehearsals, it is hardly possible to offer any kind of extrinsic motivation for the musicians. They practice because they enjoy it; otherwise (and it happens sometimes), they simply leave the rehearsal. Music must become an intrinsic experience for these musicians. Playing music with these simple instruments is so captivating for the members of the orchestra that they are able to rehearse more than an hour, sometimes even two hours. According to Mihály Csíkszentmihályi, making music holds the potential to experience flow, the self-forgetting enjoyment of a given activity.[41] Joy with making music is a key factor of success in the Nádizumzum concerts.

In contrast, a devastating consequence of being lost in a competitive and achievement-oriented concept of music education is that many people label themselves as unmusical or tone deaf. Many people lose their confidence in singing because of harmful comments from their music teachers, such as being told they are unmusical, asked not to sing, or shamed in various ways in front of others.[42] In their adulthood, these people reject participation in any kind of musical activity. Thus, music education is not only important for the development of musical skills but it also plays a central role in the student's future relationship with music.[43] According to the experience of the Nádizumzum Orchestra, music is a strong motivation even for people who are labeled as unable to focus their attention for more than a few minutes. Inclusive concerts are characterized by playfulness and happiness, which seem in some cases to be disappearing from the spirit of musical training.

Conclusion

Community music therapy projects are powerful tools to make solidarity real and open up wider perspectives for music education by experiencing equality and mutuality in music, because "education is not only about the acquisition of skills, it is also about values of respect for life and human dignity required for social harmony in a diverse world."[44] As the example of the Hungarian Nádizumzum Orchestra has shown, the first impression of dependency and powerlessness in people with different disabilities can gradually change due to common shared music that can reframe social interactions. Although the orchestra members are people with visible disabilities that are usually associated with a subordinated social role, they become the heart of the musical community, the core of the performance. Students and professional musicians become co-performers, and people previously not affected become involved as audience members. Shared music is a natural platform for participation, thus strengthening interpersonal relationships, reducing the sense of difference, and facilitating acceptance, respect, and togetherness.[45] These projects develop the participants' social skills and, as the Delors report urges, "learning to live together."[46]

When sharing music is a well-prepared action, it can open space for individual reflection, or in other words "raise more questions than it provides answers" but in this ambiguity it can lead participants to a "respect for diversity and rejection of all forms of (cultural) hegemony, stereotypes and biases . . . while ensuring balance between pluralism and universal values."[47] Building friendships with those who cannot be valued for their mental capacity, workforce contribution, or beauty can help us all to understand that human life has unconditional value, regardless of an individual's abilities This perspective on humanity could increase individual self-esteem while providing freedom from competitive social systems. This can lead to "learning to be," one of the four pillars of education for the ultimate purpose of "forming whole human beings."[48] The Nádizumzum Orchestra can serve as an example of a humane approach to including minority groups, who often suffer from social exclusion, for the sake of the common good.

LUCA TISZAI is Juhász Gyula Faculty Member of Education at the Institute of Special Education at the University of Szeged, Hungary.

Notes

1. UNESCO, *Rethinking Education: Towards a Global Common Good?* (Paris: UNESCO, 2015), 36, http://unesdoc.unesco.org/images/0023/002325/232555e.pdf.

2. Ibid., 39.

3. See Iris M. Yob, "There Is No Other," in this collection.

4. Brynjulf Stige and Leif Edvard Aarø, *Invitation to Community Music Therapy* (New York: Routledge, 2012).

5. UNESCO, *Rethinking Education*, 40.

6. Rudolf Steiner, "A Modern Art of Education (Foundations of Waldorf Education)" (lectures presented in Ilkley, Yorkshire, August 5–17, 1923); Maria Montessori, *The Absorbent Mind* (New York: Holt, Rinehart and Winston, 1967); Herbert Read, *Education through Art* (1943; London: Faber, 1970).

7. Zoltan Kodály, Közösségnevelés-közönségnevelés [Education of the community—Education of an audience], in *Visszatekintés I* [In retrospect I], ed. F. Bónis (1958; Budapest: Argumentum Kiadó, 2007), 318.

8. Michael Slevin and Patrick Slevin, "Psychoanalysis and El Sistema: Human Development through Music," *International Journal of Applied Psychoanalysis Studies* 10 (2013): 132, doi:10.1002/aps.1355.

9. See, for example, smart84ps [pseud.], "Landfill Harmonic—The World Sends Us Garbage, We Send Back Music," YouTube video, 3:42, October 5, 2013, https://www.youtube.com/watch?v=c53aA9cgdtw; or Favio Chavez, "The World Sends Us Garbage, We Send Back Music," TED video, 15:48, accessed November 20, 2016, http://tedx.amsterdam/talks/the-world-sends-us-garbage-we-send-back-music-favio-chavez-at-tedxamsterdam/.

10. Even Ruud, "Music in Therapy: Increasing Possibilities for Action," *Music and Arts in Action* 1, no. 1 (2008): 48, https://core.ac.uk/download/pdf/12826296.pdf.

11. Emily Howe, André de Quadros, Andrew Clark, and Kinh T. Vu, "The Tuning of the Music Educator: A Pedagogy of the 'Common Good' for the Twenty-First Century," in this collection.

12. Stige and Aarø, *Invitation to Community Music Therapy*, 5.

13. UNESCO, *Rethinking Education*, 38.

14. Ibid., 10.

15. Ibid., 11.

16. TASH (Association for Persons with Severe Handicaps), "Definition of the People TASH Serves," in *Critical Issues in the Lives of People with Severe Disabilities*, ed. Luanna H. Meyer, Charles A. Peck, and Lou Brown (Baltimore: Brookes, 1991), 19.

17. See for example, Contact a Family, *Forgotten Families: The Impact of Isolation on Families with Disabled Children across the UK* (2011), http://www.cafamily.org.uk/media /381636/forgotten_isolation_report.pdf; MENCAP, *No Ordinary Life: The Support Needs of Families Caring for Children and Adults with Profound and Multiple Learning Disabilities* (2001; London: Mencap, 2009), https://www.basw.co.uk/system/files/resources/basw_113415 -5_0.pdf; Johannes Schädler, Albrecht Rohrmann, and Stephanie Schür, eds., *The Specific Risks of Discrimination against Persons in Situation of Major Dependence or with Complex Needs: Report of a European Study*, vol. 2 (Brussels: European Commission, 2008), accessed January 25, 2014, https://disability-studies.leeds.ac.uk/wp-content/uploads/sites/40/library /inclusion-europe-inclusion-europe-2.pdf .

18. Alex Clarke, "Psychosocial Aspects of Facial Disfigurement: Problems, Management and the Role of a Lay-Led Organization," *Psychology, Health and Medicine* 4 (1999): 127–142; Megan Oaten, Richard J. Stevenson, and Trevor I. Case, "Disease Avoidance as a Functional Basis for Stigmatization," *Philosophical Transactions of the Royal Society B: Biological Sciences* 366, no. 1583 (2011): 3433–3452, doi:10.1098/rstb.2011.0095.

19. Andrea Stier and Stephen P. Hinshaw, "Explicit and Implicit Stigma against Individuals with Mental Illness," *Australian Psychology* 42 (2007): 106–117, doi:10.1080 /00050060701280599.

20. See Yob, "There is No Other."

21. Luca Tiszai, "Consonante, the Barrier-free Method: Orchestral Work with Individuals with Severe Disabilities," *Journal of Art for Life* 8, no. 9 (2016/2017): 1–17.

22. Daniel Stern, *The Interpersonal World of the Infant: A View from Psychoanalysis and Developmental Psychology* (New York: Basic Books, 1985), 57.

23. Daniel Stern, Lynne Hofer, Wendy Haft, and John Dore, "Affect Attunement: The Sharing by Means of Intermodal Fluency," in *Social Perception in Infants*, ed. Tiffany M. Field and Nathan A. Fox (Norwood, NJ: Ablex, 1985), 263.

24. Stern, *Interpersonal World of the Infant*, 263.

25. Daniel Stern, *Forms of Vitality: Exploring Dynamic Experience in Psychology, the Arts, Psychotherapy, and Development* (Oxford: Oxford University Press, 2010), 6.

26. Janet Graham, "Communicating with the Uncommunicative: Music Therapy with Preverbal Adults," *British Journal of Learning Disabilities* 32, no. 1 (2004): 24–29; Maya Gratier, "Grounding in Musical Interaction: Evidence from Jazz Performances," *Musicae Scientiae* (March 12, 2008): 71–110; Maya Gratier and Julien Magnier, "Sense and Synchrony: Infant Communication and Musical Improvisation," *Intermédialités* 19 (2012): 45–64, doi:10 .7202/1012655ar; Maya Gratier and Colwyn Trevarthen, "Musical Narrative and Motives for Culture in Mother-Infant Vocal Interaction," *Journal of Consciousness Studies* 15, nos. 10–11 (2008): 122–158.

27. Emile Jaques-Dalcroze, *Rhythm, Music and Education* (1921; London: Riverside, 1967); Marja-Leena Juntunen and Heidi Westerlund, "Digging Dalcroze, or, Dissolving the Mind-body Dualism: Philosophical and Practical Remarks on the Musical Body in Action," *Music Education Research* 3 (2001): 203–214; Klára Kokas, "Joy through the Magic of Music" (First Art Therapy World Congress, Budapest, Hungary, April 2003), http://arttherapy .worldcongress.hu/admin/kepek/downloads/ 219kokas.doc (page no longer available).

28. Zsuzsa Pásztor, "Az egészből a részekhez—Kezdeti tapasztalatok a zenei mozgásrögtönzések elemzéséről" [From the whole to the segments: Initial experiences about musical movement improvisations], *Parlando* 45, no. 4 (2003): 2–7.

29. Luca Tiszai, "Music Belongs to Everyone: Moments of Progress in Community Music Therapy with Musicians with Severe Disabilities," *Voices: A World Forum for Music Therapy* 16, no. 3 (2016), doi:10.15845/voices.v16i3.853.

30. Johann Issartel, Ludovic Marin, and Marielle Cadopi, "Unintended Interpersonal Co-ordination: 'Can We March to the Beat of Our Own Drum?'" *Neuroscience Letters* 411 (2007): 174–179, doi:10.1016/j.neulet.2006.09.086; Sukhvinder S. Obhi and Nathelie Sebanz, "Moving Together: Toward Understanding the Mechanisms of Joint Action," *Experimental Brain Research* 211 (2011): 329–336, doi:10.1007/s00221-011-2721-0; Mercedes Pavlicevic, "Dynamic Interplay in Clinical Improvisation," *Voices: A World Forum For Music Therapy* 2, no. 2 (2002), doi:10.15845/voices.v2i2.88.

31. Cochavit Elefant, "Reflection: Musical Inclusion, Intergroup Relation, and Community Development," in *Where Music Helps: Community Music Therapy in Action and Reflection*, ed. Brynjulf Stige, Gary Ansdell, Cochavit Elefant, and Mercedes Pavlicevic (Aldershot, UK: Ashgate, 2010), 75–93.

32. Gary Ansdell, *How Music Helps in Music Therapy and Everyday Life* (Farnham, UK: Ashgate, 2015), 186.

33. Tiszai, "Music Belongs to Everyone."

34. Ars Sacra, "Special Flashmob 2015, Ars Sacra Fesztivál," YouTube video, 3:38, August 28, 2015, https://www.youtube.com/watch?v=nfoP5-vlGZc.

35. Dorothy Miell, Raymond MacDonald, and David J. Hargreaves, eds., *Musical Communication* (Oxford: Oxford University Press, 2005); Simon Procter, "The Therapeutic, Musical Relationship: A Two-Sided Affair?" *Voices: A World Forum for Music Therapy* 2, no. 3 (2002), doi:10.15845/voices.v2i3.102.

36. Kenneth Bruscia, *Defining Music Therapy*, 2nd ed. (Gilsum, NH: Barcelona, 1998), 229.

37. Even Ruud, *Music Therapy: A Perspective from the Humanities* (Gilsum, NH: Barcelona Publishers, 2010), 57.

38. A Zene Gyógyító Ereje/the Healing Power of Music, "Magyarország az én hazám," YouTube video, 5:02, March 20, 2015, https://www.youtube.com/watch?v=oBnWnfuFKig.

39. Megan Ellen Steele, "How Can Music Build Community? Insight from Theories and Practice of Community Music Therapy" *Voices: A World Forum for Music Therapy* 16, no. 2 (2016), doi:10.15845/voices.v16i2.876.

40. Zoltán Kodály, "Gyermekkarok" [For children's choir], in *Visszatekintés* [In retrospect I], *Összegyűjtött írások, beszédek, nyilatkozatok* I, ed. Ferenc Bónis (1929; Budapest: Argumentum Kiadó, 2007), 39.

41. Mihály Csikszentmihalyi, *Flow: The Psychology of Optimal Experience* (New York: Harper and Row, 1990).

42. Carlos R. Abril, "I Have a Voice but I Just Can't Sing: A Narrative Investigation of Singing and Social Anxiety," *Music Education Research* 9, no. 1 (2007): 1–15, doi:10.1080 /14613800601127494; Pamela Burnard, "'How Musical are You?' Examining the Discourse of Derision in Music Education," in *Musicianship in the 21st Century: Issues, Trends and Possibilities*, ed. Samuel Leong (Sydney: Australian Music Centre, 2003), 28–38; Eve Ruddock and Samuel Leong, "'I Am Unmusical!': The Verdict of Self-Judgment," *International Journal of Music Education* 23, no. 1 (2005): 9–22, doi:10.1177/0255761405050927; Colleen Whidden, "Hearing the Voice of Non-singers: Culture, Context, and Connection," in *Issues of Identity in Music Education: Narratives and Practices*, ed. Linda K. Thompson and Marc Robin Campbell (Charlotte, NC: Information Age Publishing, 2010), 83–107.

43. See Ruddock and Leong, "'I Am Unmusical!'"

44. UNESCO, *Rethinking Education*, 38.

45. Kay Kaufman Shelemay, "Musical Communities: Rethinking the Collective in Music," *Journal of the American Musicological Society* 64, no. 2 (2011): 349–390, doi:10.1525/jams.2011 .64.2.349; Mercedes Pavlicevic and Gary Ansdell, *Community Music Therapy* (London: Jessica Kingsley, 2004); Graham. F. Welch, Evangelos Himonides, Jo Saunders, Ioulia Papageorgi, and Marc Sarazin, "Singing and Social Inclusion," *Frontiers in Psychology* 5, no. 803 (2014), doi:10.3389/fpsyg.2014.00803.

46. UNESCO, *Learning: The Treasure Within* (Paris: UNESCO, 1996), http://unesdoc .unesco.org/images/0010/001095/109590eo.pdf, commonly referred to as the Delors report.

47. UNESCO, *Rethinking Education*, 41.

48. UNESCO, *Learning: The Treasure Within*.

11

RETHINKING VOCAL EDUCATION AS A MEANS TO ENCOURAGE POSITIVE IDENTITY DEVELOPMENT IN ADOLESCENTS

Emily Good-Perkins

GLOBALIZATION, MASS MEDIA, IMMIGRATION, AND MIGRATION ARE PROFOUNDLY impacting youth worldwide. I think of how my students in the United Arab Emirates fluidly moved between their traditional home life and their American university classroom. Similarly, fifth and sixth graders from a Midwestern urban public school in the United States spoke with me about their family backgrounds—Eritrean, Honduran, Mexican, Vietnamese, to name a few—as well as their love for hip-hop and rhythm and blues music. Whether they are living in the United Arab Emirates or the United States, today's global youth are experiencing and negotiating local and global, as well as familial and social, influences as they construct their identities. Oftentimes, it is within the in-between spaces that they develop new definitions of culture and home. This concept of hybridity is recognized by UNESCO in their 2015 document *Rethinking Education: Towards a Global Common Good?*[1] Within the culturally fluid and hybrid realities of today's youth, "we see a new public aesthetic being expressed, rich in its inherent plurality."[2] This is evident specifically within the "domains the youth inhabit, from fashion to food, music and personal relationships."[3]

In her effort to pedagogically account for the rich cultural identities of today's youth, Gloria Ladson-Billings calls for educators to "consider the global identities that are emerging in the arts . . . toward a hybridity, fluidity, and complexity never before considered in schools and classrooms."[4] She surmises that educators must strive to sustain the abundant cultural competence of today's youth as a means of perpetuating and encouraging cultural plurality. Culturally sustaining pedagogy seeks to sustain culture in both a traditional and an evolving way according to students' lived experiences by "support[ing] young people in sustaining the cultural and linguistic competence of their communities while simultaneously offering access to dominant cultural competence."[5]

Both the UNESCO document and Ladson-Billings reconsider ways to make equitable the broad field of education to better serve the needs of today's youth. Interestingly, both sources also recognize the salient roles music and the arts play in this process. Despite the literature and the rich abundance of culture represented by American K-12 students, postsecondary music teacher education in the United States continues to be primarily Eurocentric and focused on the Western classical music tradition. In particular, vocal education for postsecondary music education majors focuses primarily on the Western classical bel canto vocal technique. This education fails to prepare teachers to teach students from diverse backgrounds and musical traditions. Because music plays an important role in adolescents' identity formation, teachers who are unprepared to recognize and teach diverse vocal styles may unknowingly alienate or silence their students.

Silenced Singer

The need for inclusivity within the voice teaching profession is important not only because of American diversity but also because of the phenomenon of the "silenced singer."[6] Both Victoria Moon Joyce and Susan Knight studied adults who, as adolescents, had been silenced from singing. Joyce found that the prioritization of a Western classical vocal sound over other vocal aesthetics was the main culprit for exclusion. Teachers who demonstrated "correct" and "incorrect" singing inadvertently devalued other vocal aesthetics. The adults with whom Knight spoke described the humiliating experience of being silenced in school singing ensembles. They had "accepted the attribution unquestioningly," carrying this "diagnosis into adulthood." Yet, as Knight illuminated, they "all longed to be able to sing and regretted that they could not."[7]

Knight and Joyce's studies illuminate the power of vocal teaching. Musical identity and ethnic identity have been shown to be intertwined and play a significant role in a child's identity development.[8] Conversely, negative vocal experiences have lifelong implications.[9] The diversification of vocal education would allow for a more humane approach to voice teaching in which each student's vocal "funds of knowledge" are celebrated, sustained, and recognized as worthy.[10] In their descriptions of humane education and culturally sustaining pedagogy, Django Paris, H. Samy Alim, and Iris M. Yob recognize the simultaneous need for student empowerment and the "dismant[ling] of barriers that would prevent anybody from full participation."[11] Humane music education, therefore, provides students with the opportunity to sustain the musical and vocal competencies of their communities "while simultaneously offering access to [and critique of] dominant" musical competence.[12]

Humane voice teaching—teaching that contributes to the "global common good"—recognizes students' vocal "funds of knowledge" as part of an educational "participatory process . . . which takes into account a diversity of contexts, concepts of well-being and knowledge ecosystems."[13] University students who will teach K-12 music classes should be prepared to sustain their students' vocal "funds of knowledge" while "simultaneously offering" them "access" to dominant vocal knowledge.[14] The question that arises is, how might music teacher education better prepare music teachers for humane vocal education?

Bel Canto Vocal Technique and White Bourgeois Culture

Joyce's study illuminated the repercussions of an exclusive "white bourgeois" approach to singing and a binary between "good" and "bad" singing.[15] The advent of a bourgeois singing technique can be traced back to Victorian Britain and the rise of the middle class.[16] This new style of singing was initiated by Manuel Garcia's *Traité complet de l'art du chant*.[17] His treatise, which addressed laryngeal position as well as diaphragmatic breathing, marked the beginning of the bel canto vocal technique and the operatic voice as we know it today. Bel canto vocal technique became an exclusive approach to singing and listening. Those with "refined" tastes were able to distinguish between a good bel canto sound and a bad other. These elite tastes were not only associated with upward mobility, but "the embourgeoisement of the singing voice brought the idea of othered voices into play."[18]

Historically, bel canto singing was intertwined with colonialism.[19] In nineteenth-century Britain, vocal pedagogy was referred to as "'voice culture,' where 'culture' in the 19th century was synonymous with 'civilisa-tion.'"[20] The "othering" of singing voices justified the use of vocal teaching to "civilize" and refine those who were not a part of white bourgeois culture for the betterment of society. This manifested both in Britain itself with the working classes as well as being part of Britain's colonialist mission in Africa. "Voice culture provided the opportunity for re-forming the voice, for colonizing yet more of the other's body."[21] Hegemonic vocal culture was rooted in Victorian Britain. The "harsh" timbre of the African voice and the "rough" grain of the working-class song provided the opportunity for seemingly innocent domination. The singing voice, intimately linked to a person's identity and culture and oftentimes a person's only means of self-expression became the vehicle for "symbolic violence."[22]

Symbolic violence is a "'gentle, invisible' form of coercion by which dominant classes enforce hegemony through the operation of institutions in which people 'collaborate in the destruction of their instruments of ex-pression.'"[23] Although Pierre Bourdieu is not specifically addressing the singing instrument, the ways in which he discusses language purification in nineteenth-century French schools is similar to the singing culture in Britain. In an effort to unify society, the French bourgeois encouraged "lin-guistic unification."[24] Working-class French citizens who used other dia-lects were forced to abandon their linguistic identities. The refined French language was imposed and much like in Britain, hegemony was apparent as citizens took part "in the destruction of their instruments of expression." Bourdieu and John Potter show how nineteenth-century French and British bourgeois societies appropriated the voices of the marginalized under the guise of refinement and a more cultured society.[25]

Bel Canto Technique and American Music Education

Much like that in Britain and France, nineteenth-century music educa-tion in the United States focused on refining the child. "Public school vocal instruction promised to distinguish bona fide citizens from those who, a priori, lacked the requisites for liberty."[26] The bel canto singing tradition became the distinct white sound to which other "unrefined" singing was compared. In the early twentieth-century, psychoacoustics allowed music educators to analyze and compare different singing styles. The racialization of the singing voice was justified through the "objectivity" of science. "*Bel canto*'s ties to processes of exclusion in public school music teaching and postsecondary education lie in its authority to judge and rank comportment, diction, ornament, and register, among other qualities as musical values."[27]

The use of the bel canto singing technique as a means to civilize both a person's voice and a person's ear did not end in the twentieth-century. The specificity and complexity of the bel canto technique allows for a narrow and exclusive definition of correct singing. James Stark describes bel canto singing to be the "art of the few and not of the many."[28] "Such singing requires a highly refined use of the laryngeal, respiratory, and articulatory muscles in order to produce special qualities of timbre, evenness of scale and register, [and] breath control. This kind of singing requires a different vocal technique than 'natural' or untrained singing."[29]

Bel canto technique allows a singer to optimize resonance and therefore projection. This technique is invaluable for operatic and solo concert performers. However, to learn the intricacies of bel canto technique, a singer must develop an acute awareness of a specific vocal timbre. This specific tone becomes the singer's status quo. Therefore, bel canto technique is not merely a study of vocal production, it is also a prioritization of a specific vocal sound.

Those who are able to recognize a good sound are said to have a "good ear."[30] Postsecondary music education allows students in both performance and education to develop and fine-tune skills in listening and singing. How pitch and timbre are defined by the Western classical tradition frame the sound for which music educators strive and inform the ways that they assess singing. Music teachers in K-12 classrooms may not necessarily teach the nuances of bel canto technique; however, the ways that they assess singing as good or bad are inadvertently informed by their postsecondary vocal training.

Much like Ruth Gustafson and Stark, Grant Olwage recognizes that the aurality of the bel canto technique manifested in colonialist Africa.[31] "Teachers monitoring singers were instructed to be on the alert for the chest register and the associated use of too loud and harsh a voice."[32] African vocal sound listened to with bel canto ears sounded "savage." Vocal colonialism, in essence, took place both with the voice and the ear.[33] The discussion about bel canto aurality from different perspectives emphasizes the specificity and exclusivity of a bel canto sound.[34] It requires that educators look more closely at bel canto vocal training in our music universities. Does this technique hinder K-12 music educators' ability to affirm and recognize diverse vocal tones? Are music teachers with trained voices and trained ears inhibiting the success of America's diverse student population? Hegemonic oppression is volatile because the marginalized are made to believe and participate in the "destruction of their instruments of expression."[35] If K-12 students' "instruments of expression" sound foreign to K-12 music teachers, is bel canto vocal teaching contributing to a form of "symbolic violence?"[36]

Where Are We Today?

"Listening for Whiteness" is the provocative title of an article by Julia Koza that peers into the postsecondary vocal audition process.[37] She describes the narrow criteria, based on bel canto principles, which are used to admit or reject students with "no pretense of welcoming diverse musical genres, styles, or experiences."[38] The students who are being excluded from music education programs are the ones who possess musical talents outside of the narrow audition criteria. These students may have the ability to provide relevant musical experiences for K-12 schools; however, university training is "the only available pipeline to K-12 music teaching."[39] By broadening the audition criteria, students with diverse backgrounds will have more opportunity to access music education programs.

Culturally Sustaining Vocal Pedagogy

In addition to access, practically speaking how might the field of vocal pedagogy evolve to meet the various needs of a diverse student population? To answer this question, we must address the specific principles of bel canto vocal training that hinder a democratic approach to voice teaching. For the purposes of this chapter, I will focus on one specific element of bel canto technique that I believe is problematic for an equitable approach to vocal teaching. It is the concept of chiaroscuro or resonance. A singer achieves this "light-dark" aesthetic with a relatively low laryngeal position and firmly sealed glottis.[40] This approach allows for optimal projection and produces a specific sound, oftentimes referred to as the "operatic ping." According to Stark, this sound "can hardly be confused with vernacular styles of singing."[41] Therein lies the fundamental problem with chiaroscuro. Music educators who are solely taught the bel canto technique, develop a specific timbral bias. This is problematic because darker, brighter, more nasal, or swallowed aesthetics are not explored or understood. A narrow understanding of and exposure to timbre limits teachers and marginalizes students. For many cultures, timbre is the most important element of a musical tradition.[42] Oftentimes, Western ears are guilty of "'pitchcentrism' or 'timbre deafness,' a perceptual proclivity on the part of western listeners, including ethnomusicologists, to focus on melody in music where the dominant parameter is timbre."[43] The timbral representation of a culture's music and language strongly distinguishes it from the next. "Each language has a distinctive palette of vocalic timbres."[44]

Voice teachers who are steeped in the Western classical tradition are susceptible to biased listening. The act of listening is more an act of perceiving, which "is constructed not only from ongoing sensory information but also from previous sensory experiences."[45] Therefore, the act of listening to singing involves both the external objective sound and the internal subjective perception.[46] Externally, "timbre is the primary ingredient for source identification . . . and it is perceived more quickly and directly than other parameters of music."[47] Internally, the sound is perceived according to the person's experience and cultural and social context.

Zachary Wallmark's study explored the ways that people perceive and appraise timbre. Empirically, he accounted for participants' "behavioral responses" to specific timbral representations as well as "the brain activity underlying those conscious appraisals."[48] His findings indicate that the appraisal of timbre is an instantaneous demarcation of good and bad sound. In addition, he found different brain activity for perceived good and bad sounds. "Timbre is often perceived with the accompaniment of covert motor mimesis (subvocalization). . . . It can be conceived as something we do with our voices."[49] Wallmark found a correlation between subvocalization and timbral perception; however, subvocalization was only present when the timbre was perceived to be a good sound. Conversely, when the sound was perceived to be bad, other motor areas of the brain were active.

Patrik Juslin and Petri Laukka describe the process of listening and perceiving sound as a "decoding" process.[50] The person singing uses specific "codes" to communicate. To interpret the sound, the listener uses codes while listening. If the codes from the listener and the singer are the same, then the listener perceives the sound as good. *Mirroring, matching,* and *empathizing* are all words used by Juslin, Laukka, and Wallmark to describe the process of listening to a recognized sound and appraising it as good.[51]

Timbral perception is complex and involves both conscious and subconscious responses. A person hears and appraises a sound based on her experience and culture. The immediate classification of timbre into good and bad categories is culturally mediated and subconscious. When a sound is perceived to be good, the listener sympathetically mirrors the sound with subvocalization; however, if the sound is perceived to be bad, the listener is not vocally engaged. These findings indicate that if voice teachers diversify their exposure to multiple singing timbres and approaches, they may be more sympathetic and therefore empathetic toward their students from diverse backgrounds.

With this in mind, one might ask, why might vocal educators be hesitant to encourage vocal exploration? Perhaps this is due to the misconception that experimentation with one's timbral palette might lead to "unhealthy" singing. Unfortunately, discussions about the "healthy" singing voice, although seemingly unproblematic, have been rarely critically analyzed, allowing for the continued "exaltation"[52] of the bel canto technique and the justification of its superiority. Nicole Becker and Jeanne Goffi-Fynn, on the other hand, use tenets of the bel canto technique to encourage a "healthy, *flexible* vocal technique"[53] as a means of attending to students' cultural and musical identities as well as the development of their vocal instrument. In doing so, students are empowered to become agents of their own singing voices.

Bel canto technique as one way to sing is unproblematic and certainly meaningful for many, myself included; however, it is the discourse of superiority, rarely questioned within schools of music, that allows for the marginalization of other singing styles and impedes teachers' preparation for culturally sustaining vocal teaching. Paris and Alim reiterate that culturally sustaining pedagogy calls for teachers to both empower their students to sustain the cultural competence of their communities as well as equip their students with knowledge of the dominant cultural competence.[54] By attending to both knowledge systems, one that recognizes a students' identity and another that offers access to the dominant culture, culturally sustaining pedagogy might also be described as a humane education that "promotes the highest development of every individual."[55]

Practical Suggestions

Typically, postsecondary applied voice lessons and studio classes are taught with classical vocal performance in mind. Applied voice teachers usually have performance degrees and teach with the same philosophy and methods they encountered in their undergraduate and graduate training, geared toward performance. Most often, they do not have music education degrees and may not be familiar with the vocal needs of K-12 music teachers.

Ideally, the applied voice lessons and voice studio class would be different for music education majors than for voice performance majors. This, however, may not be realistic in the short term. In the curriculum, there are ways in which the current approach can be supplemented or altered to encourage a more equitable vocal education. In place of the vocal studio class that is traditionally performance based, one suggested alternative is a case-based, critically reflective voice class. This course incorporates discussion, singing, teaching as well as Skype instruction from voice teachers around the world. Units begin with the presentation of particular singing styles from around the world with video clips and recordings. These cases provide a catalyst for class discussion which I frame with the following questions:

> Why do university music programs only teach Western classical vocal technique to music education students who will be encountering K-12 students from many backgrounds and musical cultures?
> What are the implications of these limitations?
> What do you observe from the different cases (vocally)?
> What were your initial emotional and vocal reactions to each musical example?
> How might we diversify vocal teaching?

This discussion provides a framework for the singing and teaching that follow. First, Skype sessions with singing teachers who specialize in non-Western classical singing styles provide interactive, diverse instruction and perspectives. One example of the many resources available for this type of instruction is the Complete Vocal Institute, whose teachers specialize in teaching diverse vocal techniques and are available for group Skype sessions.[56] After the case studies, class discussion, and Skype lessons, I ask students to choose one singing technique with which they are unfamiliar and to practice this vocality for the following class session. In addition, each student is asked to prepare a short melody from the vocal technique they chose and a lesson plan to work with the class on this melody and vocality. Once the students have completed this project, we repeat the process of case study, discussion, vocal instruction, practice, and teaching. This continues throughout the semester.

The intent of the course is to encourage students to consider alternative vocal paradigms, both theoretically and practically and perhaps the ways that a limited paradigm is exclusive. This is fostered with critical reflection as well as empathic engagement with diverse vocalities, both as a singer and as an educator. The intent of the course is not for students to become experts but rather for them to be exposed to a wide range of singing styles and vocal resources that they can pursue with more depth in the subsequent semesters. The engagement with diverse vocalities and auralities helps to broaden students' concepts of "correct" and "incorrect" singing timbres. In addition, as students grapple with new vocalities in the practice room, they become more in tune with their own vocal instruments. When combined with students' individual voice lessons, which are typically focused on learning the bel canto technique, this case-based studio class both expands and deepens students' knowledge and understanding of the singing voice.

Oftentimes, curricular changes seem impossible to implement, particularly when the changes require that educators develop new skills. This has been the case with vocal departments and the incorporation of contemporary commercial music singing techniques. However, the curricular suggestion that I am proposing in the vocal education of music education majors is possible to implement without hiring full-time faculty who are experts in every specific singing style. The format for the course is not a traditional master-apprentice model but rather an exploratory, democratic introduction to the vast world of singing timbres using online resources and Skype sessions with singing teachers around the world. The instructor of this course must be well versed with the singing voice and able to facilitate the classroom vocal explorations and discussions. Although it is not necessary that she be an expert in each specific singing style, it is imperative that she establish the course as a multicentric vocal approach, rather than a Western classical–centric approach in which all other vocalities are compared to Western classical vocalities. If done, I believe this can be a meaningful step toward diversifying postsecondary vocal education to better meet the needs of our changing society.

Conclusions and Future Directions

According to the UNESCO document, "cultural diversity is humanity's greatest source of creativity and wealth."[57] Especially within a globalized, pluralistic world, education must recognize and address the multidimensional realities with which youth are faced. Because singing is so intimately tied to culture and self, vocal education can be used to silence or empower. Culturally incongruent vocal teaching has the potential to inflict severe harm. However, by rethinking vocal pedagogy, vocal teaching can be used to promote "an environment of greater awareness and understanding of other cultures and an engagement with issues of aesthetics worldwide, leading to a recognition of the importance of other knowledge systems."[58]

Postsecondary vocal education for music educators should include multiple vocalities with a wide range of timbral aesthetics. Bel canto technique can be taught as one tradition among many, rather than the status quo to which all traditions are compared. Music educators can be better prepared to teach and affirm their students' voices if they are exposed to and can produce nasal, twangy, dark, and belted—to name a few—vocal sounds. In fact, the field of vocal pedagogy lacks terminology that can adequately describe the vibrancy of Chinese operatic singing, the strength of Congolese songs, the beauty of Vietnamese Ca trù, and the passion of Mariachi singing.

Vocal educators need to expose music education students to a wide range of vocalities and teach students to use their voices to produce a wide range of timbres. What is the position of one's larynx when singing an Arabic folk song? How can one achieve the strident resonance needed to sing a Native American powwow or potlatch song?[59] The discovery of diverse auralities and vocalities can take place in spaces outside of the studio and may be a part of new teacher training. The teacher must ask herself, "Where and how might I learn Mariachi singing, hip-hop, gospel singing, and Brazilian folk singing? What musical funds of knowledge are available within the community in which I teach? What vocal timbres are most relevant for the K-12 students I teach?"

Through careful study, exploration, and listening, this type of study has the potential to teach students more about the voice as they develop an acute awareness of their own vocal instrument and the possibilities of the human voice. As students simultaneously situate their own voices within the vocalities of "others," they are taking part in what Yob, in this collection, describes as "the way forward."[60] She further states, "The way forward is by recognizing and validating the Other, the individual who is different from us and at the same time, it is by fully appreciating and striving for the commonalities and the wholeness of humankind, as if there is no Other."[61] Educators who are well versed in diverse singing timbres and vocal funds of knowledge are better equipped to recognize the individual value of each student while simultaneously creating a collective space for each voice to be heard. A more equitable and humane approach to vocal teaching and the ideology in which it is steeped, better prepares teachers, empowers students from all cultural backgrounds, and allows for a more vocally democratic approach.

The vocal palette that surrounds global youth is full of vitality, expression, history, originality, and character. Educators should be equipped to sustain and encourage their students' vocal identities. As stated in the UNESCO document, "An endless array of different worldviews is available for the enrichment of all, if we are willing to abandon our certainties and open our minds to the possibilities of different explanations of reality."[62] By recognizing and harnessing students' "endless array of [vocal] worldviews" as "funds of knowledge" within the classroom, vocal education can contribute to UNESCO's vision of broadening education for "the global common good."[63]

EMILY GOOD-PERKINS is a Visiting Scholar at Indiana University, Indiana.

Notes

1. UNESCO, *Rethinking Education: Towards a Global Common Good?* (Paris: UNESCO, 2015): 1–85, http://unesdoc.unesco.org/images/0023/002325/232555e.pdf.

2. Ibid., 29.

3. Ibid., 29.

4. Gloria Ladson-Billings, "Culturally Relevant Pedagogy 2.0. a.k.a. the Remix," *Harvard Educational Review* 84, no. 1 (2014): 82.

5. Django Paris, "Culturally Sustaining Pedagogy: A Needed Change in Stance, Terminology, and Practice," *Educational Researcher* 41, no. 3 (2012): 95.

6. Victoria M. Joyce, "Bodies That Sing: The Formation of Singing Subjects" (doctoral diss., University of Toronto, Ontario, Canada, 2003); Susan Knight, "Exploring a Cultural Myth: What Adult Non-singers May Reveal about the Nature of Singing," *Phenomenon of Singing* 2 (2013): 144–154.

7. Knight, "Exploring a Cultural Myth," 145.

8. Raymond A. MacDonald, David J. Hargreaves, and Dorothy Miell, eds., *Musical Identities* (Oxford: Oxford University Press, 2002); Jean S. Phinney, "Stages of Ethnic Identity Development in Minority Group Adolescents," *Journal of Early Adolescence* 9, nos. 1–2 (1989): 34–49.

9. Knight, "Exploring a Cultural Myth," 144–154.

10. Luis C. Moll, Cathy Amanti, Deborah Neff, and Norma Gonzalez, "Funds of Knowledge for Teaching: Using a Qualitative Approach to Connect Homes and Classrooms," *Theory into Practice* 31, no. 2 (1992): 132–141.

11. Django Paris and H. Samy Alim, eds., *Culturally Sustaining Pedagogies: Teaching and Learning for Justice in a Changing World* (New York: Teachers College Press, 2017); Iris M. Yob, "There Is No Other," in this collection.

12. Paris, "Culturally Sustaining Pedagogy," 95.

13. Moll et al., "Funds of Knowledge for Teaching"; UNESCO, *Rethinking Education*, 11.

14. Paris, "Culturally Sustaining Pedagogy," 95.

15. Joyce, "Bodies That Sing," 153.

16. John Potter, *Vocal Authority: Singing Style and Ideology* (New York: Cambridge University Press, 2006).

17. Manuel P. García, *Traité complet de l'art du chant en deux parties* (Paris: Heugel, 1847).

18. Grant Olwage, "The Class and Colour of Tone: An Essay on the Social History of Vocal Timbre," *Ethnomusicology Forum* 13, no. 2 (Fall, 2004): 206.

19. Ibid., 203–226.

20. Ibid., 207.

21. Ibid., 208.

22. Pierre Bourdieu and Jean-Claude Passeron, *Reproduction in Education, Society and Culture* (London: Sage, 1990), 34, quoted in Potter, *Vocal Authority*, 190.

23. Bourdieu and Passeron, *Reproduction in Education*, 34, quoted in Potter, *Vocal Authority*, 191.

24. Pierre Bourdieu, *Language and Symbolic Power*, ed. John B. Thompson, trans. Gino Raymond and Matthew Adamson (Cambridge, MA: Harvard University Press, 1991), 47.

25. Ibid; Potter, *Vocal Authority*.

26. Ruth I. Gustafson, *Race and Curriculum: Music in Childhood Education* (New York: Palgrave MacMillan, 2009), 3.

27. Ibid., 128.

28. James Stark, *Bel Canto: A History of Vocal Pedagogy* (Toronto: University of Toronto Press, 2003), xxi.

29. Ibid.

30. Gustafson, *Race and Curriculum*.

31. Ibid; Stark, *Bel Canto*; Olwage, "Class and Colour of Tone."

32. Ibid., 216.

33. Ibid., 217.

34. Gustafson, *Race and Curriculum*; Olwage, "Class and Colour of Tone"; Stark, *Bel Canto*.

35. Bourdieu, *Language and Symbolic Power*, 49.

36. Bourdieu and Passeron, *Reproduction in Education*, 34, quoted in Potter, *Vocal Authority*, 191.

37. Julia E. Koza, "Listening for Whiteness: Hearing Racial Politics in Undergraduate School Music," *Philosophy of Music Education Review* 16, no. 2 (2008): 145–155.

38. Ibid., 148.

39. Ibid., 152.

40. Stark, *Bel Canto*.

41. Ibid., 34.

42. Cornelia Fales, "The Paradox of Timbre," *Ethnomusicology* 46, no. 1 (Winter 2002): 56–95.

43. Ibid., 56.

44. Aniruddh D. Patel, *Music, Language, and the Brain* (New York: Oxford University Press, 2010).

45. Jamie Ward, *The Student's Guide to Cognitive Neuroscience* (New York: Psychology Press, 2015), 231.

46. Zachary T. Wallmark, "Appraising Timbre: Embodiment and Affect at the Threshold of Music and Noise" (doctoral diss., University of California, Los Angeles, 2014).

47. Ibid., 163.

48. Ibid., 103.

49. Ibid., 26.

50. Patrik N. Juslin, and Petri Laukka. "Communication of Emotions in Vocal Expression and Music Performance: Different Channels, Same Code?" *Psychological Bulletin* 129, no. 5 (Fall 2003): 770.

51. Ibid; Wallmark, "Appraising Timbre."

52. Sunera Thobani, *Exalted Subjects: Studies in the Making of Race and Nation in Canada* (Toronto: University of Toronto Press, 2007).

53. Nicole Becker and Jeanne Goffi-Fynn, "Discovering Voices: Expanding Students' Musical and Vocal Ideals in an Urban Community Children's Choir," *Choral Journal* 56, no. 7 (2016): 10 (my emphasis).

54. Paris and Alim, *Culturally Sustaining Pedagogies.*

55. Yob, "There Is No Other."

56. Complete Vocal Institute, accessed September 17, 2019, http://completevocal.institute/.

57. UNESCO, *Rethinking Education.*

58. Ibid., 28.

59. Natalie Kuzmich, "Making Connections Part 4: Native North Americans—When I Hear the Drums and Singing I Begin to Feel Good," *Canadian Music Educator* 44, no. 4 (Summer 2003): 10.

60. Yob, "There Is No Other."

61. Ibid.

62. UNESCO, *Rethinking Education*, 30.

63. Moll et al., "Funds of Knowledge for Teaching"; UNESCO, *Rethinking Education.*

12

RETHINKING EDUCATION

The Four Pillars of Education in the Suzuki Studio

Blakeley Menghini

I N RETHINKING EDUCATION: TOWARDS A GLOBAL COMMON GOOD?, UNESCO identifies four pillars of education from the 1996 Delors report: learning to know, learning to do, learning to be, and learning to live together.[1] "Beyond education's immediate functionality, [the Delors report] considered the formation of the whole person to be an essential part of education's purpose."[2] Regardless of background or status, education is for the benefit of the whole person and every person. The four pillars uphold education as a child-centered common good. UNESCO shares a definition of common goods: "Those goods that, irrespective of any public or private origin, are characterized by a binding destination and necessary for the realization of the fundamental rights of all people."[3] Music educator and pedagogue Shinichi Suzuki believed that "advanced ability can be nurtured in any child," and not just musical ability.[4]

Most educational practices tend to prioritize the first two pillars of information and vocation. Although Suzuki never identified the four pillars of education, his philosophy validates the importance of all four areas. The Suzuki method provides a unique opportunity for students to grow in knowing, doing, being, and living together through playing the violin. Not only do the students develop skill in music theory, knowledge of instrument, repertoire (knowing) and playing violin (doing), but when they grow in a nurturing environment, they develop a sense of identity, owner-ship, and responsibility (being), and they acquire characteristics that help them function in a society (living together). While many violin pedagogues only accept the best and most gifted into their studios, Suzuki wrote "any child can develop in any way," musically, emotionally, or socially.[5] Fostering character development and good citizenship through education is crucial, especially for students who have a less-than-ideal home environment. In these cases, teachers must rethink their role and act accordingly, taking re-sponsibility for the child's flourishing. This chapter will propose techniques for nurturing and educating children regardless of their parental situations rather than excluding them from the Suzuki method. Above all, the purpose of this chapter is to inspire an intentional educational philosophy, putting the flourishing child at its center, where "full opportunities are provided for their full development," no matter their environment.[6] Child-centered education requires the teacher to fulfill this most considerable role.

Rethinking the Four Pillars of Education

At their core, the four pillars of education are for everyone and for the bene-fit of everyone. While I believe this to be true, the Delors report's language of "learning to" places weighty responsibility on children and can enable a passive approach from their teachers. By simply rethinking and rephrasing the language of those pillars, greater responsibility is placed on educators, where it belongs.

If we are willing to rethink and rephrase the four pillars, we may be more willing to take more responsibility for the flourishing of our students. After all, the ultimate goal of humane education is "the highest develop-ment of every individual."[7] Simple language adjustments can drastically shift our educational philosophy. Instead of "Learning to Know," the first pillar could state "Inspiring to Know." "Learning to Do" becomes "Equip-ping for Action," "Learning to Live Together" becomes "Providing Oppor-tunities to Engage in Community," and "Learning to Be" transforms into "Allowing to Be." Although they may no longer be as catchy or concise as before, this new language places more responsibility on educators and frees students from the bondage of expectations and pressure to succeed. With the original phrasing, the child is the one actively participating, but this chapter will focus more heavily on what educators can do for the sake of children.

Ideal Suzuki Community

Suzuki founded his method in the mid-twentieth century. First called the "mother tongue method" (based on language learning), the approach is known today as the "Suzuki method." The original name, along with the decade of its birth, give us a glimpse into Suzuki's view of the family unit. Suzuki admired Western culture and typical Western midcentury two-parent families composed of a father who worked and a mother who raised children. Although he recalled examples of fathers bringing their children to violin lessons, the mother typically attended the lessons and practiced with the child at home. In today's economy, many families find it impossible for one of the parents to stay home. Furthermore, many women are pursuing careers and denying the stereotypical gender roles of earlier generations. Even though families do not look and function like they did in the 1950s, the Suzuki method still relies heavily on the parent-teacher-student triangle. Stated simply by the Suzuki Association of Americas (SAA), the role of the parent is to provide the environment, the role of the teacher is to provide the lessons, and the role of the student is to practice.[8] While this may be a good starting place, more clarification better nurtures the children involved.

The parent is responsible for the child in emotional, musical, and financial ways. As the primary caregiver of the child, the parent creates a loving environment in which the student can flourish into his or her best self. Whether a musician or not, the parent is expected to be the home practice partner, especially for younger children. This requires the parent's presence in every lesson, so they understand the assigned concepts and exercises. As the practice partner at home, the parent must respect the teacher's authority. For instance, parents should not decide when the child is ready to begin or finish a piece; they must only guide the child in the assignment the teacher gives. If close supervision is not needed, say, for an older child, the parent still enforces the habit of practice. Financially, the parent must provide transportation to and from the lesson, the means for owning or renting an instrument, and payment for the lessons, books, recordings, and other materials.

It should be noted that the Suzuki method does require resources such as instruments and lessons. As understanding about common goods and social justice moves forward, many socially conscious organizations offer scholarships for students with financial hardship. Many great and inspiring recordings of Suzuki repertoire can also be found on YouTube free of charge. The Suzuki method is for every child, no matter the ability level or personal development. This is a major difference between Suzuki and other leading pedagogies, for instance the bel canto technique of singing. As Emily Good-Perkins identifies, this singing technique is for "the few and not . . . the many."[9] While famous pedagogues like Ivan Galamian taught musical geniuses and influenced the conservatory sphere, Suzuki influenced families in their own homes and communities.

The SAA describes the student's role as simply "practicing."[10] While a primary facet of their role, practicing is not the whole picture. The students are expected to listen to their recordings and other students' performances and they themselves are expected to perform semi-regularly. The student is also expected to respect the authority of the teacher and parent and to trust both. If trust and respect are lacking, the lessons and home practice will suffer. Trust and respect, however, are not given, they are earned. In the most basic way, the child's role falls more under the adults' responsibilities. Left to a six-year-old child, practicing would consist of playing the newest, most fun song once or twice. The teacher and parent can work to provide the child with opportunities to make better decisions in their practice.

The teacher's responsibility is to give the violin lessons, which involves a gamut of duties. They must equip the child with the knowledge needed for musicality, listening, music theory, aural skills, violin technique, and physical care for the instrument and bow. The teacher also has the critical responsibility of making sure their students avoid injuries caused by poor technique. They should foster a love of music and other arts. They also must be flexible, solving problems in the moment, as well as in-advance lesson planning. Teachers must also practice hospitality, welcoming *all* students "across the threshold," providing opportunities and acceptance.[11]

While revision of language is on the table, Suzuki's parent-teacher-student triangle could also benefit from some rephrasing. The concept of a triangular relationship evokes ideas of shared responsibility and cooperation, split evenly into three. The Suzuki relationship, however, should center around the child, for the child. I argue for leaving the triangular language behind and using "Suzuki community" in its place. Suzuki community also suggests a broad, hopeful image for children with absent parents or unstable home environments. Suzuki community exists to benefit, care for, and support the child at its center, where others might fulfill the role of absent or ineffective members of the triangle. Instead of a triangle as its grounding metaphor, a solar system image may better illustrate the Suzuki community.

When Suzuki community is healthy and properly functioning, the Suzuki method thrives and the child flourishes. Parents benefit from this relationship because they feel involved and important. By attending the lessons, they maintain a relationship with the teacher, freeing them to contact the teacher about any issues at home. Suzuki community also helps the parent and teacher feel like a united front when it comes to practice. If parents are uninvolved in lessons, they may just tell their child to "go practice your violin," without clear expectations for the child. Requests like "time for review, and then three minutes of vibrato practice" are much more effective. The teacher can teach more effectively because the parents can more accurately report the home practice than a young child. The parent can explain that an assignment was unclear, or that the student had trouble staying on task. This information is key to making better assignments in the future. Perhaps most of all, the child benefits from a well-functioning community. He is nurtured and cared for by multiple adults who have his well-being in mind. The information he learns at the lesson is reinforced throughout the week, making the concepts more accessible. Finally, students and adults alike benefit from developing cross-generational relationships built on mutual trust and respect. However, the parent-teacher-student triangle is an oversimplified concept that places too much responsibility on the child. If teachers are willing to accept responsibility for building community with the flourishing child at its center, the Suzuki method can have a greater impact on education.

The Suzuki method's focus on relationships sets it apart from other methods and emphasizes the common good. According to *Rethinking Education*, "the common good is . . . inherent to the relationships that exist among the members of a society tied together in a collective endeavour."[12] Violin lessons focused on technique, talent, and virtuosity tend to weigh a student's worth by their inborn abilities and their hours of private practice. A much more humane approach, however, is focused on community, where all children in the community are valued and equal. The teacher and parent(s) work together to give the child a nourishing experience through music. The only way to go about this is to adopt a humane approach to music education: child-centered, not violin-centered. The child can simply "be," and by being, they are worthy of growing, developing, and learning. Every child can "be" and therefore no child is excluded from this type of education.

Suzuki for Today

The ideal Suzuki environment is hard to find. Poor conditions are sometimes the direct fault of the parent, but very often are out of the parent's control. A common problem is absent parents: the child is raised by grandparents or another relative, or the child is an orphan. Occasionally, the parent is physically or emotionally unavailable to the child. At times, financial hardship requires the parents to be absent.

Other poor conditions can hinder the child's flourishing. For example, some music programs do not allow the students to take the instruments home to practice. The students play their instruments a couple of times a week as a part of their music program, but home practice is impossible. In some cases, lessons are only available during the school day, therefore eliminating the parent's involvement. I previously taught at a school where the parents paid the school their lesson fees and the school paid me. I had no contact whatsoever with the parents. Similarly, through many community programs, only group lessons are available. While group lessons are extremely helpful, a weekly private lesson is necessary to help students individually flourish. Some families can simply hire a private teacher, which may not be possible for other families. Other more severe conditions include financially and emotionally unsupportive parents or a hostile home environment. When the ideal conditions are impossible, the teacher must fill the gap for the child. In these cases, the teacher should be willing to adapt their main purpose: to help the child flourish, not to create a prodigy.

When dealing with nonpresent parents, teachers should widen the scope of the Suzuki community, include the alternative caregiver; inviting them to the lessons or sending home evaluations. If parents seem uninterested, teachers should reach out—repeatedly, if needed—to the parent. Sending email updates and providing reading materials is an easy way to invite the parent's involvement. *Nurtured by Love*, by Suzuki, and *Helping Parents Practice*, by Edmund Sprunger, are examples of inspiring resources.[13] Most of all, in the case of a nonpresent parent, the teacher must earn the child's trust.

Students in less-than-ideal conditions often lack the encouragement that so easily grows in the Suzuki method. The teacher should support the child in as many ways as possible, including being present for the child. This could translate to something as simple as listening to the child. When students come in for their lessons, it can help them feel valued if their teacher listens intently to the stories they share. Teachers can also musically support students with absent parents by providing and attending as many performance opportunities as possible. Teaching by ear keeps the cost of materials down and it also empowers the students because they memorize so many pieces. They can feel comfortable playing their violin anywhere without a music stand and they can draw from any piece in their mental library. Instilling positivity in students like this is crucial; hopefully they will practice positivity in everyday life. If a student is not allowed to bring their instrument home to practice, teachers should give listening assignments and physical activities the children can do at home without a violin and without supervision. When group lessons are the only option, teachers should try to meet the needs of every child. This can be quite difficult and at times frustrating, because it means the entire class will have to take a slow to moderate pace. This slower pace, however, provides peer-teaching opportunities for advanced students.

Living in an imperfect world and teaching in less-than-ideal situations, music teachers should always instruct with the nurtured child in mind. They must equip the child with the knowledge needed for musicality, listening, music theory, aural skills, proper technique, and physical care for the instrument. They should foster a love of music and other arts. Beyond this, the teacher may also need to compensate for whatever is lacking in the student's home environment so they can flourish musically, relationally, and emotionally, being supported by growth in knowing, doing, being, and living in community. Fostered through relationships, students not only learn practical knowledge such as performance and instrument care, but they also grow in their character. Suzuki's view that "the purpose of music education is to develop noble human beings in order to make the world more peaceful and loving," can guide music educators of all varieties toward a philosophy that treats education as a common good, deserved by all and benefitting all.[14] In order for Suzuki's vision to be fulfilled and for music education to be a true common good, teachers must work toward musical, interpersonal, and intrapersonal goals.

Musical Aims: Inspiring to Know and Equipping to Do

The Suzuki teacher's most obvious task is of a musical nature. The first goal is to help the student learn by ear. This enables the child to focus on technique instead of being buried in a music book. Furthermore, teaching by ear encourages learning socially. To do this successfully, however, the student must listen to her Suzuki recording at home so the music grows more familiar. Learning aurally is done most easily in small musical sub-phrases, which helps the child notice patterns in the compositions. Teaching students to play by ear is practical, inspiring, and effective, especially for younger students. This enables them to learn music in the same way they learn language—first hearing, then making sounds, then forming words, then sentences, then reading and writing.

Another musical aim is proficiency in the core repertoire, where the child demonstrates understanding of important concepts in each piece. Some of these concepts are taught explicitly; for example, in "Chorus from Judas Maccabeus" in *Suzuki Book 2*, the student should know that the piece is for creating beautiful tone. Each note should ring and resonate. Other concepts are not as explicit. For example, the rhythmic variations for "Twinkle, Twinkle, Little Star" (the first piece in *Book 1*) are intended to develop the child's bow arm technique. I do not let my beginning students pass these variations until they produce a beautiful sound with a coordinated, relaxed bow arm in the correct position. I do not, however, explain all of this to the students. Instead, I encourage them to focus on their posture and sound. True proficiency in Suzuki violin is the ability to demonstrate understanding through playing. Sometimes this understanding is subconscious ("Twinkle") and other times at the forefront of the performer's mind ("Chorus"). Either way, students demonstrate they can think like a violinist.

Proficiency has many benefits, including simplified collaboration and interaction with other students, ease in performing and sharing music, and feelings of accomplishment and ownership. The method books determine the core repertoire, so proficiency comes from *how* the pieces are taught, practiced, and performed. The teacher equips the student with practice tools to conquer difficult passages (slow practice, stop-bow practice, unit practice, one- two- and three-track thinking, and repetition) as well as expressive tools (dynamics, bow speed, phrasing, and breathing). Even though Suzuki teacher trainers can explain the main teaching points of each piece, proficiency is neither objective nor consistent among teachers. Instead, each one must decide his or her own personal requirements for proficiency.

A further musical aim is proper technique. The Suzuki method books contain very few descriptions or pictures of posture and left-hand position, so most technique is explained, evaluated, and corrected by the instructor. Many different views of technique exist. For example, Suzuki himself was instructed in Germany to hold a book under his bow arm while playing to restrict movement of the upper arm. As pedagogy evolved, teachers discovered a frozen upper arm leads to tension and inhibits use of the whole bow. Opinions differ on everything from the position of the left thumb to the tilt of the bow. Some teachers argue small children should have "pinky houses" (small pinky-sized cups made of tape and attached to the bow), and others believe it weakens the small finger. Some teachers believe the left foot should be slightly forward to support the instrument and others believe this twists the spine in a damaging way, so the feet should be directly across from one another. These ideas vary teacher-to-teacher and evolve over time.

Since Suzuki materials contain little instruction for technique, the teacher is responsible for gaining knowledge from other teachers, performers, and other resources. Occasionally the SAA will publish new pedagogical findings in their journal and on their website, only to be seen by subscribing teachers. In all my pedagogical studies, I have yet to encounter a pedagogue who argues against a stable, neutral, aligned posture or a tension-free grasp of the bow and instrument. Broadly, it is the teacher's responsibility for the student to play with great posture and minimal tension.

The instructor must play with excellent technique so they model for the child. The teacher's warm, full sound should inspire the child in their own playing. The instructor must also understand the components of technique, not as a prescribed recipe, but as an individualized solution to individual issues.

Interpersonal Aims: Providing Opportunities to Engage in Community

The most basic engagement in community is through Suzuki community, our revised parent-teacher-student triangle. With this adaptation, teachers should be careful not to view the child's role as unimportant or passive. The child should be central to the Suzuki community, benefitting from all activities and relationships. The child actively participates by attending lessons, practicing, listening, performing, caring for their instrument, and giving creative input and personal expression. Everything the teacher does should support and encourage this participation.

On a larger scale, Suzuki teachers help their students engage in community by teaching group classes. Especially in classes for beginners, the parents should be active listeners and audience members. Children interact with their peers and other children of varying skill. These classes also give them an opportunity to listen to, enjoy, and encourage the accomplishments of others. The more experienced children help the less experienced, which provides a teaching opportunity. On an even larger scale, Suzuki families from around the world collaborate at Suzuki summer institutes. This, I believe, gives children a taste of what it means to be citizens in the world. When empathy, attention, listening, and encouragement are practiced in musical group environments, they hopefully transfer to life outside of music. Suzuki's vision for education was that "no one will be left behind; and based on love, [education] will foster truth, joy, and beauty as part of a child's character. If nothing else, it will at least teach children . . . to be warmhearted and to enjoy doing kindnesses to others."[15]

Intrapersonal Aims: Allowing to Be

The most complicated and unclear set of aims are the intrapersonal aims. The Suzuki teacher's intrapersonal aims are to instill a love of music, to develop good character in their students, to nurture them, and, as Suzuki believed, to develop "the whole child."[16] These are the least understood and monitored aims, possibly because they cannot be forced. No child can have good character forced upon them, it must be allowed to grow from within.

A love of music often develops naturally, but a few specific practices can help. First, the way the teacher talks about music and being a musician can have a huge impact on a student. My viola professor Sally Chisholm often talks of loving composers, being excited to play with her colleagues, and listening to transcendent recordings. She has encouraged me to develop relationships with composers I study and thus my love of music and performing has increased. Secondly, teachers should provide positive experiences for their students. For instance, making sure recitals are celebratory, encouraging, and nonjudgmental events. Having pleasurable performances creates a snowball effect that cultivates passion and drive.

According to *Rethinking Education*, "in all societies, extreme inequalities are a source of social tension and a potential catalyst of political instability and violent conflict."[17] Music educators can address inequalities in their own spheres of influence. Despite background, finances, or talent, every student should be given the equal opportunity to play, enjoy, and experience music in their schools and communities. Suzuki urges educators to consider the following: "Art exists for the human species. I think that all of the people who love art, those who teach art, and all of you, should burn with the obligation to save the world. It is necessary to be concerned about the importance of educating a really beautiful human spirit. . . . Teaching intonation, and teaching technique will never be more than a method. We are burning with a deeper mission that we must do something for the future."[18] A love of music can draw people closer together and provide all types of communities with beauty they can experience.

An all-important intrapersonal aim of a Suzuki teacher is allowing good character traits to develop in her students. Suzuki often discussed developing good character in students, but these discussions lacked concrete information. His writings on this topic are frequent enough for us to know he was deeply concerned with his students' character, however, he uses vague language (such as reference to "life force").[19] The Suzuki community clings to equivocal phrases such as "beautiful tone, beautiful heart."[20] However inspiring, this vague language is not particularly helpful in developing an educational philosophy. It is better to specify desired character traits, including but not limited to dedication, focus, openness, sensitivity, and responsibility. With specific goals in mind, teachers can more effectively communicate goals with parents and focus on them in their teaching.

Suzuki believed his method should be used to develop the "whole child." He emphasized nurturing, and this is still stressed by Suzuki-inspired pedagogues. For instance, leading violin pedagogue Mimi Zweig prioritizes what she calls the "nonjudgmental environment," where mistakes are just "neutral information that will be used to solve problems."[21] If the tone is scratchy, the student is not a bad person or a bad violinist, but merely not focused, not using the correct amount of bow speed, or not using a helpful area of the bow. Students are more hopeful and motivated when their issues can be remedied. Teachers should clarify that the home should also be a nonjudgmental environment. If a student believes they are simply a poor violinist, they will probably not become an open, sensitive performer. However, if a student understands any difficulties in their playing can be tackled by intentional practice and focus, they are far more likely to be responsible and reap the benefits of violin playing.

Music educators have the tremendous responsibility and opportunity to critically consider their personal teaching philosophies. If humane education is the goal, educators must be "human-centered [and] human-focused."[22] The Delors report's four pillars of education are worded in such a way that the child is given full responsibility for their own learning and the educator's agency is absent from the equation. Rephrasing these pillars not only gives agency to the educator and removes the weighty responsibility from the child, but it can be a first step on a long journey toward humane education. This step will lead teachers to take responsibility and even stand in the gaps for children who lack support at home, whether financial or emotional. The Suzuki method stresses the importance of the parent-teacher-student triangle, which also implies that the child is at least one-third responsible for their music education. In another powerful rephrasing, "Suzuki community" gives more responsibility to those surrounding the child and simply allows the child to be. Suzuki believed that "a truly civilized human being is thoughtful of others, pours his love on others, knows all the joy of living, and enjoys working for the happiness of all. Such a person loves other people and other people love him in return. Raising children to become such people is the best gift we can give them, and it will help in civilizing this world."[23]

BLAKELEY MENGHINI is Violist of the Griffon String Quartet, in residence at Midsummer's Music in Door County, Wisconsin.

Notes

1. UNESCO, *Rethinking Education: Towards a Global Common Good?* (Paris: UNESCO, 2015), http://unesdoc.unesco.org/images/0023/002325/232555e.pdf, 39; UNESCO, *Learning: The Treasure Within* (Paris, UNESCO, 1996), http://unesdoc.unesco.org/images/0010/001095/109590eo.pdf (commonly referred to as the Delors report).
2. UNESCO, *Rethinking Education*, 15.
3. Ibid., 77.
4. Shinichi Suzuki, *Ability Development from Age Zero*, trans. Mary Louise Nagata (1969; Miami: Summy-Birchard, 1981), 1.
5. Ibid., 28.
6. UNESCO, *Rethinking Education*, 25.
7. Iris M. Yob, "Introduction: Education for the Common Good in a Diverse World," in this collection.
8. Suzuki Association of the Americas, "About the Suzuki Method: Video Overview," accessed May 21, 2017, https://suzukiassociation.org/about/suzuki-method/.
9. Emily Good-Perkins, "Rethinking Vocal Education as a Means to Encourage Positive Identity Development in Adolescents," in this collection.
10. Ibid.
11. Jacob Axel Berglin and Thomas Murphy O'Hara, "Working with Transgender Students as a Humane Act: Hospitality in Research and in Practice," in this collection.
12. UNESCO, *Rethinking Education*, 78.
13. Suzuki, *Nurtured by Love: A New Approach to Talent Education*, trans. Waltrud Suzuki (1069; Miami: Summy-Birchard, 1983); Ed Sprunger, *Helping Parents Practice: Ideas for Making It Easier*, vol. 1 (St. Louis: Yes Publishing, 2005).

14. Karin S. Hendricks, "The Philosophy of Shinichi Suzuki: 'Music Education as Love Education,'" *Philosophy of Music Education Review* 19, no. 2 (Fall 2011), 142.

15. Suzuki, *Nurtured by Love*, 58.

16. International Suzuki Association, "The Suzuki Method," accessed July 29, 2017, http://internationalsuzuki.org/method.htm.

17. UNESCO, *Rethinking Education*, 23.

18. Suzuki, *Ability Development*, 61.

19. International Suzuki Association, "Shinichi Suzuki (1898–1998): A Short Biography," accessed December 12, 2015, http://internationalsuzuki.org/shinichisuzuki.htm.

20. Martha Shackford, "Beautiful Tone, Beautiful Heart," *American Suzuki Journal* 24, no. 4 (August 1996): 25.

21. Mimi Zweig, String Pedagogy, "Introduction: Philosophical and Pedagogical Approach," accessed July 29, 2017, http://www.stringpedagogy.com/members/?submit=START&submissionGuid=67799eac-19f6-4950-a958-ddc042d2d8a4.

22. Yob, "Introduction."

23. Suzuki, *Ability Development*, 29.

13

MUSIC EDUCATION IN SACRED COMMUNITIES

Singing, Learning, and Leading for the Global Common Good

Mary B. Thomason-Smith

MUSIC EDUCATORS WHO LEAD CHOIRS AND CONGREGATIONS IN the twenty-first century Christian church are positioned to cultivate compassionate listening within community, to educate intergenerational communities through hymns of justice, to sing theology addressing present-day global crises, and to artistically inspire action to benefit the global common good. Choral conductors, organists, instrumentalists, and singers are needed as artist-prophets of our time, keenly informed in the intersections of music, theology, and justice. Musical artists in the church bear responsibility to resound the voices of the oppressed and, through song, to guide faith communities into fresh visions of compassion, justice, and peace. Skilled in acute listening, adept to embolden the human voice through song, and attuned to the rhythm of life around us, musicians are crucial to employ humane music education for the global common good.

Will our current musical landscape within the Christian church include timely voices that sing of suffering, those that cry and lament? Will musical expressions of hope, despite adversity, yet resound? Such questions invoke the spiritual dimension of the integrated education that is called for in UNESCO's *Rethinking Education*.[1] Thus, the spiritual component is explored in this chapter, illustrating music and spirituality as channels through which humanistic education may flow. It is a vision of music education conceived from UNESCO's call for humanistic education that "integrates the multiple dimensions of human existence."[2] Learning spaces alternative to conventional academic institutions are considered, as is learning beyond traditional academic measurement.[3] Furthermore, the discussion that follows strives to answer UNESCO's appeal to consider how the "commodification of public education be countered by stronger partnerships with community associations and non-profit organizations."[4]

Consider the climate and environmental crisis as just one challenge for which humane music education generates advocacy and action, thereby benefitting the global common good. Hymnody and theology provide ample stores for education and reflection on the environmental crisis through music. What musical opportunities would create fresh spaces to cultivate healthy relationship with the natural world? The paradigm for this search is UNESCO's call for curriculum that "raises more questions than it provides answers."[5] In the discussion to follow, spirituality and music education are illumined as complements for humanistic inquiry, well suited to ask probing questions that impact the global common good and bolster UNESCO's humanistic vision to "reaffirm universal ethical principles."[6]

Our discussion focuses on three tenets of humane music education within a Christian setting. First, within each person is a spiritual dimension to be valued, cultivated, and affirmed through music. Second, music within a spiritual community provides a construct to nurture healthy relationships with neighbors, with God, and with the natural world. Third, music that celebrates the natural world will foster appreciation and care for the environment. These three values thus underpin a concept of humane music education wherein human relationships and environmental sustainability experience beneficial impact.

The environmental crisis serves as the touchstone on which I build a case for music educators in the Christian church to embrace their vital role in benefitting the global common good. To that end, I call on them to equip themselves with a robust understanding of ecotheology, a burgeoning branch of theology examining the relationship between God, humanity, and the environment. I draw on a historical model who integrated music and theology for the purpose of reform in his own time: J. S. Bach, a music educator who rigorously applied theological concepts through music, resulting in a thriving musical community. Next, I introduce the modern field of ecotheology, surveying it from a wide lens in contemporary ecojustice statements by the Christian church. Finally, I offer an example of humane music education for the global common good, specifically promoting environmental stewardship and sustainability while celebrating humane values within community.

J. S. Bach, Theology, and Reform

"But without theology, music cannot fulfill its prophetic purpose in worship," aptly states Bach scholar Robin Leaver.[7] The year 2017 marked the five hundredth anniversary of Martin Luther's ninety-five theses of 1517 and the birth of the Protestant Reformation—a timely occasion on which to reflect on the music of the Christian church in our era. Transforming the musical landscape of the Protestant church, J. S. Bach synthesized Luther's theology with music, propelling reform and providing us a model of a music educator whose theology determined and shaped his life's creative work. While a consummate composer, Bach was also a music educator, a role of his that will serve well for us to consider. There are similarities of circumstance we share with Bach; as music educators we work amid rapid societal change, needing reform, seeking artistic renderings to interpret our times. How might Bach's example of theological study and musical application inform the work of modern music educators in the church? Further, drawing on Bach's example, how might musicians in the church synthesize music education with the theology of contemporary justice issues, with significant implications for the common good, and bring this synthesis into the current musical landscape of the Christian church?

Bach's personal library reveals a musician with resources for theological study at his fingertips, including writings of Luther, sermons, Bible commentaries, and the Cavlov Bible.[8] Prior to his post as Thomaskantor in Leipzig, Bach was required to complete an examination of Lutheran theology, as was customary. This was conducted by a professor of theology in Leipzig, Johann Schmidt, who assessed Bach's knowledge of the *Book of Concord*, a collection of Lutheran confessional documents.[9] Robin Leaver highlights that music and theology were studied in conjunction in Bach's time, further evidenced by Bach's required teaching of Luther's small catechism combined with musical responsibilities.[10] Paul Brainard argues evidence of Bach's working understanding of theology is found in his masterful musical interpretations of scripture and theology.[11] Michael Marissen sums Bach's role in Leipzig as "a 'musical preacher' for the city's main Lutheran churches."[12] How might modern church music educators adopt a similar multidisciplinary approach to their work, with potential outcomes of positive reform and relevant musical offerings?

I posit Bach's understanding of theology informed and contributed in significant ways to the artistic achievement of his music; Marissen affirms, "Bach's musical settings of church cantata poetry can project significant Lutheran theological meanings that are not identical to those arrived at by simply reading the librettos; that is to say, Bach's music can *interpret*, not only reflect, the words."[13] As music educators in the heritage of Bach, how will musicians more fully encompass the rich tradition passed down to us by Bach, a music educator steeped in the theology of his time? How may music educators in the church adapt their role to include facets of theological study, composition, artistic development, and music education, all valuable components contributing to a thriving musical community? What timely synthesis of music, theology, and artistry needs to spring forth? As one answer to these questions, our focus will presently narrow to a specific modern challenge addressed by theologians and primed for the contributions of modern musical artist-prophets: the environmental and climate crisis.

Ecotheology and Music Education in the Christian Church

Ecotheology studies the relationship between God, the natural world, and humanity, considering environmental ethics within a spiritual perspective.[14] Theologian Willis Jenkins seeks to inform environmental ethics with grace, providing context for Christian communities to "rediscover new roots of practical engagement and find fertile ground for the seed of new witness."[15] Kevin W. Irwin's case for a creation-focused liturgy served as a foundation for my example that follows.[16] He asserts, "to use creation in liturgy is to show reverence for creation through, with, and in which the incarnate God is disclosed and discovered."[17] Ecotheological reading of the Bible as explored by Richard J. Clifford, SJ; Bernhard W. Anderson; and Roger S. Gottleib seeks sustainable and hopeful ecological paths based on scripture.[18] Hilary Marlow considers how "an ecological hermeneutic might interact with and inform the concerns of contemporary environmental ethics."[19] Indeed, ecotheology provides fertile ground for musical interpretation for education, advocacy, and action. Refrains of ecological lament, confession, and ultimately hope are ripe with artistic potential for expression.[20] What music of the church will inform and inspire the implementation of humane values in the environmental crisis, celebrating the natural world, and advocating for environmental justice?

Three examples will serve for our introduction to ecotheology: Pope Francis's *Encyclical on Climate Change and Inequality: On Care for Our Common Home*; the Evangelical Lutheran Church of America's *Caring for Creation: Vision, Hope, and Justice*; and *Social Principles: The Natural World* of the United Methodist Church.[21] From a wide lens, we can now examine common themes that emerge from these three statements that may facilitate humane music education.

Resonating within each of the three statements are the following ideas: the environment is in crisis as a result of human degradation and exploitation of the natural world; a spiritual response to the environmental crisis is called for; stewardship of the environment is a value of Christian faith; and humanity shares connectedness and relationship with all that is living. Exploring such ideas within a spiritual and artistic context addresses "new knowledge horizons that we need to consider" as a result of "new levels of complexity, tensions and paradoxes," as cited in *Rethinking Education*.[22] Implications for the global common good reach far and wide when students navigate tensions of spiritual and material or the value of socioeconomic development with the preservation of the environment. Such dichotomies, probed through a spiritual and artistic lens, usher students to the heart of UNESCO's challenge to "explore alternative approaches to progress and to human well-being."[23]

The encyclical of Pope Francis is a thorough and developed ecotheology, acknowledging pollution of the natural environment, specifically as it relates to global inequality and, as an issue of justice, how it intersects with the spiritual life. Next, it examines biblical narratives in relation to the environment and a discussion of the origin of the environmental crisis follows, citing the role of technology and globalization. Ecology as a matter of justice and the common good is examined; a call for dialogue between science and religion and for the development of ecological spirituality through education concludes Pope Francis's compelling argument.[24]

Caring for Creation: Vision, Hope, and Justice, from the Evangelical Lutheran Church of America, is smaller in scope than the encyclical and begins its discussion with biblical references that speak to humanity's relationship to creation, highlighting stewardship and responsibility as hallmarks of a biblically grounded response. A confession follows, acknowledging the realities of humanity's responsibility to the environmental crisis, including pollution of air and water and the exploitation of forests and soil. Citing further biblical references, hope is offered as a premise for a forward path. Finally, affirming statements of commitment by the church include: justice through participation, solidarity, sufficiency, and sustainability; creating awareness in congregations through education and programing; and ecological advocacy in the private and public sector.[25]

Social Principles: The Natural World, by the United Methodist Church, is a concise ecotheology, introduced by a call to stewardship and sustainability, followed by detailed ways that the United Methodist Church will respond. The statement is organized categorically by water, air, soil, minerals, plants; use of energy resources; animal life; global climate stewardship; space; science and technology; food safety; and food justice. Within each subheading are declarations of actions through which members may seek to improve conditions, such as by saving energy, supporting sustainable agriculture, and reducing the use of hazardous pesticides. With clarity and brevity, this ecotheological statement of the United Methodist Church depicts a community responding to the needs of the natural world.[26]

Each of these three statements provides a springboard on which musicians may cultivate fresh intersections of music and ecotheology. Provided within them are distinct values and clear arguments that may be explored and interpreted through musical expression. Through such, these tenets may be further disseminated into a broader intergenerational audience, affirming learners of all ages, generating dialogue, reform, and justice. These resources provide music educators a richly defined ecotheology that celebrates humanistic values. I call for music educators in the church to develop curriculum that gives voice to ecotheology, manifesting Pope Francis's challenge: "Environmental education should facilitate making the leap towards the transcendent which gives ecological ethics its deepest meaning. It needs educators capable of developing an ethics of ecology, and helping people, through effective pedagogy, to grow in solidarity, responsibility and compassionate care."[27] To this end, I offer an example of humane music education beyond the formal sector, conducted in learning spaces that engage the natural world, championing social and environmental harmony, and inviting students on a search for the global common good.

Hymns of Ecojustice: An Example of Music Education for the Global Common Good

The following example of a humane music education curriculum introduces ecotheology through the music of the Christian church, exploring implications for justice and the common good while enriching the students' relationship with the natural world. It provides a musical pathway for a spiritual response to the ecotheological values students choose to embrace. Through inquiry and reflection, this curriculum strives for the balanced approach advocated by Hanne Rinholm and Öivind Varkøy, providing experiences that invite (not prescribe) music to "shake, disquiet, and challenge us in relation to conventional 'truths' and values."[28] For experiential learning, the classroom expands from the confines of choir room and sanctuary into the prayer garden and beyond, mingling music and nature. Four sessions are organized by an overarching theme and introduce an ecotheological principle extracted from modern statements of the Christian church. Intended for an intergenerational classroom, the concepts presented are adaptable to the abilities of the individuals in the setting. Incorporating meditation, prayer, and silence—educational opportunities unique to the setting of spiritual community—provides valuable opportunity for discussion, reflection, affirmation, and growth. Implementation may be framed in a variety of formats, adaptable for established choral settings for children or adults, as seasonal experience for intergenerational engagement such as a weekly summer choir school, or as a focused retreat occasion.

The theme of the first session is *relationship*; the goal is to enhance students' connection to the natural world and to foster their appreciation for the relationship they share with all things living. Facilitate the session outdoors, utilizing transportable instruments and engaging students with the natural world. Two principles from ecotheology are taught. First, Pope Francis states, "Nature cannot be regarded as something separate from ourselves or as a mere setting in which we live. We are part of nature, included in it and thus in constant interaction with it."[29] Second, from the Evangelical Lutheran Church of America, we are told that "humanity is intimately related to the rest of creation" and "scripture speaks of humanity's kinship with other creatures."[30] For inquiry and reflection, invite students to listen to sounds of nature around them, encouraging their reflection on the following: What is the music of the natural world? Who is singing? How may I join nature's song? What relationship do I share with the natural world around me?

St. Francis of Assisi's "All Creatures, Worship God Most High" gives voice to an ecotheology of our familial relationship with the natural world.[31] Begin with a soloist offering the hymn, inviting students to listen for phrases that convey relationship, inviting students to signify each time an element of the natural world is named as sister or brother. Set to "Lasst Uns Erfreuen," the refrain of alleluias provides an accessible starting point to teach the melody, while verses may be offered by a soloist. Alternatively, for a choir of skilled musicians, the hymn may be taught in its entirety. The repetitive alleluias in "Lasst Uns Erfreuen" may further engage students to observe similar repetitive melodic or rhythmic patterns in the sounds of nature.

Invite students to respond through movement as the hymn is played on an instrument or sung; ask students to use motions to depict brother wind, brother fire, sister water, or sister moon. Finally, invite concluding reflections and response: How may our shared relationship with the natural world transform the way we care for it? Invite students to reflect in silent meditation, listening attentively to the songs of the natural world around them.

Session two establishes the theme *stewardship*. In ecotheological terms, stewardship may be introduced through the United Methodist Church's *Social Principles*: "Water, air, soil, minerals, energy resources, plants, animal life, and space are to be valued and conserved because they are God's creation and not solely because they are useful to human beings. God has granted us stewardship of creation. We should meet these stewardship duties through acts of loving care and respect."[32] *Caring for Creation* highlights stewardship as the work of justice: "When we act interdependently and in solidarity with creation, we *do* justice. We serve and keep the earth, trusting its bounty can be sufficient for all, and sustainable."[33] Outlined by Pope Francis is the aspect of stewardship that considers future generations: "Since the world has been given to us, we can no longer view reality in a purely utilitarian way, in which efficiency and productivity are entirely geared to our individual benefit. Intergenerational solidarity is not optional, but rather a basic question of justice, since the world we have received also belongs to those who will follow us."[34] Invite students' to reflect on how stewards are different from consumers: What are ways we may, as stewards, care for natural resources? How do our actions sustain or suppress the natural world?

Shirley Erena Murray's hymn "Touch the Earth Lightly" highlights themes of stewardship, acknowledging the earth as gift, calling for respect and care of its resources, and affirming that these gifts must last for a new generation.[35] Observe these themes in the words of the first verse: "Touch the earth lightly, use the earth gently, nourish the life of the world in our care: gift of great wonder, ours to surrender, trust for the children tomor-row will bear." A pointed confession is offered in the second verse: "We who endanger, who create hunger, agents of death for all creatures that live, we who would foster clouds of disaster, God of our planet, forestall and for-give!" Paired with Swee-Hong Lim's tune "Ai Hu," a lilting 3/4 melody with sequencing phrases, this hymn is accessible to varied levels of musical abil-ity. Given the slow waltz-like tune, invite students to form a circle, moving together as the hymn is sung by the group or an individual. Invite students to imagine themselves as a circle of life, of protection, of respect for one an-other and the earth. Invite response and reflection: How will I encircle with protection and respect, the natural resources that sustain my life? How may I touch the earth lightly? Conclude with silent meditation in a circle.

In the third session, *lament* is the overarching theme. Acknowledg-ing harmful actions and their effects is explored in the United Methodist Church's *Social Principles: The Natural World*: "Economic, political, so-cial and technological developments . . . have led to regional defoliation, dramatic extinction of species, massive human suffering, overpopulation, and misuse and overconsumption of natural and nonrenewable resources, particularly by industrialized societies. . . . Therefore, let us recognize the responsibility of the church and its members to place a high priority on changes . . . to support a more ecologically equitable and sustainable world leading to a higher quality of life for all creation."[36] Pope Francis highlights misguided values that result in oppression: "While some are concerned only with financial gain, and others with holding on to or increasing their power, what we are left with are conflicts or spurious agreements where the last thing either party is concerned about is caring for the environment and protecting those who are most vulnerable."[37] *Caring for Creation* states, "Not content to be made in the image of God, we have rebelled and disrupt-ed creation. . . . Our sin and captivity lie at the roots of the current crisis."[38] Students may explore the theme of lament by reflecting on questions such as the following: For what aspects of the natural world do I share respon-sibility? What results when there is over consumption, rather than steward-ship, of natural resources?

Ruth Duck's hymn "Creative God, You Spread the Earth" resonates an ecotheology of lament and confession: "Forgive us for each flow'r and bird now vanished by our hand," "Forgive us, that, the last to come, we threaten sea and air," and "Forgive us that we grieve your heart, destroying what you do."[39] In response, a positive action is offered as reply: "Teach us simpler, gentler ways to live on earth with you," and "Teach us to tend life's fragile web with wise and tender care." The lamenting melody, "Kingsfold," by Ralph Vaughan Williams, provides a fitting musical pairing to the text, set in a slow 4/4 meter, with a descending three-note melodic pattern evoking the contrition of a humble confession. Invite students to discuss which phrases of the text are words of confession; highlight phrases that affirm acts of justice.

To experience lament and confession through movement, invite students to assume a posture of lament and confession, kneeling or sitting down. Direct students to tap an ostinato rhythm of quarter, quarter, half-note on their heart or knee. Instruct students to imagine the ostinato representing lament for repetitive harmful actions to the environment. Play the melody of "Kingsfold" on an instrument, while students maintain the tapping ostinato. Maintain a period of silent reflection and meditation at the conclusion of the hymn. Ask students to reflect on what emotions are experienced when singing lament and confession. As we sing hymns of lament in community, how may this act propel our progress from negative choices to actions of justice, stewardship, and peace?

Building on the previous themes of *relationship, stewardship,* and *lament,* session four culminates with *hope.* In *Caring for Creation,* the Evangelical Lutheran Church of America cites hope through affirming its commitments: "We celebrate the vision of hope and justice for creation, and dedicate ourselves anew." In practical terms, the challenge extended is for congregations to assume the role of a "Creation Awareness Center," wherein theological foundations of creation care are explored through education, annual observances, programming, and advocacy.[40] Hope through dialogue is encouraged by the ecotheology of the United Methodist Church: "Science and theology are complementary rather than mutually incompatible. We therefore encourage dialogue between the scientific and theological communities and seek the kind of participation that will enable humanity to sustain life on earth and, by God's grace, increase the quality of our common lives together."[41] Finally, the *Encyclical on Climate Change and Inequality* concludes with hope for an "ecological conversion," a commitment to the environment that integrates spirituality, inspiration, and protection. Citing the "lack of awareness of our common origin, of our mutual belonging, and of a future to be shared with everyone," this call to conversion envisions that a "great cultural, spiritual and educational challenge stands before us, and it will demand that we set out on the long path of renewal."[42]

Engage in dialogue with students, inviting them to imagine hopeful visions for the natural world. How may we, as musicians and students of ecotheology, invite a multidimensional dialogue that includes science, faith, and advocacy? How may an "ecological conversion" be supported and inspired through music?

Mary Kay Beall's text "The Lord of Life, a Vine is He" is rich with vibrant imagery, evoking a healthy and hopeful greening of the natural world and our connected spirituality within it.[43] Images of vine, fruit, and branches weave through Beall's text that calls for pruning, grafting, shaping, yielding, and growing in the "Source Divine," the "Lord of Life," and the "call of Christ." Using inclusive language, an experience of community emerges through word pictures of branches joined and grafted: "The Source Divine calls us to come, with him entwine" and the hopeful "Word sown deep in us will be both sun and rain, sufficiency." Paired with John Carter's tune "Latham," the joy of the text is reflected in the simple, dance-like, motivic tune, four phrases in an accessible AA'BA phrase structure.

Invite students to reflect on ecological conversion in light of the hymn: How is the support of a singing and musical community helpful in making positive ecological changes? To incorporate movement and action with musical expression, plant a tree, vine, or other planting, as a culminating action of hope and community. Following the planting, encircle it, singing the four hymns from each session. Conclude with silence, allowing the community space and time to appreciate the gifts of music, the environment, and the new life planted.

Conclusion

Exploring fresh applications for humane music education, I consider the Christian church as a setting where intersections of music, ecotheology, and spirituality converge to influence the global common good. Fundamental to my example are humane values explored through music, organized by four themes: relationship, stewardship, lament, and hope. Within this construct, learners reflect on the human need for connection to the natural world. They explore the spectrum of human emotion, express human desire to be heard and to contribute, and acknowledge human vulnerability to discouragement. Affirming that the whole of human experience includes both intellect and spirit, this curriculum example values learning that extends beyond the mind and into the heart. By design, this example provides hymns by contemporary female composers and theologians amid historical and male counterparts, aiming to flesh out a multidimensional and humanistic perspective of its themes. The inclusion of both Roman Catholic and Protestant ecotheology respects humanity's diverse needs to engage in a varied spectrum of religious traditions, symbolism, and ritual. My interpretation of humanistic music education within the Christian church aims to grow the human spirit, to allow for its creative expression, and to engage with that which is beyond and greater than our humanity.

Finally, I proposed an example engaging students in a quest to discover ethical values, environmental stewardship, and social harmony as advocated in *Rethinking Education*.[44] Revealed were possibilities to integrate humanistic education within spiritual and artistic dimensions, supporting UNESCO's depiction of the global common good: it is "not only the 'good life' of individuals that matters, but also the goodness of the life that humans hold in common."[45] Furthermore, this example intends to serve as a threshold on a trajectory of continued exploration of the "transformative and reconciling power of music," called for by Alexandra Kertz-Welzel in this collection.[46]

Through humane music education in the Christian church, connections between environmental health and the spiritual journey may be explored, our responsibility to ecological well-being defined, and God's loving action for the natural world celebrated. In conclusion, I offer Pope Francis's benediction: "Let us sing as we go. May our struggles and our concern for this planet never take away the joy of our hope."[47]

MARY B. THOMASON-SMITH researches intersections of sacred music and music education, drawing on her experience as a choral director, organist, and private studio instructor in Bloomington, Indiana. She holds a doctor of music in organ from the Jacobs School of Music at Indiana University.

Notes

1. UNESCO, *Rethinking Education: Towards a Global Common Good?* (Paris: UNESCO, 2015), 38.

2. Ibid., 11.

3. Ibid., 37.

4. Ibid., 81.

5. Ibid., 41.

6. Ibid., 37.

7. Robin A. Leaver, *J. S. Bach as Preacher: His Passions and Music in Worship*, ed. Carl Schalk (St. Louis: Concordia, 1982), 7.

8. Robin A. Leaver, *Bachs Theologische Bibliothek / Bach's Theological Library* (Neyhausen-Stuttgart: Hänssler-Verlag, 1985).

9. Robin A. Leaver, "Music and Lutheranism," in *The Cambridge Companion to Bach*, ed. John Butt (New York: Cambridge University Press, 1997), 35.

10. Ibid., 42.

11. Paul Brainard, "Bach as Theologian?" in *Reflections on the Sacred: A Musicological Perspective*, ed. Paul Brainard (New Haven, CT: Yale Institute of Sacred Music, 1994), 7.

12. Michael Marissen, *Bach and God* (New York: Oxford University Press, 2016), 152.

13. Ibid., 5.

14. Robert Booth Fowler, *The Greening of Protestant Thought* (Chapel Hill: The University of North Carolina Press, 1995), 91–107.

15. Willis Jenkins, *Ecologies of Grace: Environmental Ethics and Christian Theology* (Oxford: Oxford University Press, 2008), 227.

16. Kevin W. Irwin, "The Sacramentality of Creation and the Role of Creation in Liturgy and Sacraments," in *Preserving the Creation: Environmental Theology and Ethics*, ed. Kevin W. Irwin and Edmund D. Pellegrino (Washington, DC: Georgetown University Press, 2007), 67–111.

17. Ibid., 73.

18. Richard J. Clifford, SJ, "The Bible and the Environment," in *Preserving the Creation: Environmental Theology and Ethics*, ed. Kevin W. Irwin and Edmund D. Pellegrino (Washington, DC: Georgetown University Press, 2007), 1–26; Bernhard W. Anderson, "The Sacredness of the Earth," in *Preserving the Creation: Environmental Theology and Ethics*, ed. Kevin W. Irwin and Edmund D. Pellegrino (Washington, DC: Georgetown University Press, 2007), 27–32; Roger S. Gottlieb, *A Greener Faith: Religious Environmentalism and Our Planet's Future* (New York: Oxford University Press, 2006), 21.

19. Hilary Marlow, *Biblical Prophets and Contemporary Environmental Ethics: Re-reading Amos, Hosea, and First Isaiah* (Oxford: Oxford University Press, 2009), 245.

20. Jenkins, *Ecologies of Grace*, 230.

21. Pope Francis, *Encyclical on Climate Change and Inequality: On Care for Our Common Home* (Brooklyn: Melville House, 2015); Evangelical Lutheran Church of America, *Caring for Creation: Vision, Hope, and Justice*, accessed March 1, 2017, https://www.elca.org/en/Faith/Faith-and-Society/Social-Statements/Caring-for-Creation; United Methodist Church, *Social Principles: The Natural World*, accessed March 1, 2017, http://www.umc.org/what-we-believe/the-natural-world.

22. UNESCO, *Rethinking Education*, 21.

23. Ibid., 21.

24. Pope Francis, *Encyclical on Climate Change*, 16–38; 39–62; 63–84.

25. Evangelical Lutheran Church, *Caring for Creation*.

26. United Methodist Church, *Social Principles*.

27. Pope Francis, *Encyclical on Climate Change*, 129.

28. Hanne Rinholm and Øivind Varkøy, "Music Education for the Common Good? Between Hubris and Resignation: A Call for Temperance," in this collection.

29. Pope Francis, *Encyclical on Climate Change*, 86.

30. Evangelical Lutheran Church, *Caring for Creation*, 2.

31. Francis of Assisi, "All Creatures, Worship God Most High!," in *Evangelical Lutheran Worship* (Minneapolis: Augsburg Fortress, 2006), 835.

32. United Methodist Church, introduction to *Social Principles*.

33. Evangelical Lutheran Church, *Caring for Creation*, 6.

34. Pope Francis, *Encyclical on Climate Change*, 98.

35. Shirley Erena Murray, "Touch the Earth Lightly," in *Worship and Song* (Nashville: Abingdon Press, 2011), 3129.

36. United Methodist Church, introduction to *Social Principles*.

37. Pope Francis, *Encyclical on Climate Change*, 121.

38. Evangelical Lutheran Church, *Caring for Creation*, 3.

39. Ruth Duck, "Creative God, You Spread the Earth," in *Chalice Hymnal*, ed. Daniel B. Merrick (St. Louis: Chalice, 1995), 697.

40. Evangelical Lutheran Church, *Caring for Creation*, 9.

41. United Methodist Church, "Science and Technology," in *Social Principles*.

42. Pope Francis, *Encyclical on Climate Change*, 125.

43. Mary Kay Beall, "The Lord of Life, a Vine Is He," in *Worship and Song*, (Nashville: Abingdon Press, 2011), 3155.

44. UNESCO, *Rethinking Education*, 21.

45. Ibid., 78.

46. Alexandra Kertz-Welzel, Leonard Tan, Martin Berger, and David Lines, "A Humanistic Approach to Music Education: (Critical) International Perspectives," in this collection.

47. Pope Francis, *Encyclical on Climate Change*, 148.

14

WORKING WITH TRANSGENDER STUDENTS AS A HUMANE ACT

Hospitality in Research and in Practice

Jacob Axel Berglin and Thomas Murphy O'Hara

Introduction

In the summer of 2017, philosopher Anne Dufourmantelle jumped into the waters of Pampellone Beach near St.-Tropez, France, in an attempt to save the lives of two children whom she'd never met.[1] While the children survived, Dufourmantelle was unable to be resuscitated. As a student of Jacques Derrida, Dufourmantelle's dedication to hospitality and risk makes her decision to sacrifice her life unsurprising.[2] Still, how does an individual come to this decision? How does a parent and spouse make the decision to place the lives of others—of strangers—before her own? What responsibility does an individual have to the greater (or common) good and, for that matter, who decides what constitutes that good?

These questions are explored in *Rethinking Education*, the UNESCO document that undergirds this collection of essays.[3] While the authors are direct in their repudiation of educational systems that "alienate individuals and treat them as commodities, and of social practices that divide and dehumanize people," their exploration of the relationship between individual protections and the common good is more nuanced.[4] As detailed in the introduction to this work, the emergence and development of the "common good" from the Faure and Delors reports and throughout *Rethinking Education* suggests an impetus in educational settings to honor both the individual as constituent part and individuals as the sum of the whole.[5] Indeed, improper use of terms like *global good*, *greater good*, or *common good* might justify the exclusion of exactly the individuals the UNESCO documents purport to include. Thus, as with Dufourmantelle's work—and her actions in life—there is an inherent risk in seeking to honor the members of society who are traditionally underrepresented in education while also attending to the constituent whole. Ultimately, the authors of *Rethinking Education* suggest a curricular balance between pluralism and universal values.[6] How might music educators and researchers strike a balance?

In this essay, we seek to frame the exploration of this balance through the lens of hospitality—the invitation and acceptance of a guest by a host.[7] To accomplish this task, we will explore hospitality both in the music classroom—through a metaphor of welcome to a transgender student into the music classroom—and in music research and scholarship. In school music, and in school vocal music in particular, welcoming the student who is transgender—an umbrella term used to describe people whose gender identity mismatches with their sex assigned at birth—has become a topic of conversation at conferences and in publication.[8] In light of fluctuating national and international policies regarding the rights of transgender students—rights that we hope UNESCO addresses in future publications concerning gender equality—we certainly want to suggest that welcoming the transgender student into school music is an important consideration. Building from that foundation of inclusion, however, we hope to explore hospitality more generally as it might apply to all students in a music program and to music research publication.

How might hospitality toward the transgender student change the music classroom into which the student is invited? What does the inclusion/exclusion of transgender students mean, not only for those students but also for their cisgender peers? How are different forms of hospitality mirrored in music research, where a host (author) welcomes a guest (participant)? Reconciling Jacques Derrida's conceptions of hospitality with Nel Noddings's ethic of care, Donna Haraway's concept of the cyborg, and several other writings examining the role of transgender individuals within queer theory and beyond, we will explore not only how and why a guest might be welcomed into school music and music research space but also the risks and vulnerabilities associated with each type of welcome and how acts of hospitality might necessitate changes to the spaces themselves.

To that end, we would like to offer for further consideration three forms hospitality might take: hospitality-after-the-fact, hospitality-as-assimilation, and hospitality-as-boundary-weakening. Our presentation throughout this chapter of the words of Thomas, a transgender opera performance major at the University of California, Long Beach—and the coauthor of this chapter—should be taken at face value as an exploration of the ways a transgender musician might be welcomed into a musical space. Ultimately, however, we would like to investigate the strengths and limitations of each form of hospitality more broadly and to suggest how music educators and researchers might incorporate each form into their work, and the implications each form might have toward both humane education and the common good.

It is worth noting that one of the overarching tenets in *Rethinking Education* is on reaffirming an educational approach that focuses on "sustaining and enhancing the dignity, capacity and welfare of the human person in relation to others."[9] The task of working toward a space that welcomes the individual without classifying and separating, that recognizes a connection across identity boundaries while resisting difference erasure in service of populism, is challenging, especially against the backdrop of musical systems that may seem unfit to the task. Still, by opening the musical space to the guest—the already-invited guest and the unforeseen guest to come—we not only prepare that space for new guests, but reaffirm that opening for those already invited.

(Un)Conditional Acceptance: Hospitality-After-the-Fact

In our first invitation of Thomas's text into this essay, we begin with the type of hospitality that requires the least amount of risk—through direct, attributed quotations.

> I am uncharted territory, in a field as heavily gendered as choral music. Not only do tenor/bass choirs as yet lack a gender-neutral moniker that makes an adequate answer to the soprano/alto "treble choir" label, but the repertoire is inundated with testosterone-laden sea shanties and bawdy barbershop. Gendered choirs' repertoire tends to assume the masculinity or femininity of those singing it, rather than exploring the fuller range of colors and emotions present in mixed choir repertoire.[10]

Hospitality is a welcoming of the stranger, of the guest, and it is most often bound within the law and, as such, has limits. Most frequently, hospitality involves a domain or space, owned by a host, into which the guest is invited. The host may insist that a guest "make themselves at home," but that is a (necessarily) limited invitation: a guest might be allowed to use the bathroom or change the channels on the television, but a guest cannot stay indefinitely or take the television home.[11] For Derrida, hospitality in the world is always conditional, always existing within a set of limits and boundaries. While limitless hospitality can be theorized, hospitality in practice is a greeting of the Other with conditions, so that the host maintains some amount of authority.[12]

While hospitality might be understood as an invitation from a host to a guest, to a stranger who becomes a friend, it is important to note that this simplified definition only scratches the surface of the limitless impossible potential of hospitality. We choose the word *impossible* here to underline the idea that hospitality always exists within the world and always comes with limits. Unless an individual is willing to give away all rights to possessions, hospitality is always limited. This is not meant as a cynical indemnification of hospitality—"If one can't be unconditionally hospitable, why even try?"—but is in fact the nature of hospitality itself, always working toward an impossible unconditional, yet understanding that state can never be reached. Indeed, as Derrida continued to explore the concept throughout his career, hospitality became more and more a fundamental concept, joining ethics and democracy and justice as ideas that ultimately have limits in the world, reproducing the "aporia of the gift" that served as the foundation of Derrida's philosophy of deconstruction.[13]

The work of hospitality in an educational space is in the putting into practice and in the stretching of the boundaries between host (the teacher) and guest (the student). These boundaries, however, are always already present. Though a hospitable host might seek to welcome a guest, the welcome only exists when there is a space over which the host asserts some amount of control. Patrick Schmidt employs Derridean hospitality as a method toward understanding *aporia* as applied to pedagogy in an educational setting.[14] Like hospitality, Schmidt finds aporia to serve best as the "necessary tension" between instructional ideals of shared identity on one side and authority on the other.[15] Though hospitality to the guest involves some amount of risk, we would like to suggest that different levels of hospitality represent different amounts of risk.

It is worth noting from the outset that our intention in presenting Thomas's text in three ways is not to suggest that one method is superior to the others. All three have their use, especially when applied more literally to an educational setting. While it may be tempting to apply a framework such as Haraway's "unity-through-domination" and "unity-through-incorporation" to compare the ways that a stranger might be welcomed into a school classroom and to therefore suggest that one method of hospitality is more preferable than others, it would be irresponsible to suggest there is only one way that the student/guest can be invited in to the classroom by the teacher/host, especially when that classroom has thirty, or fifty, or more guests, all with different and often contradictory needs.[16]

This first form of hospitality, which we will call *hospitality-after-the-fact*, demonstrates a welcome to the guest's ideas and words, if not a bodily welcome. This can be a very helpful form of hospitality. The attribution is clear—who is speaking and to what end is unmistakable. Given the relative lack of risk, it is not surprising that this remains the most common way scholarly writers invite the "guest" into their space.

In a classroom setting, this form of welcome may manifest as sharing the story of some Other—a transgender individual or someone from a political, social, or cultural group unfamiliar to the majority—and allowing space for that story to be shared. While the welcome may be brief and may involve very little risk on behalf of the host, there was nonetheless a welcome where one need not have occurred. Still, in a musical space and otherwise, hospitality toward the guest when the guest is not—or is no longer—present is obviously limited. Are the words and ideas of the guest used with proper intention, or appropriated to the host's needs? In the classroom, teachers—who are also acting as hosts to their students—may invite a guest's words into the space, but educators should interrogate the intention behind the use of those words.

Educators may seek to honor individual identities not outwardly represented in the classroom in order to humanize the uninvited guest, but an invitation after the fact can only contribute to the common good inasmuch as the members of that classroom represent the multiplicity of individual experiences in a society. An invitation of the words or experiences of a guest that is not a bodily invitation is, then, a limited one. Similar questions must be asked by music researchers who use the words of a guest in their "space," the scholarly essay. While hospitality-after-the-fact may allow more permanent guests—the students in a classroom or the essay reader—an opportunity to reflect on the guest's circumstances and how they might relate to their own, it does not represent a permanent invitation into the space.

(Im)Possible Futures: Hospitality-as-Assimilation

In the second invitation of Thomas's text into this essay, his words have been repurposed, and added to the body of the chapter—meant to be read alongside the rest of the essay, but offset here for emphasis. The ideas and words written by the guest are included, but attribution of those words to the guest is gone. While we may attempt to internalize the meaning in Thomas's words, he is missing from the result:

> In a field often centered as heavily on the director as choral music, hospitality is uncharted territory. Not only do we tend to assume that acceptance means assimilation, rather than exploring the fuller range of individuals present in our choirs, we find the simple remapping of masculinity or femininity onto another body to be an adequate answer.

This form of hospitality, hospitality-as-assimilation, involves a guest welcomed by the host into the existing structures of the space, so long as the guest adheres to existing rules. In the choral classroom, hospitality-as-assimilation likely manifests as an invitation to transgender students to participate in the existing organization of the choir. A well-meaning educator may invite gender nonconforming students to sit with the voice part that aligns with their gender identity. There may even be a shift to allow the student to dress in traditionally "male" or "female" clothing for concerts or to adjust room assignments for trips. Similarly, music researchers may embed themselves within the circumstances of the guest, collecting overheard phrases, concepts, and ideas, before reporting the results in publication or presentation. The final result may be more genuine than a simple block quotation, due to prolonged exposure, but direct attribution back to a guest may be removed, in favor of anonymization or collecting multiple stories into an abstract whole.

As stated previously, we hesitate to suggest that hospitality-as-assimilation—an invitation that allows for space but not attribution—is wrong or worse than other forms. There is a value and a risk for both the host and the guest, in the invitation across the threshold.[17] As Derrida notes, "in order to be hospitable, the host must rid himself of security and invite the new arrival."[18] Much of his deconstruction of hospitality is rooted in historical relationships between the state and foreigners, a relationship that was often mutually beneficial. Mark Westmoreland notes that "the foreigner was placed inside the law, under the law, essential to the law. The foreigner occupied an integral space within the city. Indeed, the foreigner was essential because he provided that to which citizens could compare themselves."[19] Without the host, there can be no hospitality, no domain to invite the guest into, and no threshold to cross. Without a teacher as host in an educational setting, there is no ensemble classroom. Without a researcher as host in a scholarly setting, there is no essay in which to share the guest's story. The same can be said, however, about the guest. Both are necessary: the host, the guest, the space, the threshold, and the invitation are all necessary components.

Hospitality, then, shares many qualities with Noddings's ethic of care, which similarly requires a relationship between a subject and an object. In an ethic of care, one measures caring not as an esoteric virtue, but as a "quality of the relation" between the subject (the carer) and the object (the cared-for.)[20] Even before soliciting a text from Thomas, we met virtually to discuss the concept of the essay and to explore not only the presentation, but the manipulation, of his words. An element of caring between guest (Thomas) and host (Jacob) was necessary, both in our collaboration itself and the way that his words were ultimately used.

In a scholarly setting, caring may be questioned when the words and stories of the guest are presented without attribution. While there is value in these vignettes and anecdotes being shared, there is also personal bene-fit in the publication of these stories—even in the seemingly simple act of authorship—that can, in the wrong hands, border on exploitation. Here, reciprocation—the acknowledgement from the Other that caring has occurred—is crucial to the publication process.[21]

Pedagogically, caring extends in the classroom from the teacher to the student in much the same way that hospitality begins with an invitation. In the case of the transgender student, some school music teachers may be re-luctant even to extend the invitation. Ultimately, this may have something to do with an aversion to risk. To explore this aversion, hospitality becomes a more helpful model. While there are boundaries to caring, reciprocation is the ultimate measure of whether an educator can claim an ethic of care in the classroom—there must be some sort of minimal response from the cared-for (the Other) for the relationship "to be described as caring."[22] In this way, the teacher (the Subject) remains centered.

This is not the case with hospitality, as it moves, always, toward its un-conditional ideal. What Claudia Ruitenberg deems an "ethic of hospitality" "is not about social conventions of welcoming, but about responding to an-other who arrives and who confronts the host with absolute otherness."[23] While this "other" may, at the moment, be the transgender student, it may be some *other* "other," an unknown "other" in the future. Unlike an ethic of care, which is concerned with the reciprocal relationship between the subject and the object, an educator working toward an ethic of hospitality understands that any relationship that requires a reciprocation cannot be hospitable.

As stated previously, risk is a condition of hospitality, but different forms of hospitality represent different levels of risk. An invitation of the guest's voice after the fact involves minimal risk, while an invitation of the guest that subsumes that guest into the prior structure of the whole represents a different level. Still, this form of hospitality emphasizes the needs of the common good by transplanting the previously uninvited guest into that good through the act of the invitation across the threshold. Are the needs of each individual being met? Does the preexisting structure of the classroom or the scholarly publication process allow for human flourishing?

A series of questions concerning the malleability of the musical space—physical space, pedagogy as space, norms as space—is necessary: "Does what I am about to do leave a possibility for my assumptions about knowledge and teaching and learning to be upset by a new arrival? Does it close down a space for future questioning or questioners?"[24] This aversion to risk is, we believe, an aversion to the possibility that the space will require change in order for hospitality—even in its conditional form—to occur. This is an inevitable feature of hospitality, which "does not seek to fit the guest into the space of the host, but accepts that the arrival of the guest may change the space into which he or she is received."[25] The question remains: How must showing hospitality toward the transgender student change the space of the school music classroom?

(Trans)Forming Gender: Hospitality-as-Boundary-Weakening

In this final invitation of Thomas's text into this essay, our words are presented alongside each other and intertwined.

While this may be uncharted territory in the field of music scholarship, it is heavily borrowed from Derrida himself and his student Anne Dufourmantelle.[i] I can invite Thomas's text into my space, present it in a neutral fashion alongside mine, and allow the reader to find similarities and differences, but is that an adequate answer? Is my text, inundated with his but still mine, changed in the process? Are there other impossible futures worth exploring?	I am uncharted territory in a field as heavily gendered as choral music. Not only do tenor/bass choirs as yet lack a gender-neutral moniker that makes an adequate answer to the soprano/alto "treble choir" label, but the repertoire is inundated with testosterone-laden sea shanties and bawdy barbershop parody. Gendered choirs' repertoire tends to assume the masculinity or femininity of those singing it, rather than exploring the fuller range of colors and emotions present in mixed choir repertoire.

i. Jacques Derrida and Anne Dufourmantelle, *Of Hospitality* (Stanford, CA: Stanford University Press, 2000), 10.

In accepting Thomas's words into the space of this essay it is transformed—and in this instance Thomas's identity remains. This third form of hospitality, what we call hospitality-as-boundary-weakening, is not without challenges—and risks—and should not be undertaken lightly. Exploring vulnerability in music education, Lauren Richerme asserts that a welcome "depends neither on comfort nor convenience," echoing similar thoughts in education philosophy about the risks inherent in the invitation of the stranger.[26] In the case of this essay, Thomas's name is indelibly tied to this work for the foreseeable future, both in the body of the text and as an author, indexed and searchable, and while we discussed the benefits and risks in detail as we collaborated, other informants might be more averse to the idea.

In an educational setting, the final form in this chapter manifests as showing hospitality toward the transgender student while allowing one's (the teacher's) subjecthood to be displaced and room for the space to change. Hospitality-as-boundary-weakening, which involves taking care not to lose the inherent subjecthood of the guest—is useful for two reasons. First, it allows for an educator to think of hospitality as a look forward, toward other groups as yet barred from the music space. Second, it urges a look backward, pushing educators to consider whether the space of school music is hospitable to those already invited across the threshold.

Showing hospitality toward transgender students requires a willingness to risk that the school music space might be changed in the process. An educator must question whether the underlying norms of the space—the repertoire, the structure of the ensemble, the language used, and more—preclude hospitality from taking place. One might invite the stories of transgender individuals without extending an invitation to the individual (the first example) or invite the transgender individual under the auspices of assimilation (the second)—these are important steps that should not be discouraged—but an invitation to the transgender student that allows for the possibility that the space will change moves closer toward unconditional hospitality.

For Lee Higgins, the site of this possible future hospitality is the community music ensemble.[27] While Derrida found the concept of community to be etymologically problematic—a community has boundaries and therefore delimits who is and is not part of said community, Higgins attempts a reclamation of community as a space with boundaries that are "porous, tentative, even weak."[28] Recent work in community music has applied Higgins's conception of hospitality to choral singing, demonstrating the potential for belonging and empowerment in open musical spaces.[29] We wish to assert that hospitality toward transgender students and critical examination of the space into which they are invited can serve as a measure of just how porous and weak the boundaries of the school music classroom can be. The transgender student might elucidate, for instance, other examples of body-based discrimination in the classroom, such as body size, disability, or race.[30] Indeed, in the opening section of this book, Iris Yob draws attention to the "substantial diversity" that exists with regard to all learners in an educational setting.[31] For education toward a "common good" to be truly possible, educators must understand that marginalized learners demonstrate flaws in a system not only for the marginalized themselves, but for all learners within that system.

Again, we should reiterate that our intention is not to suggest that one form of hospitality, applied either to scholarly writing or to the music classroom, is the only form worth exploring. All three forms employed in this essay have merit, and there may be other ways of showing hospitality to the Other in music scholarship and in the music classroom. Still, we do want to suggest that hospitality-as-boundary-weakening offers the richest site for a hospitality that honors the humane education of each individual through questioning whether, and to what extent, individuals are honored among the collective of the common good. As explained in the introduction of this work, the two terms—*humane education* and *common good*—are best considered complementary, the common good serving as antecedent to the consequent of truly humane education of the individual. Like hospitality and the other aporic concepts of Derrida, it might be useful to think of working toward a humane education of the common good, with the realization that educational interactions are always already situated in the world. Still, an invitation across the threshold of underserved or marginalized individuals may provide the strongest path in this direction.

These identities of marginalized embodied positions, such as "transgender" or "women of color" are, Donna Haraway suggests, "sites for critical cultural, political, and intellectual practice."[32] The myth of the cyborg in her seminal work is "about transgressed boundaries, potent fusions, and dangerous possibilities."[33] Drawing on technological advances and science fiction, Haraway's cyborg is a being that transcends essential boundaries— the boundary between human and animal, for instance, or the boundaries that have otherwise defined what constitutes maleness or femaleness.[34] The cyborg is a metaphor through which to examine the boundaries of embodiment and humanity. As such, the possible futures Haraway suggests are accessible not only through showing hospitality toward the transgender student, but in being critical of the boundaries of that hospitality even as it is taking place. Inviting the transgender student into the space, for instance, and allowing the space to be changed to admit a "third gender" can be useful, but it is not without its problems. Allowing space for "male," "female," and "transgender" simply makes the complexity of gender ternary instead of binary.[35] Similarly, the categories "transgender" and "cisgender," while useful in discussion and in critical analysis of the school music space, ultimately create another set of limiting categories.[36]

Choral music educators, for instance, might make space to allow for transgender students to participate using their "true voice," contributing to the myth that voice and identity are indelibly linked.[37] In her chapter earlier in this section, Emily Good-Perkins demonstrates the problematic nature of linking one style of vocal production with "proper" singing and we wish to suggest that linking the voice inextricably to identity might work toward similar ends.[38] While this connection between bodily identity and voice—figuratively in the classroom and literally with regard to speaking and singing—may be true for some transgender students, extant research suggests it is not true for others.[39] In this way, Lucas Crawford's "transgender without organs" might serve as an example of how slightly opening the musical space to allow for the invitation of one version of "transgender" is limiting.[40] Developed from Gilles Deleuze and Félix Guattari's concept of a body as constituted not as a prescribed set of organs but as a set of interconnected traits within and outside of the body itself, Crawford suggests that our conceptualization of "transgender" goes beyond anatomy and includes values like geography and access to resources.

While Haraway's cyborg is rooted in technological futurity and in using the cyborg to critically analyze bodies that might be excluded from feminism, we believe there is a simultaneous look backward in her work, an assertion that we are, all of us, cyborgs navigating the story of gender.[41] Extending an invitation to the excluded Other is a deeply important concern and the transgender student can aid in better understanding that invitation. So, too, can the transgender student aid in the look backward toward a critical unpacking of exclusion more generally with regard to gender and more. Is the school music space truly hospitable to those guests already invited? If all hospitality is conditional, what assumptions about gender-conforming students might be worth addressing? Hale asserts that "woman" is a set of categories and that the presence or lack of one category is not generally enough to guarantee that status.[42] Similarly, manhood, masculinity, and maleness are socially constructed.[43] Perhaps it is not some set of inherent categories, but "our method of applying information" which maintains our gender.[44]

Given these potential openings of gender, how hospitable is the school music space? Are cisgender students invited across the threshold without condition or only invited after those conditions—perhaps quite unconsciously—are met? Haraway imagines "a world without gender, which is perhaps a world without genesis, but maybe also a world without end" and suggests that the cyborg should have "*pleasure* in the confusion of boundaries and for *responsibility* in their construction."[45] We believe this simultaneity of pleasure and responsibility is possible for the hospitable music educator, that hospitable actions need not feel burdensome.

With regard to music scholarship we must ask, as Haraway asks: "who counts as 'us' in my own rhetoric? Which identities are available to ground such a potent political myth called 'us,' and what could motivate enlistment in this collectivity?"[46] Very recent research has applied an ethic of hospitality to school music settings, but there is room for much more, especially within the choral music space.[47] Inviting transgender students into the choral classroom only conditionally, when their gender identity matches a preexisting form of already-invited guest, is a limited form of hospitality-as-assimilation that should be interrogated. Allowing, for instance, transgender male students to room with cisgender male students represents a decision still made in a gender binary system. Questioning repertoire choices that reinforce that binary for the sake of transgender students is well intentioned but also fails to account for cisgender students who may feel similarly limited by the binary. It is our hope that showing hospitality toward transgender students uncovers not only ways in which these students can be dignified but also ways for their cisgender peers—and the student to come—to be similarly supported.

Conclusion

Educators and scholars will need to decide for themselves which form of hospitality works best in which situation and what strengths and limitations exist in each form. Hospitality-after-the-fact, often the first invitation, involves clear attribution of the guest and a risk to the host and to the space. This form of hospitality, though limited and fleeting, should not be discounted. Hospitality-as-assimilation, an invitation toward the guest in which the personhood of the guest is discounted in favor of allowing the guest entry into preexisting categories, is similarly limited but no less important. Finally, hospitality-as-boundary-weakening allows for the space to change in the course of the invitation across the threshold. This form of hospitality approaches the impossible, unconditional hospitality theorized by Derrida, though it is still necessarily limited by the realities of hospitality in the world.

School music programs are by no means monolithic, so the most we hope to do with this essay is to present different forms of hospitality and to generate a set of questions. These questions (the ones we end with and many, many others) are necessary if hospitality is to become "a demand for openness to the arrival of something and someone we cannot foresee; a demand that is impossible to fulfill, but that confronts all of our decisions and actions."[48] Who is "us" in the school music classroom? Are we a collective based in identity or one based in affinity?[49] Who is invited across the threshold? Does the guest become part of "us" or does the guest remain a foreigner? Scholars and educators who consider these questions, who strive toward hospitality in all interactions, have the greatest potential to honor the humanity of each individual they meet and with whom they create music.

JACOB AXEL BERGLIN is Associate Professor of Choral Music Education at Florida International University, Florida.

THOMAS MURPHY O'HARA is Vocal Performance Major in the Bob Cole Conservatory of Music at California State University, California.

Notes

1. Benoît Morene and Megan Specia, "Philosopher Who Praised Risk Died Trying to Save Children from Drowning," *New York Times*, July 26, 2017, https://www.nytimes.com /2017/07/25/world/europe/risk-philosopher-anne-dufourmantelle-dies.html.

2. Jacques Derrida and Anne Dufourmantelle, *Of Hospitality* (Stanford, CA: Stanford University Press, 2000); Anastasia Vécrin, "Anne Dufourmantelle, 'La sécurité engendre plus la peur que l'inverse,'" *Libération*, September 14, 2015, http://www.liberation

.fr/debats/2015/09/14/anne-dufourmantelle-la-securite-engendre-plus-la-peur-que-l-inverse
_1382441.

3. UNESCO, *Rethinking Education: Towards a Global Common Good?* (Paris: UNESCO, 2015).

4. Ibid., 35.

5. The "Faure report" refers to UNESCO, *Learning to Be: The World of Education Today and Tomorrow* (Paris: UNESCO, 1972), http://unesdoc.unesco.org/images/0000/000018 /001801e.pdf; the "Delors report" refers to UNESCO, *Learning: The Treasure Within* (Paris, UNESCO, 1996), http://unesdoc.unesco.org/images/0010/001095/109590eo.pdf.

6. UNESCO, *Rethinking Education*, 41.

7. Additional writing with regard to hospitality in music and music education includes Lee Higgins, "The Impossible Future," *Action, Criticism, and Theory for Music Education* 6 (2007): 74–96, http://act.maydaygroup.org/articles/Higgins6_3.pdf; Brian Sullivan, "Exploring a Theory and Ethic of Hospitality through an Instrumental Case Study of a Middle School Band Room" (PhD diss., University of Illinois at Urbana-Champaign, 2017); Chad West and Radio Cremata, "Bringing the Outside In: Blending Formal and Informal through Acts of Hospitality," *Journal of Research in Music Education* 64 (2016): 71–87.

8. While it is not within the scope of this essay to delimit the boundaries of gender, it might be helpful to provide a cursory definition of what I mean when I use the word *transgender* here and in other sections of the essay. For the purposes of this work, *sex* can be defined as the male or female assignment made at birth, usually by parents and doctors and largely based on primary sex characteristics such as genitalia, and *gender* can be defined as the set of social and cultural markers, differing over time and based on geography, that mark a person as a member of a gender category such as "man" or "woman." *Transgender* will refer to someone assigned to a sex at birth who identifies as the other gender or as gender nonbinary. Jacob Berglin, "'I Could Sing Tenor': Options, Outcomes, and Perceptions of a Transgender Student in a High School Choral Music Program" (poster presented at annual meeting, Committee on Institutional Cooperation Music Education Conference, University Park, Pennsylvania, October 10, 2014); J. Michele Edwards, "Transgender Choral Voices," (paper presented at the biannual Feminist Theory and Music Conference, Greensboro, North Carolina, 2009); Paul Caldwell and Joshua Palkki, "Creating Safe Space: LGBTQ Singers in the Choral Classroom," (paper presented at the biannual American Choral Directors Association National Conference, Salt Lake City, Utah, 2015); Jeananne Nichols, "Rie's Story, Ryan's Journey: Music in the Life of a Transgender Student," *Journal of Research in Music Education* 61 (2013): 262–279; Sarah J. Bartolome, "Melanie's Story: A Narrative Account of a Transgender Music Educator's Journey," *Bulletin of the Council for Research in Music Education* 207–208 (2016): 25–47.

9. UNESCO, *Rethinking Education*, 32.

10. Thomas O'Hara, email communication, February 1, 2017.

11. John D. Caputo, *Deconstruction in a Nutshell: A Conversation with Jacques Derrida* (New York: Fordham University Press, 1997), 110.

12. Jacques Derrida, "Hospitality," *Angelaki* 5 (2000): 4.

13. Caputo, *Deconstruction in a Nutshell*, 112.

14. Patrick Schmidt, "Authority and Pedagogy as Framing," *Philosophy of Music Education Review* 24 (2016): 12.

15. Ibid., 13.

16. Donna Haraway, "A Cyborg Manifesto: Science, Technology, and Socialist-Feminism in the Late Twentieth Century," in *The Transgender Studies Reader*, ed. Susan Stryker and Stephen White (New York: Routledge, 2006), 109.

17. Derrida, *Adieu to Emmanuel Levinas* (Stanford, CA: Stanford University Press, 1999), 27.

18. Mark W. Westmoreland, "Interruptions: Derrida and Hospitality," *Kritike* 2 (2008): 7.

19. Ibid., 2.

20. Claudia W. Ruitenberg, "The Empty Chair: Education in an Ethic of Hospitality," *Philosophy of Education* (2011): 29.

21. Nel Noddings, *Caring: A Relational Approach to Ethics and Moral Education* (Berkeley: University of California Press, 2013), 4.

22. Ibid., 4.

23. Ruitenberg, "Empty Chair," 32.

24. Ibid., 33.

25. Ibid., 32.

26. Lauren K. Richerme, "Vulnerable Experiences in Music Education: Possibilities and Problems for Growth and Connectivity," *Bulletin of the Council for Research in Music Education* 209 (2016): 37; Jen Gilbert, "'Let Us Say Yes to Who or What Turns Up': Education as Hospitality," *Journal of the Association for Curriculum Studies* 4 (2006), 25–34.

27. Higgins, "Impossible Future," 80.

28. Caputo, *Deconstruction in a Nutshell*, 107; Higgins, "Impossible Future," 88.

29. Anne Haughland Balsnes, "Hospitality in Multicultural Choral Singing," *International Journal of Community Music* 9, no. 2 (2016): 171.

30. Riki Anne Wilchins, "What Does It Cost to Tell the Truth," in *The Transgender Studies Reader*, ed. Susan Stryker and Stephen White (New York: Routledge, 2006), 547.

31. Iris M. Yob, "There Is No Other," in this collection.

32. Haraway, "Cyborg Manifesto," 103.

33. Ibid., 107.

34. Ibid.

35. Evan B. Towle and Lynn M. Morgan, "Romancing the Transgender Native: Rethinking the Use of the 'Third Gender' Concept," in *The Transgender Studies Reader*, ed. Susan Stryker and Stephen White (New York: Routledge, 2006), 109.

36. A. Finn Enke, "The Education of Little Cis: Cisgender and the Discipline of Opposing Bodies," in *The Transgender Studies Reader* 2, ed. Susan Stryker and Aren Z. Aizura (New York: Routledge, 2013), 235.

37. Wayne Koestenbaum, *The Queen's Throat: Opera, Homosexuality, and the Mystery of Desire* (Boston: Da Capo, 2001), 155.

38. Emily Good-Perkins, "Rethinking Vocal Education as a Means to Encourage Positive Identity Development," in this collection.

39. Joshua Palkki, "'My Voice Speaks for Itself': The Experiences of Three Transgender Students in Secondary School Choral Programs" (PhD diss., Michigan State University, 2016).

40. Lucas Cassidy Crawford, "Transgender without Organs? Mobilizing a Geo-affective Theory of Gender Modification," in *The Transgender Studies Reader* 2, ed. Susan Stryker and Aren Z. Aizura (New York: Routledge, 2013), 479.

41. Haraway, "Cyborg Manifesto," 103.

42. Jacob Hale, "Are Lesbians Women?" in *The Transgender Studies Reader*, ed. Susan Stryker and Stephen White (New York: Routledge, 2006), 290.

43. Patrick Califia, "Manliness," in *The Transgender Studies Reader*, ed. Susan Stryker and Stephen White (New York: Routledge, 2006), 438.

44. Suzanne J. Kessler and Wendy McKenna, "Toward a Theory of Gender," in *The Transgender Studies Reader*, ed. Susan Stryker and Stephen White (New York: Routledge, 2006), 177.

45. Haraway, "Cyborg Manifesto," 104, emphasis in the original.

46. Ibid., 107–108.

47. Sullivan, "Exploring a Theory," 153–154.

48. Ruitenberg, "Empty Chair," 33.

49. Haraway, "Cyborg Manifesto," 108.

PART IV

ELABORATIONS AND EXPANSIONS

15

NOURISHING THE MUSICALLY HUNGRY

Learning from Undergraduate Amateur Musicking

Susan Laird and Johnnie-Margaret McConnell

THIS CHAPTER'S RESPONSE TO UNESCO'S *RETHINKING EDUCATION: TOWARDS a Global Common Good?* puts forward a vision of humane music education that resists exclusive focus on professional music education to value amateur musicking for the common good. Our conceptual inquiry focuses on amateur musicking within higher education. Diverse US cultures have valued amateur musicianship's contribution to the common good since the early republic, when its communal role was more prominent.[1] People universally create and use music to express lived (and remembered) human experiences, suggesting its value in a holistic student-centered undergraduate curriculum.[2] Music expresses diverse identities and can engage people together in a common cause.[3] Diverse university students have aimed to satisfy their own "musical hunger" as amateurs since Harvard's beginnings, albeit often without formal institutional recognition that music is a "lifelong and life-wide" learning pursuit.[4]

Susan Laird's concept of musical hunger signifies metaphorically a felt human need to engage in musical creation, as performer or listener or both, for personal fulfillment.[5] Musical hunger initially stimulates one to seek musical nourishment; therefore music educators should respect it. Ignored or suppressed, musical hunger can signal musical miseducation. Unfed, musical hunger can compromise a person's ability to participate in musicking as performer or listener. If chronically underfed, force-fed, or overfed (to the exclusion of other vital learning), musical hunger can become harmful, as it may reflect musical malnourishment—which students may experience variously, as cultural narrowness evident in their musical taste and as kinds of musical insecurity, starvation, or gluttony. Musical hungers are not singular, but plural, diverse in both kinds and intensities. One may hunger to hear, listen to, or know music; to make music or dance with it; to claim the identity of "musician"; and to live well and serve the common good with music. The musical hunger concept shines metaphoric light on a problematic political economy governing access to music education and on the spiritual cost to students denied adequate means to satisfy their musical hunger. Collegiate amateur musicking practices share and nurture musical knowledge based on students' various musical hungers for musical engagement.[6] Humane music education that nourishes amateur musicking offers students means to satisfy their various kinds of musical hunger.

Amateur musicians choose to feed their musical hunger, often investing personal time and money. The etymology of "amateur" in both French (*ameour*, as written in the sixteenth-century) and Latin (*amator*) signifies the root meaning that amateurs are committed to a "loving pursuit."[7] The "amateur musician" designation can become complicated, however, when someone has been educated for professional musicianship, as Johnnie-Margaret McConnell has been in clarinet performance, but then turns to another profession in higher education, student affairs leadership, while teaching clarinet to children and adolescents (which makes her a professional music educator), organizing a summer intergenerational clarinet choir camp (at no profit to herself) and playing clarinet only as an amateur performer. Is she a professional musician or an amateur one? Luckily, we need not answer that to be conceptually clear about amateur musicking. We propose side-stepping such analytic difficulties surrounding what it means to engage in amateur musicking by applying "amateur" to undergraduates who have not undertaken any training for professional musicianship or earned money by making music or teaching but still pursue some form of musicking.

This chapter undertakes a conceptual inquiry on humane higher education for the common good, prompted by McConnell's interviews at a public university with three musicking students who were not music majors.[8] We have here renamed them Emma, Scott, and Joan. A communications major, Emma participates in her university's marching band to satisfy the musical hunger that playing clarinet in her high school's band aroused. Engineering major Scott and microbiology major Joan have sustained their musical hungers aroused by private piano lessons, church choir, and teen karaoke. They have made their own amateur musicking lives on campus— he as a pianist in everyday residence life and she as a singer who has organized a community-service ensemble. Their testimonials demonstrate how amateur musicking practices can ground humane higher education.

Amateur Musicking's Educative Value

Amateur musicianship played a central role historically in communities diverse with regard to race, gender, and ethnicity.[9] The same is true of collegiate amateur musicking.[10] Yet, little attention is given to the educative and miseducative roles informal musical experiences play in supporting and developing undergraduate students' social, emotional, spiritual, and cognitive needs or their institutional, civic, and moral commitments.[11] To breach this gap, we will amend UNESCO's explanation of humane education by retheorizing that concept's "four pillars of learning" in light of what we have learned from Emma, Scott, and Joan's undergraduate amateur encounters.[12] We have viewed them through the conceptual lens of the late Christopher Small's *Musicking*.[13] We suggest renaming UNESCO's four pillars the *four encounters of musical learning*, which we propose as a vital means for humane higher education that values both musical diversity and lifelong learning.

Small theorized musicking broadly: "To music is to take part, in any capacity, in a musical performance whether by performing, by listening, by rehearsing or practicing, by providing the material performance (what is called composition) or by dancing."[14] Small wanted people to understand music as an aesthetic experience that, as John Dewey theorized, requires both doing and undergoing.[15] Musical performance is a multidimensional social act existing within all known cultures, thereby raising questions why one musical style should be valued over another. UNESCO reminds us that learning is contextual and opens the door to knowledge acquisition. Individuals and communities engaged in amateur musicking undergo the process of learning through relationships that engage in, with, and through music with self and others. Musical hunger is satisfied and potentially new knowledge is acquired through both the process and results of learning.

Philosopher and amateur classical pianist Jane Roland Martin's theory of education as encounter represents education as an interaction between an individual and a culture in which both parties change."[16] What Small calls musicking is such an encounter; we therefore think of amateur musicking as a kind of learning that feeds musical hunger and may foster humane education. When amateur musicking fails to change the individual or the culture with a view to the common good, it may contribute little to humane education. When, however, amateur musicking changes students and their communities' cultures with a view to the common good, it can become integral to humane higher education.

Undergraduates can come to know a variety of music through diverse musicking encounters with others toward a common goal of making music. UNESCO's four pillars of learning address learning to know, to do, to be, and to live well. We reframe each of these "pillars" to propose four "encounters" of musical learning: to know music, to make music, to be a musician, and to live musically for a good life and the common good. We name each encounter of musical learning, and the musical hunger that each feeds, accordingly: *epistemological* encounters through which students learn to know music; *practical* encounters through which students learn to make and perform music; *ontological* encounters through which students learn to become and see themselves as musicians; and finally, *axiological* encounters through which students learn music's value for living well and serving the common good. Encounters of musical learning can arouse and feed epistemological, practical, ontological, or axiological musical hungers, each of which demands nourishment.

Professional musicians may experience such encounters of musical learning through formal studio work and performance employment and often they participate in amateur musicking as teachers, guides, accompanists, composers, and conductors. Our chapter instead focuses on undergraduates' access to amateur musicking as a vital contribution to their humane higher education. Curricular and cocurricular college amateur musicking ensembles directly supported by colleges and universities—like Emma's marching band—offer generous participation guidelines and public performances, whereas various ad hoc forms of amateur musicking—like Scott's piano playing and Joan's community-service ensemble—experience little institutional oversight and may or may not reach public audiences. Can institutional and ad hoc amateur musicking offer students all four encounters of musical learning that make humane higher education possible?

Four Encounters of Musical Learning: Feeding
Musical Hungers

Rethinking Education calls for "new approaches to learning for greater justice, social equity, and global solidarity. Education . . . must be about cultural literacy, on the basis of respect and equal dignity."[17] McConnell's investigations suggest that amateur musicking in undergraduates' everyday living exemplifies often what music educator and philosopher Estelle Jorgensen has designated as "feminine" informal practices, which aim to honor diversely gendered humans' dignity, equality, social justice, diversity, and collective responsibility. Jorgensen explains, "In the feminine view, art is a part of life, whereas in the masculine view, art is a discrete entity apart from life. The feminine approach to art is holistic, contextual, and thereby unified, whereas the masculine approach is logocentric, decontextualized, and therefore alienating."[18]

The 1968 Tanglewood Symposium reflected similar educational values in its declaration that music education should focus on the "art of living, the building of personal identity, and nurturing creativity" for all ages, and because music develops such aims, it should be central within curriculum.[19] This chapter asks whether the four encounters for musical learning that amateur musicking can offer may also hold educational value for democratic aims that promote a "shared way of life" through knowing, being, and doing music together.[20] We aim to clarify each encounter's meaning as nourishment for undergraduate amateurs' musical hunger, which renders higher education humane by focusing on their appreciation for the common good rather than on personal professional achievement.

Epistemological Hunger, Epistemological Encounters: Learning to Know Music

Like the garage band teenagers English music education theorist Lucy Green studied, Emma, Scott, and Joan all experienced Western-based music education before college.[21] Emma satisfied her hunger to play the clarinet within her university's marching band. By continuing the same musicking focus from her high school, her amateur musicking exemplifies what music educators refer to as "carryover."[22] However, Emma's continued musical encounters offer a counter case of humane music education because, by following a known marching-band track grounded in what Jorgensen would call "masculine" competitive practices, she may have missed epistemological encounters through which she might have broadened her knowledge of diverse musical cultures and their music-making practices.

Scott and Joan's ad hoc amateur musicking practices are clear cases of epistemological encounters that nourished both their own and their campus culture's underfed musical diversity while also fulfilling their other personal and social aims. They engaged their peers in such encounters as fellow music-makers or as listeners, sometimes as both, by performing diverse music they may not have known previously. Following classical piano instruction, Scott's musical hunger found nourishment through amateur musicking that he pursued accidentally. Through informal performances for culturally diverse student-peers, he learned a variety of culturally diverse and intergenerational popular tunes.

Similarly, having sung in church choirs and played with a home karaoke machine, Joan's musical hunger led her into amateur musicking that sustained her delight in singing, where it became a means of broader cultural and musical learning. She founded a local campus chapter of Music is Medicine (MiM), which pairs song writers with critically ill pediatric patients to create songs about their lives. Such patients and the musical knowledge on which their collaborative song-writing draws had origins in ethnically diverse American cultures. Thus, through creative amateur musicking that reflected idiosyncratic kinds of carryover from their earlier musical learning, Scott and Joan experienced epistemological encounters through which they met culturally diverse genres of music new to them, for culturally diverse strangers.

Epistemological encounters allow undergraduates, with or without previous music education, experiences as amateur performers and listeners. Contemporary amateur musicking collegians learn when they seek encounters with diverse music through a cappella groups, gospel choirs, Taiko drumming circles, or other kinds of student-led ensembles. Many enroll also in elective courses such as Native American flute or world music. Such diverse epistemological encounters may expose undergraduates through listening to a variety of musical traditions and styles, which may arouse new musical hungers while potentially also nourishing a student's knowledge about what is music, what is music making, and what are its social purposes.

Practical Hunger, Practical Encounters: Learning to Make Music

Practical encounters build on students' musical knowledge, however limited it may be, and nourish their musical hungers for developing music-making skills, for producing music with and for others. Emma's university choice was based on her musical hunger to participate in marching band, which she viewed as a way to keep making music. As she noted, "Now I don't have the pressure of having to perform at a contest or having to perform a solo. I'm in [marching band] to . . . continue myself . . . continue growing by learning and . . . just having a goal, very collectivist goal." Emma's university marching band participation has sustained her musical nourishment, potentially enlarging her knowledge of marching-band clarinetists' performing practices.

In contrast to Emma's institutionally managed experience of amateur musicking, Scott and Joan are engaged in self-initiated practical encounters. Scott discovered his practical musical hunger by happenstance, playing the piano in residence halls' public spaces. His peers recognized tunes he was playing and became engaged as listeners. Scott realized his piano music was "something that other people can access." These regular nightly encounters nourished Scott's desire to make music while developing his musical skills through playing with and for others.

Joan sought an outlet that would intertwine her professional aspirations as a premedical student with her musical avocational practices of designing and performing YouTube videos. Founding MiM, she embarked on practical encounters to make music for and with others. Joan did not want musical ignorance to stop her peers from participating, so the local chapter is open to anyone interested in becoming a medical professional or in learning to create music. All chapter meetings include practical encounters, which often become impromptu music-making sessions. Both Scott and Joan created their own amateur musicking spaces to move from making music in isolation (Jorgensen's masculine view) to nourishing their musical performance skills (Jorgensen's feminine view) with and for others. Within the context of humane education, their musicking aims for the common good rather than just their professional development.

All three musicians' amateur musicking outlets feed their practical musical hunger, to make music for everyday aims, not commercial consumption. Yet, Scott and Joan's practical hunger leads them to encounters that change how, for whom, and why they create music, as well as what music they create. Such practical encounters redirect students' music-making skills in ways that may awaken or intensify their ontological hunger and offer opportunities to reconstruct their own musical self-concepts.

*Ontological Hunger, Ontological Encounters: Learning
to be Musicians*

Philosopher of education and conservatory-educated amateur pianist Deanne Bogdan, author of chapter 16 in this collection, argues that music is a "form of practical wisdom" which individuals reflect through musical engagement with self and others, "embracing the psychological, ethical, and spiritual introspection that comes with critical engagement of the arts and its discourses."[23] Undergraduates exhibit various kinds and degrees of cultural self-consciousness influenced through musical engagement as seen through the multimusicalities found on many campuses.[24] These musicking communities can nourish undergraduates' musical ontologies by developing and defining their status as amateur musicians.

Small believed musicking is a projection of self. Adrian North, David Hargreaves, and Susan O'Neil surveyed almost 2,500 American and English teenagers and found that self-identification with a specific musical genre becomes a "badge" for students to express their inner life to both themselves and others.[25] The survey also revealed that music's importance for most teenagers primarily developed outside the music classroom. Creating music through the university marching band affirms and sustains Emma's status as a musician with the badge "clarinetist." Scott and Joan's amateur musicking enriches their practical knowledge in ways that offer ontological encounters that enable them to see themselves as musicians, not just as music-makers. Playing the piano for his peers became an ontological encounter insofar as this amateur musicking made it possible for Scott to claim the piano as his "voice" and to call himself "the piano guy." Joan also discovered a musical identity for herself that supported her professional development as a premedical student by capturing critically ill patients' lived experiences in cocreated songs. MiM helped her find an entirely new audience for her YouTube video-making skill and its activity of composing songs with a healing intent that fed both her professional ontological hunger (to be a healer) and her spiritual ontological hunger (to be a musician). All three undergraduates interviewed by McConnell found amateur musicking opportunities for "sustaining and enhancing the dignity, capacity and welfare" of their overall lives.[26] Scott and Joan's musicking experiences show how amateur musicking goes further in developing their "creative powers" for the common good.[27]

*Axiological Hunger, Axiological Encounters: Learning to Live
Musically for the Common Good*

Music's value can be not only artistic and aesthetic, but also social, ethical, political, or religious. A performer desires a listener and a listener desires a performer. Axiological encounters help students learn how to live an inter-dependent human existence as they share their cultural, social, spiritual, democratic, and emotional lives. Jorgensen explains that regardless of cul-ture, people utilize music to "celebrate, to mourn, to encourage, to pray, and to remember their lived experiences."[28] Therefore, we take seriously Small's view of musicking as storytelling. Each musical story gives form to feelings wrought by lived experiences.[29] Undergraduates bring diverse musical hun-gers to diverse campuses and thus impart to amateur musicking a variety of narratives that make axiological encounters possible.

Evidencing social benefits akin to those that Luca Tiszai has stud-ied, Emma, Scott, and Joan explained how cocurricular amateur musick-ing helped them develop peer relationships, engage their musical passion, relieve stress, and provide a space for fun.[30] Joshua Duchan concluded un-dergraduate a cappella ensembles foster "social support" systems where stu-dents explore their individual identities, develop membership within the larger collegiate community, negotiate relationships with others, and de-velop leadership and time management skills creating a sense of community within and direct connection to their respective educational institutions.[31] Green observed similar teenage-run garage bands were idiosyncratic, per-sonally creative attempts at copying music enjoyed in everyday living, often by ear, with peers: "in friendship groups, [students] listen, discuss, select, copy, arrange, rehearse and perform the music as an ensemble."[32] Such axiological encounters through collegiate cocurricular musicking practices often exemplify Laird's concept of "befriending . . . as an educational life-practice" insofar as they foster students' relationships with music(s) and with one another. Their musical friendships—an intimate mutuality among undergraduates, through shared devotion to music—enables a community of support to form during the liminality of collegiate years.[33] Amateur mu-sicking students may thus learn interdependence, including a "particular set of capacities for learning to love, survive, and thrive in the face of dif-ficulties."[34] Thus they learn to value music itself "as a learner's responsibility (practice, practice, practice) or as an artful means of claiming responsibil-ity (voice); as a non-human object of love, as a source of self-respect, and a means of expressing love for others; as a means of spiritual survival and an expression of thriving; or even as a trouble (frustration, performance anxiety)."[35] Within cocurricular musicking practices, undergraduate students befriend each other as they create and experience encounters of musical learning in, with, and through the music as well with one another.

Emma described marching band music as "collective" in nature, requiring everyone to play a role through instrumental representation: "*Stars and Stripes* . . . you take the euphoniums out and you're missing a lot. You take the clarinets out and you are missing the trio. Everyone plays a role in every song." Emma's marching band participation sustains her devotion to her university and to American patriotic culture, but her interview gave no signs that she, or the ensemble, experienced any transformative learning for the broader humane common good, a concept that Iris Yob has analyzed.[36]

At first, Scott sought to play on the residence hall pianos merely to soothe his own loneliness. Then playing became a "fun way to just meet other people . . . 'cause a lot of times people will just come up to me and go 'that's cool, I recognize that song.'" Joan stumbled on a way to unite her medical aspirations with her musical creativity through MiM. She aimed intentionally to bring her peers together who have "musical passions and may have passions in health care fields" to create music. Collegiate amateur musicking communities such as Scott and Joan's can offer axiological encounters where altruism and collaboration are valued over egotism and achievement, thereby earning Jorgensen's label "feminine" and advancing an ethic of care through befriending music and one another, whether for audience members or for performers.[37] Befriending as a life practice undertaken through all these diverse encounters of amateur musical learning can become for undergraduates an artful approach toward educating themselves to live well.

Collegiate Amateur Musicking for Humane Education

UNESCO's *Rethinking Education* describes humane education as developing "respect for life and human dignity, equal rights and social justice, cultural and social diversity, and a sense of human solidarity and shared responsibility for our common future."[38] Taking undergraduates' unexamined musical hunger seriously, we propose music educators should collaborate with higher education leaders and heed Tanglewood II's declaration to develop "broad musicianship in all of their students for lifelong learning" that may nourish musical hunger for the common good ranging from personal to communal. Small believed that through "musicking we have a tool by means of which our real concepts of ideal relationships can be articulated, those contradictions can be reconciled and the integrity of the person affirmed, explored and celebrated."[39] We have theorized four kinds of encounters of musical learning as a normative conceptual framework for imagining, investigating, evaluating, and encouraging forms of amateur musicking responsive to undergraduates' diverse musical hungers. The question this raises is how can different forms of amateur musicking become pedagogically strategic for developing humane education?

Elliot, Silverman, and Bowman's artistic citizenship concept ultimately locates artistry in the public sphere activity like Emma's marching band commitment, dismissing the value of domestic musicking encounters like Scott and Joan's.[40] McConnell's ongoing research recommends institutional concern to feed undergraduates' musical hunger by enacting a transformative pedagogical strategy to encourage musicianship for communal and individual well-being. Emma, Scott, and Joan did not engage in musicking for equal rights or social justice, but history offers examples such as the Highlander Folk School worthy of research.

Jorgensen suggests that twenty-first century "centers of advanced learning" are optimal sites for transforming all levels of music education from a predominant competitive masculine value system toward a collaborative feminine approach.[41] Collegiate amateur musicking groups' "feminine" approach to music making opens the doors for all students potentially to experience the encounters of musical learning for humane education. Through amateur musicking, as performers or listeners, students may gain access to musical knowledge (epistemological), engage in musical creation (practical), (re)develop personal and social identities (ontological), and befriend others for a common cause (axiological). Our three musicians' amateur musicking experiences caution educators that learning may vary from one ensemble to another, and recommend that music educators and higher education administrators should, as authors such as Emily Howe, André de Quadros, Andrew Clark, and Kinh T. Vu allow themselves to be tuned by the worlds of undergraduates, learning from them how best to support and encourage student-led amateur musicking as a kind of humane education.[42]

Emma's marching band experiences failed to arouse her epistemological and axiological musical hungers for living with an appreciation of musical diversity and an urge to serve the common good. If Emma had chosen to attend a historically black university, perhaps its marching band's differently styled sound and movement, pride in black identity, and explicit educational purpose as "a laboratory that provides hands on leadership experiences for aspiring band directors and students" could have offered her encounters of musical learning that might have fulfilled those purposes.[43] But her marching band at a predominantly white university, whose self-promotion highlights the band's academic and musical excellence by listing its participants' various prominent awards and distinctions, reflected a familiar societal vision that Jorgensen might recognize as masculine, hierarchical, and competitive.[44]

Emma's case urges our caution to music educators working with higher education leaders, against an unquestioning assumption that any old institutional provision of amateur musicking opportunities will produce humane higher education. To avoid such a trap, universities should consider the addition of musical student affairs professionals and departments to support and encourage the development of student-led cocurricular amateur musicking experiences similar to Scott and Joan's for all students. Support may include, but not be limited to: designating funds, providing instruments, securing rehearsal spaces, partnering with professional musicians. Musical student affairs programs should aim to empower and engage all students in identifying and nourishing their musical hungers.

Scott and Joan's cases exemplify what Jorgensen called a feminine approach to amateur musicking grounded in egalitarian, collaborative aims by acknowledging musicking as central to developing a well-lived life.[45] Both developed ad hoc "amateuring" spaces within the university's domestic realm for spiritual self-fulfillment, eventually bridging into the communal civic realm. Scott's amateur musicking at the residence hall piano healed his loneliness, engaged him with listeners, diversified his musical repertoire, gave him avocational purpose as well as musical identity, and transformed his campus residential culture both aesthetically and socially. Joan explains how MiM's musical creation process became a way of building multiple relationships through music: "I feel that music brings this experience to them that they are learning about themselves, they are learning about the person who is working with them; it is not necessarily just the music, its music with everything else brings this overall experience for them. The use of music, I guess, creates this greater experience." Through amateur musicking, song writer and patient are acting in the "spirit of solidarity" as both are listeners and performers.[46] The finished product, an online music video, symbolizes the "greater experience" created through their musical collaboration. MiM promotes a "shared way of life" through exploring, making, and sharing music about and for everyday lived experiences of chronic illness. Each video is a musical storytelling of human healing for the common good no longer confined by geography or time. We could hardly have asked for a clearer case of amateur musicking encounters as humane education.

Learning from amateur musicking groups and individuals can reveal to us the kinds of musical hunger that move them—and by what means, toward what ends, in what settings, with what needed resources does each encounter of musical learning move them. Continuing such narrative inquiry could inform music educators' future efforts with higher education leaders to nourish diverse musical hungers within curricular and cocurricular amateur musicking. Undergraduate musicians' befriending practices through the encounters of musical learning, responsive to their own diversely felt musical hungers, enact amateur musicking for the common good as a transformative pedagogy of humane music education.

SUSAN LAIRD is Professor Emeritus of Educational Leadership and Policy Studies at the University of Oklahoma and Value Theorist in Residence at the Center for Leadership Ethics and Change, Oklahoma. She is author of *Mary Wollstonecraft: Philosophical Mother of Coeducation*.

JOHNNIE-MARGARET MCCONNELL is a PhD graduate in Educational Studies from the University of Oklahoma, Oklahoma.

Notes

1. Alan Clarke Buechner, *Yankee Singing Schools and the Golden Age of Choral Music in New England, 1760–1800* (Boston: Boston University, 2003); Eileen Southern, *The Music of Black Americans: A History*, 2nd ed. (New York: Norton, 1983).

2. Estelle R. Jorgensen, *Transforming Music Education* (Bloomington: Indiana University Press, 2003).

3. Gregory F. Barz and Timothy J. Cooley, *Shadows in the Field: New Perspectives for Fieldwork in Ethnomusicology*, 2nd ed. (New York: Oxford University Press, 2008); Lee Higgins, *Community Music: In Theory and in Practice* (New York: Oxford University Press, 2012); Mark. Slobin, *Subcultural Sounds: Micromusics of the West* (Hanover, NH: University Press of New England, 1993).

4. Buechner, *Yankee Singing Schools*; Joshua Duchan, "Powerful Voices: Performance and Interaction in Contemporary Collegiate A Cappella" (PhD diss., University of Michigan, 2007), https://deepblue.lib.umich.edu/handle/2027.42/126676; Maurice R. Faulkner,

"The Roots of Music Education in American Colleges and Universities" (PhD diss., Stanford University, 1955); Susan Laird, "Musical Hunger: A Philosophical Testimonial of Miseducation," *Philosophy of Music Education Review* 17, no. 1 (2008): 4–21; Henry Davidson Sheldon, *The History and Pedagogy of American Student Societies* (New York: Appleton and Camp, 1901); UNESCO, Rethinking Education: Towards a Global Common Good? (Paris: UNESCO, 2015), 10, https://unesdoc.unesco.org/ark:/48223/pf0000232555.

5. Laird, "Musical Hunger," 7.

6. UNESCO, *Rethinking Education*, 41.

7. Thomas A. Regelski, "Amateuring in Music and Its Rivals," *Action, Criticism, and Theory for Music Education* 6, no. 3 (2007): 27; Robert A. Stebbins, "The Amateur: Two Sociological Definitions," *Pacific Sociological Review* 20, no. 4 (October 1977): 582–606, doi:10 .2307/1388717.

8. Johnnie-Margaret McConnell interviewed three undergraduate students, one male and two females, through purposeful sampling who elected to participate in cocurricular musicking for the purpose of learning more about practices of and reasons for participating.

9. Buechner, *Yankee Singing Schools*; Southern, *Music of Black Americans*.

10. W. J. Baltzell, "The American College Man in Music," *Musical Quarterly* 1, no. 4 (October 1915): 623–636; Buechner, *Yankee Singing Schools*; Joshua Duchan, *Powerful Voices: The Musical and Social World of Collegiate A Cappella* (Ann Arbor, MI: University of Michigan Press, 2012); Faulkner, "Roots of Music Education "; W. Imig, *Professional Music Training in Universities and Colleges in the United States*, vol. 2 (New York: International Society for Music Education Archives, 1974); Mabel Newcomer, *A Century of Higher Education for American Women*, 1st ed. (New York: Harper, 1959); Southern, *Music of Black Americans*.

11. John Dewey, *Art as Experience* (New York, Minton, Balch, 1934); John Dewey, *Experience and Education*, Kappa Delta Pi Lecture Series (New York: Macmillan, 1938); Duchan, *Powerful Voices*; David J. Elliott and Marissa Silverman, *Music Matters*, 2nd ed. (New York: Oxford University Press, 2005); Adrian C. North and David J. Hargreaves, "Music and Adolescent Identity," *Music Education Research* 1, no. 1 (1999): 75–92.

12. UNESCO, *Rethinking Education*, 39.

13. Christopher Small, *Musicking: The Meanings of Performing and Listening* (Hanover: University Press of New England, 1998).

14. Ibid., 9.

15. Dewey, *Art as Experience*.

16. Jane Roland Martin, *Education Reconfigured: Culture, Encounter, and Change* (New York: Routledge, 2011).

17. UNESCO, *Rethinking Education*, 39.

18. Jorgensen, *Transforming Music Education*, 22.

19. Robert A. Choate, "Documentary Report of the Tanglewood Symposium," in *Music in American Society* (Music Educators National Conference, Tanglewood: Music Educators National Conference, 1968).

20. Regelski, "Amateuring in Music and Its Rivals."

21. Lucy Green, *How Popular Musicians Learn: A Way Ahead for Music Education* (Aldershot, UK: Ashgate, 2001).

22. Roger Mantie, "A Study of Community Band Participants: Implications for Music Education," *Bulletin of the Council for Research in Music Education*, no. 191 (April 10, 2012): 22, doi:10.5406/bulcouresmusedu.191.0021.

23. Deanne Bogdan, "Betwixt and Between: Working through the Aesthetic in Philosophy of Education: George F. Kneller Lecture, Conference of the American Educational Studies Association, Savannah, Georgia, October 30, 2008," no. 46, 308, 292, doi:10.1080 /00131941003799886.

24. Bruno Nettl, *The Study of Ethnomusicology: Thirty-One Issues and Concepts*, new ed. (Urbana: University of Illinois Press, 2005), 55–57.

25. Adrian C. North, David J. Hargreaves, and Susan A. O'Neill, "The Importance of Music to Adolescents," *British Journal of Educational Psychology* 70 (2000): 258.

26. Jorgensen, *Transforming Music Education.*

27. Ibid.

28. Jorgensen, "A Philosophical View of Research in Music Education," *Music Education Research* 11, no. 4 (December 2009): 14.

29. Susanne K. Langer, *Feeling and Form: A Theory of Art* (New York: Scribner, 1953).

30. Luca Tiszai, "Friendship, Solidarity, and Mutuality Discovered in Music," in this collection.

31. Duchan, *Powerful Voices*, 95.

32. Lucy Green, *Music, Informal Learning and the School: A New Classroom Pedagogy*, Ashgate Popular and Folk Music Series (Aldershot, UK: Ashgate, 2008), 194.

33. Laird, "Musical Hunger," 10.

34. Ibid.

35. Ibid.

36. Iris M. Yob, "There Is No Other," in this collection.

37. Patricia Hill Collins, *Black Feminist Thought: Knowledge, Consciousness, and the Politics of Empowerment*, 10th ed. (New York: Routledge, 2000); Carol Gilligan, *In a Different Voice: Psychological Theory and Women's Development* (Cambridge, MA.: Harvard University Press, 1993); bell hooks, *Feminism Is for Everybody: Passionate Politics* (Cambridge, MA: South End Press, 2000).

38. UNESCO, *Rethinking Education*, 38.

39. Small, *Musicking*, 221.

40. Elliot, Silverman, and Bowman define artistic citizenship as engaging individuals and communities in artistic acts for "improving human well-being" for human flourishing; see David James Elliott, Marissa Silverman, Wayne D. Bowman, eds., *Artistic Citizenship: Artistry, Social Responsibility, and Ethical Praxis* (New York: Oxford Press, 2016), 89.

41. Jorgensen, *Transforming Music Education*, 134. "Feminine" and "masculine" gender (not sex) designations on the surface appear to assume cisgender formation. That is not our stance. We use these binary categories to show differing cultural gender norms illustrated through public and private music-making practices. Music making through drag shows and other gender-bending performance practices challenges cisgender assumptions, but Jorgensen's gender designations reflect what Carolyn Korsmeyer has called "deep gender."

42. Emily Howe, André de Quadros, Andrew Clark, Kinh T. Vu, "The Tuning of the Music Educator: A Pedagogy of the 'Common Good' for the Twenty-First Century," in this collection.

43. "Marching Pride," Langston University, accessed July 15, 2017, http://www.langston .edu/marchingpride.

44. Jorgensen, *Transforming Music Education.*

45. Ibid., 134.

46. UNESCO, *Rethinking Education*, 23.

16

DISSOCIATION/REINTEGRATION OF LITERARY/MUSICAL SENSIBILITY

Deanne Bogdan

THIS CHAPTER APPROACHES THE THEME OF HUMANE MUSIC education by using a brief survey of literary criticism as a heuristic for exploring the dissociation of literary/musical sensibility and its possible reintegration in a "decentered" world, with its attendant aesthetic, social, and political values of "difference." In so doing, it both supports the UNESCO principle that "knowledge is the common heritage of humanity" and that "like education, [it] must . . . be considered a global public good." Further, the chapter responds directly to UNESCO's concern regarding "how a plurality of worldviews [can] be reconciled through a humanistic approach" to education, here, specifically, through the dual lenses of literature and music education.[1]

Reintegration of sensibility springs from T. S. Eliot's *dissociation of sensibility*—the disjuncture between thought and feeling that he deemed had occurred following the advent of the seventeenth-century metaphysical poets, who possessed a "mechanism of sensibility that could devour any kind of experience." Eliot's exemplar of a poetic integrated sensibility is John Donne, for whom a "thought . . . was a [felt] experience" that "modified his sensibility. When a poet's mind is perfectly equipped for its work, it is constantly amalgamating disparate experience . . . always forming new [aesthetic] wholes" such that the poetic construct infuses the reader with a corresponding balance between thought and feeling.[2] Lines from Donne that spring to mind are, "Batter my heart . . . and bend / Your force, to break, blow, burn, and make me new."[3]

The assumption of the potential for a unification of sensibility underlay Eliot's own theory of literary response, as it did for his fellow New Critics in England and the United States.[4] A reaction against nineteenth-century historicist, biographical, and sociological criticism, New Criticism posited a "science" of literature, the educational objective of which was to train students in the theory and method of literary analysis in terms of aesthetic principles such as the inseparability of form and content, the priority of poetic convention, internal coherence, and organic unity. The resulting unified sensibility was set within a modernist context in which the literary work, contemplated as a self-contained, self-referential aesthetic object, was assumed to democratize education by making poetry available to everyone, "everyone" presumed to be a white, heterosexual, able-bodied, Oxbridge/ Ivy League–educated male.[5]

Enter the Anglophone academic equivalent of Sputnik in 1957— *Anatomy of Criticism*, authored by Canadian literary theorist Northrop Frye, whose prodigious critical imagination extended the solipsistic logocentrism of the New Critical "verbal icon" into a universalist, archetypal "order of words,"[6] in which an anagogic, quasimystical critical perspective created a "cultural envelope" of verbal hypothetical constructs so broad that it entailed the veritable "swallowing" of life by literature, thereby effectively resolving Eliot's dissociation of sensibility.[7] Although integrated sensibility was for Frye a theoretical ideal, he foreclosed on its practical realization: within his synoptic vision, "dissociation" became the default position of sensibility in literary reading because of the apparent psychological impossibility of simultaneously participating in and being consciously aware of experience.[8] For him, readers tend toward an integrated sensibility through "the participating response" to literary works, but habitually either overintellectualize—lacking feeling—or sentimentalize— lacking objectivity. Thus the detached critical response had to ground the transfer of literature's imaginative energy to the reader.[9] In face of his belief that the direct experience of literature cannot be taught, Frye unwittingly reinscribed Eliot's dissociation of sensibility by making criticism logically prior to experience, the legacy of which has been the predominant pedagogical mode in postsecondary English classes throughout most of the twentieth and twenty-first centuries.[10] Under the rubric of dissociated sensibility, "humane reading," that is, reading for enjoyment, pleasure, or a sense of individual well-being, is subsidiary to the determinants of an inhumane Humanism, surely an unlikely *means* to the *goal* of education for the common good, as set out in UNESCO's *Rethinking Education*, in which the integrated intellectual, emotional, and spiritual health of readers would be paramount.[11]

The normalization of dissociated literary sensibility began to change in the 1960s, 1970s, and early 1980s with the advent of reader-response criticism and poststructuralist literary theory.[12] By 1985, questions of "the Other" became germane to reintegrating the literary sensibilities of readers in terms of race and gender, with two landmark publications of "standpoint theory": Elaine Showalter's *The New Feminist Criticism: Essays on Women, Literature, and Theory*, which became for me and others a core class text in Women's Studies; and Henry Louis Gates Jr.'s introduction to his famous edition of *Critical Inquiry*, in which he traced the past and then current history of black literary sensibility.[13] As examples of seeing "from below," Showalter and Gates bridged the modernist and poststructuralist discursive worlds of late twentieth-century efforts at reintegrating sensibility, thereby giving voice to women and other Others through feminist criticism as resistance to identifying against oneself (the personal having become the political) and postcolonial criticism as writing "the Black race" into existence.[14] Gates confronted head on the intrication of race with the formalist basis of Eliot's dissociation of sensibility, which Gates noted was shot through with the glaring Eurocentrism of "the human condition" that New Criticism purported to espouse. He saw Eliot's literary dissociation of sensibility as inextricable from its historical/political context, as accruing from "the fraternal atrocities of the First World War," while "for many people with non-European origins . . . dissociation of sensibility resulted from colonialism and slavery."[15] To counteract being othered by the literary canon, Gates offered a twofold vision for reintegrating black literary sensibility: standpoint "autobiographical 'deliverance' narratives" in dialogue with discursive accoutrements as a "wide variety of critical approaches" included in his special issue of *Critical Inquiry*.[16]

What does my own current "situated sensibility" as a Canadian academic within a culture of "otherness" make of "dissociation" and "reintegration" of literary sensibility today in rethinking education for the common good?[17] As I hope to show in the remainder of my chapter, standpoint theory and postmodern considerations of "otherness" interplay with the democratic ideals embedded in the terms *humane education* and *the common good*: standpoint theory as an individual's right to aesthetic experience and expression with the concomitant awareness of and accountability for the ethical implications of the material effects on others who are differently situated.

The infamous problem of the "residential schools" for indigenous peoples living in Canada's north/west provides a salient example. Cited below is an excerpt from *Wenjack*, a novella by celebrated Canadian author Joseph Boyden, which strikes me as positively John Donne–like in its immediacy and intensity:

> Ash snow and its cold . . . maybe . . . is
> Sent to me from teachers at the
> School, from the men the colour of a fish
> belly who hunt me to take me back. They
> won't find me. . . . I won't go
> back to that place.[18]

Wenjack is a poeticized version of the foreshortened life of Chaney (a.k.a. Charlie) Wenjack, a twelve-year-old Ojibway boy who did not survive escaping from his "school," having frozen to death trying to find his way home, four hundred miles distant. Boyden's work is a stark wake-up call for Canadians to confront one of the most shameful stains on our history. For me, consciously taking in Boyden's words is a transformational "felt experience," in Eliot's terms, a fusion of thought and feeling that touches the soul aesthetically and politically. (In fact, Boyden's work has been foundational to the 2015 Truth and Reconciliation Commission in my country.) Here the simple act of literary reading can be in itself a kind of social justice education, even without Gates's discursive accoutrements.

Yet *Wenjack* did in fact generate its own accoutrements—in the form of newspaper articles concerning the furor around Boyden's ethnicity and the questions it raised in both the literary establishment and the general public about identity and representation. Belying his claims to be part Ojibway, part Nipmuc, Boyden ultimately confessed to being just "a white guy from Willowdale [a Toronto suburb] with native roots."[19] As author and as Other, Boyden ultimately othered himself in his zeal to further the cause of there being no Other.[20] Although he was eventually welcomed back into Canada's indigenous community and despite his own retraction of claiming blood ties to it, his readers continue to dwell in the tension between exhortations to study his unanimously lauded work and Boyden's own voluntary stifling of his literary commitment to indigenous causes, to "keep quiet" and just "listen" for a while—a listening in the service, perhaps, of the common good?[21]

In "Thinking in Dark Times," a 2006 speech delivered to university professors, psychoanalyst and cultural scholar Julia Kristeva asserted that, as "public intellectuals," their mandate is to "reconstruct the new humanism we need." Rather than integrate knowledge, for Kristeva, the humanities currently "*fragment* human experience. . . . Transdisciplinarity does not in itself" suffice. "What matters is that from the outset the thinking subject connects . . . thought to . . . being in the world through affective, political, and ethical transference."[22] That is, something has to move, to shift, "in the Aristotelian sense of thought as act, the actuality of intelligence."[23] The Boyden controversy accomplished just that: by entering the public consciousness, the social role of literature was no longer "simply academic." Perhaps Canadians are now reintegrating their sensibility in the hindsight of our collective state of national dissociation of sensibility—by thinking harder in dark times, as the daily press documents the burden of belated retributive justice for our historical demons—from the Japanese- and Italian-Canadian internment camps to the 2016 Quebec City mosque massacre.[24]

Can literature really accomplish the work of reintegrating sensibility, of making readers think deeply—transferentially and transformationally—in a globalized, technocentric world? Can it reconcile the means-end twin aspirations to a truly humane education and the common good? Perhaps.[25] In his introduction to a 2016 Special Issue of the *Publications of the Modern Language Association* dedicated to "World Literature," editor Simon Gikandi (paralleling Gates in his 1985 *Critical Inquiry* issue on race) reframes the problem by asking whether literature itself may have "a curious ontological status" or whether it must always be referential to the world's "exigencies."[26] "Literature, like the world, is both immanent (by virtue of its literariness) and relational (because it always exists in relation to the nonliterary). The intersection of the immanently literal and the inherently relational . . . accounts for what Derrida . . . [calls literature's] 'paradoxical structure.'" Especially pertinent to this paradox is pedagogy, which now addresses the margins of "Euro-American cultural centers in a world defined by conflicted literary histories and their competing publics."[27]

The Joseph Boyden dilemma illustrates the Derridean paradox cited by Gikandi as one example of the impasse in the current relationship between dissociation and reintegration of literary sensibility. Boyden is caught in undecidability, a no-win dilemma of speaking/not speaking, writing/not writing, othering/being othered, thus epitomizing the larger conundrum of the arts and education for the common good. In the remainder of this chapter, I draw upon Northrop Frye's modernist literary theory as well as salient postructuralist thinkers to explore the tension between immanence and referentiality in music and music education with respect to reintegrating sensibility as the condition of there being no Other.

I begin with the question, "What might count as an instance of unified musical sensibility equivalent to Eliot's "constantly amalgamating disparate experience" into "new [aesthetic] wholes" both in the performer and respondent? For me, it is performances (and their reception) of the young Russian pianist Daniil Trifonov, winner of *Gramophone*'s 2016 Artist of the Year award: "the astonishing thing about him . . . has been the ready achievement of and *ideal balance of feeling and intellect*. . . . You sense the acuteness of his listening, which guides him towards a precise ideal of the sounds he requires and their realization."[28] Here there seems to be no Other in the identification between the musical object and its reception. Such instances of unified sensibility or musical immanence, however, are not limited to those performed by professional artists. Recently I witnessed a choir of twenty-five culturally diverse Florida state-funded secondary school students publicly perform complex sixteenth-century Italian and English madrigals. Their Latino choir director refused to engage in "musical malnourishment" by consigning his students to "cultural narrowness"— keeping them culturally "ignorant" of Western art music, even though these works may have been for them what Frye would have called "alien structure[s] of the imagination, set over and against [them], strange in its conventions and . . . values."[29] Frye regarded these conventions as initiating a "death and rebirth process" in learners that would be a precondition for their genuine "possession" of music. For him, just as criticism is logically prior to the participating response, the intellectual work of *understanding* becomes "the ground base" for the *undergoing* of music. It is through the educated imagination that music "revives within [students], as something now uniquely [theirs] though still itself." The Other, then, is no Other, but integrated within the self "though still also itself."[30]

Frye's modernist espousal of privileging form over content (inherited from Eliot) permeated his musical aesthetics. An ardent amateur pianist, Frye championed music to the point where it became foundational to his literary theory.[31] Reintegrating musical sensibility entailed the apprehension of "pure . . . design,"[32] which he regarded as more readily discernible in music than in literature or the visual arts, where the perception of form is weakened by the greater susceptibility of the other arts to point to the world.[33] That music seems not to be primarily about anything other than the properties and materials intrinsic to it—musical immanence—was what made music for him the paradigmatic art, and thereby ontologically superior to what Paul Ricoeur called "the fleeting character of the literary event."[34] Accordingly, Frye valorized the structural components of music—counterpoint and the organization of sound—for him best embodied by the fugues of Bach and the sonatas of Mozart, which "cannot exist outside music."[35] Here Frye's *Anatomy* resonates with *The Well-Tempered Clavier*: both Frye's "order of words" and Bach's "Great Forty-Eight" epitomize the self-referentiality of musicologist Peter Kivy's "music alone,"[36] in which the musical object is none other than itself.

The Frye-Kivy musical ontology may augur well for the possibility of the indwelling of immanence, but is conditional upon the logical priority of understanding and its attendant risk of furthering a hegemonic Humanistic musical education. Philosopher of aesthetics Richard Shusterman, however, privileges undergoing over understanding by invoking Martin Buber's assertion that the most profound aesthetic experiences "are not those that we have but rather those that have us, overwhelming the experiencer to the point where one cannot properly talk about the appreciative knowledge of the experience," a phenomenon some call ineffability.[37] I would argue that it is the sonic force of musical undergoing that confers its ontological validity. Here poststructuralist theory comes to the fore by opening up a space for a humane musical sensibility. Musical undergoing inheres in the very nature of sound, which invokes the relational aspect of music as inseparable from its immanence by virtue of the unique power of sound over the unconscious. Roland Barthes writes that the listener is constituted by musical sound such that the very "injunction to listen," in creating an instantaneous connection with the unconscious other within the self, "is the total interpolation of one subject by another."[38] Thus, while the listening experience aspires to the condition of pure aesthetic presence, its ineluctable, ethical implication with the other is inherent in the exchange of acoustical spaces. This nontransparency of immanence is even more complex in playing because of what Barthes insists is the textual, discursive nature of performance, in which "the body itself must transcribe what it reads: it *fabricates* sound and sense."[39]

Immanent and relational aspects of music are thus interdependent. Both indwelling and textuality can be accommodated within what Estelle Jorgensen has termed the ongoing "dialectics" of music education.[40]

Reintegrating musical sensibility, then, becomes a work-in-progress that entails nonhierarchical, recursive instances of understanding and undergoing—experiential direct experiences and textual learnings about music and its relation to the humanities. The practice of music as encompassing the fine arts and cultural theory, including philosophy, has an august history dating back to the ancients' concept of *mousike techne*, an activity that must ever remain unfinished.[41] As with literary sensibility, musical sensibility encompasses textual learnings about gender and race that can be seen as counterparts to Gates's accoutrements, and, as such, part of cultural theorist Edward Said's "worldliness," in which music is made accessible and attainable, its necessary "embeddedness . . . in networks of nonmusical forces" an advantageous condition for resolving dualisms between Others.[42]

Mousike techne would include my own feminist standpoint analysis of Frye's archetypal cosmos as derogating the material, sometimes negative, effects of his universalist literary theory on real readers reading in my classrooms.[43] My critique of Frye coincided with the somewhat belated incursions of poststructuralism and postmodernism into the discipline of music as "the new musicology." Here, among others, Marcia Citron gendered the canon; Karin Pendle performed second-wave "excavations" of women in music history; and music educationists Lucy Green and Charlene Morton addressed patriarchal musical meaning and the feminization of music in the curriculum, respectively.[44] One of the most powerful statements concerning canon in terms of race comes not from a music theorist but from *literata* Toni Morrison, who, echoing Gates, reconsidered the implications for American letters of the codependence of the Enlightenment and the institution of slavery: "How does literary utterance arrange itself when it tries to imagine an Africanist other?[45] I would ask, "What conceptions of the 'not-me' make possible and sustain a theory and practice of humane music education for the common good in which there is no Other?" My response interweaves themes of the canon, artistic excellence, socially conscious musical projects, pedagogy, and political will.

One example of widening the canon to include world music (akin to Gikandi's in World Literature) is cellist Yo-Yo Ma's recent documentary on his Silk Road project, *The Music of Strangers*.[46] Ma speaks from a nonacademic humanist standpoint of trying to find his "place in the world," of wanting "to contribute without having to justify myself."[47] So he traversed the globe, gathering together talented musicians who speak and play in different musical tongues. Here Ma seems to embody the quintessential codependence of a humane musical sensibility and dedication to the common good. His project attests to the ontological superiority of music in undergirding its social value through his fervency about the power of world music to turn fear of the Other into joy. His hope for changing the world through music extends to Silk Road's pedagogical project—*mousike techne* as a 125-page interdisciplinary curriculum guide. Not the statutory "integration" of music into the curriculum as a "hand-maiden" to nonmusical subjects, in which music becomes what Frye would have called "a *rhetorical analogue* to . . . truth," this document, a kind of mandala with music at the center, radiates outwards to pertinent related historical, geographical, and other transdisciplinary cognate disciplines precipitated by the Other within the music itself.[48]

Does the purported ontological authority of music help to dissolve the paradoxes of "otherness"? No, if educators expect definitive answers or ignore potential hegemony inherent in the power of music. Yes, if the symposium on "Charting the Future of Music Learning in the 21st Century," held in June, 2007, for nearly a week at Williams College, Massachusetts, which I had the privilege of attending, is any indication. Comprising thirty-two international delegates, sponsored by Boston University's Department of Music, Tanglewood II became *mousike techne* writ condensed and intense: participants listened, witnessed, and deliberated on change in music learning within the transdisciplinarity of cognitive science, anthropology, evolutionary theory, neurobiology, and cultural history, along with the praxis of drumming and singing African music under indigenous musical leaders. Together we formulated a "Declaration" to reintegrate musical sensibility within an expanded notion of musicianship, by striking a balance among established traditions and innovations, espousing high aesthetic standards, and foregrounding the musicality of all children as their birthright while honoring cultural differences and the principles of social justice.[49]

More recent inclusionary music projects here at home are further signs of "hard thinking in dark times." In early 2017, a CD, "Going Home Star: Truth and Reconciliation," won a Juno award for Best Classical Composition of the Year 2017. Its title song featured a collaboration between The Northern Cree singers and the Winnipeg Symphony Orchestra.[50] Its composer extolled the work's significance for a broader concept of classical music that would include throat singing and powwow, while also noting the underrepresentation of both musical genres within musical culture generally.[51] Further examples of *mousike techne* include philosopher of education Susan Laird's keynote address to the Philosophy of Music Education Society almost a decade ago; prominent piano chamber musician and pedagogue Patricia Parr's recent memoir and cofounding of a registered charity to provide high-quality music lessons for students in an "at risk" part of town; a panel discussion at my home university in 2016 addressing the philosophical and sociological status of music as social justice education; and of course, this present volume.[52]

The work-in-progress of reintegrating sensibility literally progresses as leaders in the music industry and academe do their part, but in order for their efforts to be truly transformative beyond music's status as one of the decorative arts, their mandate needs support by a collective principle that regards music as "a primary human need."[53] This in turn must be underwritten by a "will-ful," imaginative conception of what kind of society we want to be. To wit, a community outreach project recently launched by Mervon Mehta, Executive Director of Performing Arts at the Royal Conservatory of Music in Toronto, a mecca of music learning and performance, demonstrates aesthetic and political vision for the common good. A pioneer in curating upwards of more than a hundred concerts annually in classical, jazz, and world music for several years, Mehta has founded the New Canadian Global Music Orchestra (whose name has recently been changed to KUNÉ, meaning "together" in Esperanto) to celebrate Canada's Sesquicentennial Anniversary of Confederation in 2017. In residence at The Royal Conservatory of Toronto, twelve young Torontonians—all recent immigrants—made their concert debut on June 4, 2017, in a program collectively composed entirely by the orchestra members themselves. Representing the musical cultures of Canada-Métis, Iran, Ukraine, Cuba, Pakistan, Burkina Faso, Mexico, Brazil, Greece, Peru, Tibet, and China, most of these young musicians play both traditional instruments and an array of "other" kinds unknown to most Toronto concert-goers.[54] The press release for this initiative was accompanied by a personal email from the director, in which, lauding Toronto's multicultural diversity, he asserted that this ensemble would "look and sound like [our city] in 2017." His message concluded with a 1971 quotation from former prime minister Pierre Elliott Trudeau, "which has become a mantra for the project": "Every single person in Canada is a member of a minority group. . . . There is no such thing as a model or ideal Canadian. . . . A society which emphasizes uniformity is one which creates intolerance and hate. . . . What the world should be seeking, and what in Canada we must continue to cherish, are not concepts of uniformity but human values: compassion, love, and understanding."[55] Whether my country/city can live up to this ideal is an open question. If it can, it could help realize music's telos as a primary need within a society in which there would be no Other, in which music education's default "humane" raison d'être would be furthering the common cause of all humanity.

Acknowledgments

The author acknowledges the advice of the editor and reviewers as well as the invaluable support of Susan Laird and Guopin Zhao in an earlier version of the first half of this chapter, presented at the conference of the Philosophy of Education Society in Seattle, March 2017.

DEANNE BOGDAN is Professor Emerita in the Department of Social Justice Education at the Ontario Institute for Studies in Education of the University of Toronto, Canada.

Notes

1. UNESCO, *Rethinking Education: Towards a Global Common Good?* (Paris: UNESCO, 2015), 80, 84, http://www.unesco.org/fileadmin/MULTIMEDIA/FIELD/Cairo/images /RethinkingEducation.pdf.

2. T. S. Eliot, "The Metaphysical Poets," in *Criticism: The Major Texts*, ed. Walter Jackson Bate (1952; New York: Harcourt, Brace Jovanovich, 1970), 532. The balance between reason and emotion is thought to be intrinsic to *Bildung* (aesthetic education). See Alexandra Kertz-Welzel, Leonard Tan, Martin Berger, and David Lines, "A Humanistic Approach to Music Education: (Critical) International Perspectives," in this collection.

3. John Donne, "Holy Sonnets, XIV," *Poems of John Donne*, vol. 1, ed. E. K. Chambers (London: Lawrence and Bullen, 1896), 165.

4. For example, I. A. Richards, William Empson, John Crowe Ransom, William K. Wimsatt, René Wellek, and Robert Penn Warren.

5. For definitions of the terms *modernist*, *postmodernist*, and *poststructuralist*, see Iris M. Yob, "Introduction: Education for the Common Good in a Diverse World," in this collection.

6. W. K. Wimsatt, *The Verbal Icon: Studies in the Meaning of Poetry* (Lexington: University Press of Kentucky, 1954); Northrop Frye, *Anatomy of Criticism: Four Essays* (Princeton, NJ: Princeton University Press, 1957), 17.

7. "Anagogically . . . poetry unites total ritual, or unlimited social action, with total dream, or unlimited individual thought" (Northrop Frye, *Anatomy of Criticism* [Princeton, NJ: Princeton University Press, 1957], 120). See also, "human life [is] contained within a cultural envelope that insulates it from nature" (Northrop Frye, *Creation and Recreation* [Toronto: University of Toronto Press, 1980], 27); and "literature does not reflect life . . . it swallows it" (Northrop Frye, *The Educated Imagination—Second Series* [Toronto: Canadian Broadcasting Corporation Publications, 1963], 33).

8. Northrop Frye, *T. S. Eliot* (Edinburgh: Grove, 1963), 33, 81–82.

9. Northrop Frye, *The Well-Tempered Critic* (Bloomington: Indiana University Press, 1963), 145: "The more we know about literature, the better the chances that intensity of response and the greatness of the stimulus to it will coincide."

10. See Gerald Graff, *Beyond the Culture Wars: How Teaching the Conflicts Can Revitalize American Education* (New York: Norton, 1993).

11. In this chapter, I follow Iris Yob's distinction between uppercase *Humanism* as a "narrow philosophic tradition" and lowercase *humanism* as "human-centered, human-focused." See Yob, "Introduction." Yob notes, "The common good is . . . understood as common goods, indicating that it is made up of what is good for each individual. And what is good for the individual is a humane education that promotes and nurtures his or her human potential. . . . [within a certain] codependence between humane education and the common good." These two notions, on the other hand, are distinguished in that "humane education points more to the means of achieving the common good . . . [which in turn is] is the goal of humane education, its 'foundation' and 'outcome.'"

12. See especially David Bleich, *Readings and Feelings: An Introduction to Subjective Criticism* (Urbana, IL: National Council of Teachers of English, 1975) and Louise M. Rosenblatt, *The Reader, The Text, The Poem: The Transactional Theory of the Literary Work* (Carbondale: Illinois University Press, 1978).

13. Randall Everett Allsup underscores the integral relationship between knowledge of the Other and the importance of difference. See his "On the Perils of Wakening Others," in this collection. See also Elaine Showalter, ed., *The New Feminist Criticism: Essays on Women, Literature, and Theory* (New York: Pantheon, 1985); Henry Louis Gates Jr., "'Race,' Writing, and Difference," *Critical Inquiry* 12, no. 1 (Autumn 1985): 1–20.

14. Donna Haraway, "Situated Knowledges: The Science Question in Feminism and the Privilege of Partial Perspective," *Feminist Studies* 14, no. 3 (Autumn 1988): 584. For Haraway's concept of the "cyborg" in addressing difference, see Jacob Axel Berglin and Thomas Murphy O'Hara, "Working with Transgender Students as a Humane Act: Hospitality in Research and Practice," in this collection. See also Judith Fetterley, *The Resisting Reader: A Feminist Approach to American Fiction* (Bloomington: Indiana University Press, 1978); and Gates, "'Race,' Writing, and Difference," 6: "Literacy . . . is the emblem that links racial alienation to economic alienation."

15. Gates, "'Race,' Writing, and Difference," 2, 4, 5.

16. Ibid., 11, 13, 15.

17. See Deanne Bogdan, "Situated Sensibilities and the Need for Coherence: Musical Experience Reconsidered," one of four papers addressing the theme "Art and Aesthetic Education in Times of Terror: Negotiating an Ethics and Aesthetics of Answerability" for the inaugural symposium section of *Philosophy of Music Education Review* 10, no. 2 (Fall 2002): 124–128.

18. Joseph Boyden, *Wenjack* (Toronto: Penguin Random House, 2016), 64.

19. Shree Paradkar, "Boyden Not the Victim in Saga over Heritage," *Toronto Star*, January 16, 2017, E3.

20. Yob defines there being no Other as taking "everybody into account regardless of their differences." Yob, "There Is No Other," in this collection.

21. Marsha Lederman, "Defending His Story," *Globe and Mail* (Montreal and Toronto), January 7, 2017, R11. See also Eric Andrew-Gee, "The Making of Joseph Boyden," *Globe and Mail* (Montreal and Toronto), August 5, 2017, F1–F5, F8.

22. Julia Kristeva, "Thinking in Dark Times," *Profession 2006* (New York: Modern Language Association, 2006), 14, http://www.jstor.org/stable/25595824 (my emphasis).

23. Ibid. In 1579 Sir Philip Sidney termed *architectonic knowledge* "the ethic and politic consideration, with the end of well-doing and not of well-knowing only." Sidney, *A Defence of Poetry*, ed. J. A Van Dorsten (London: Oxford University Press, 1966), 29.

24. See Les Perreaux and Eric Andrew-Gee, "Quebec City Mosque Attack Suspect Known as Online Troll Inspired by French Far-Right," *Globe and Mail* (Montreal and Toronto), January 30, 2017, http://www.theglobeandmail.com/news/national/quebec-city-mosque-attack-suspect-known-for-right-wing-online-posts/arcticle33833044/04/04/2017. In June 2019, Canada's National Inquiry into Missing and Murdered Indigenous Women released their 1,200-page report, which raised the issue as to whether its findings evidenced commission of a "genocide." To wit, one public press account deemed that the inquiry's report, together with the acknowledged "cultural genocide" precipitated by the residential schools, as found by the Truth and Reconciliation Commission, had the effect of "driv[ing Indigenous people] away from their communities." See Gloria Gallaway and Wendy Stueck, "PM Vows Action on Indigenous Inquiry," *Globe and Mail* (Ontario), June 4, 2019, A1, A8.

25. The danger of music educators' "hubris" in their often uncritical belief in the unconditional power of the arts to protect the common good from "barbarism" is expressed by Hanne Rinholm and Øivind Varkøy in "Music Education for the Common Good? Between Hubris and Resignation—A Call for Temperance," in this collection. See also Eleni Lapidaki, "Toward the Discovery of Contemporary Trust and Intimacy in Higher Music Education," in this collection.

26. Pheng Cheah, *What Is a World? On Postcolonial Literature as World Literature* (Durham, NC: Duke University Press, 2016), 4, as quoted in Simon Gikandi, "Introduction: Another Way in the World," *Publications of the Modem Language Association* 13, no. 5 (October 2016): 1200.

27. Gikandi, "Introduction: Another Way," 1200, 1202; Jacques Derrida, "This Strange Institution Called Literature: An Interview with Jacques Derrida," *Acts of Literature*, ed. Derek Attridge (New York: Routledge, 1992), 46, as cited in Gikandi, "Introduction: Another Way," 1200.

28. Stephen Plaistow, "Artist of the Year, Winner Daniil Trifonov," in "Gramophone Classical Music Awards Special Issue 2016," special issue, *Gramophone Magazine*, September 2016: 18 (my emphasis).

29. See Johnnie-Margaret McConnell and Susan Laird, "Nourishing the Musically Hungry: Learning from Undergraduate Amateur Musicking," in this collection. On the other hand, music educators must guard against the hegemonic potential of "timbral bias" associated with some Western monolithic methods of teaching voice. See Emily Good-Perkins, "Rethinking Vocal Education as a Means to Encourage Positive Identity Development in Adolescents," in this collection; Northrop Frye, *The Stubborn Structure: Essays in Criticism and Society* (London: Methuen, 1970), 77.

30. Northrop Frye, *Spiritus Mundi: Essays on Literature, Myth, and Society* (Bloomington: Indiana University Press, 1976), 119.

31. See Deanne Bogdan, "Musical/Literary Boundaries in Northrop Frye," *Changing English: Studies in Reading and Culture* 6, no. 1 (March 1999): 57–79.

32. Frye, *Stubborn Structure*, 63.

33. Frye, *Spiritus Mundi*, 118.

34. Frye, *Stubborn Structure*, 46–47; Paul Ricoeur, *Interpretation Theory: Discourse and the Surplus of Meaning* (Fort Worth: The Texas Christian University Press, 1976), 9.

35. Northrop Frye, *The Bush Garden: Essays on the Canadian Imagination* (Toronto: House of Anansi Press, 1971), 173. Cf. the claim that Bach's music is inextricable from his theological "program" in Mary Thomason-Smith, "Music Education in Sacred Communities: Singing, Learning, and Leading for the Global Common Good," in this collection.

36. Peter Kivy, *Music Alone: Philosophical Reflections on the Purely Musical Experience* (Ithaca, NY: Cornell University Press, 1990).

37. Richard Shusterman, "Aesthetic Experience: From Analysis to Eros," *Journal of Aesthetics and Art Criticism* 64, no. 2 (Spring 2006): 223; Martin Buber, *The Knowledge of Man: Selected Essays*, ed. Maurice Friedman (London: Allen and Unwin, 1965), 44, as cited in Shusterman, "Aesthetic Experience," 223. See Vladimir Jankélévitch, *Music and the Ineffable*, trans. Carolyn Abbate (Princeton, NJ: Princeton University Press, 1983). For the connection between the ineffable and the "messiness" of felt inquiry-based learning experience, see Betty Anne Younker, "Inquiry-Based Learning: A Value for Music in Education with Aims to Cultivate a Humane Society," in this collection. See also Allsup, "On the Perils," on the ineffable present and its relationship to searching as a guide for music education.

38. Roland Barthes, "Music's Body," in *The Responsibility of Forms: Critical Essays on Music, Art, and Representation*, trans. Richard Howard (New York: Hill and Wang, 1985), 251. One aspect of extraordinary sonic musical power is its capacity to create "liminal space, challenging linear chains of cause and effect . . . and examining what is and could be." See Kevin Shorner-Johnson, "Doing the Common Good Work: Rebalancing Individual 'Preparation for' with Collectivist Being," in this collection. Luca Tiszai cites Zsuzsa Pásztor in arguing that "responding to sound . . . is phylogenetically much older than intellectual concepts"; see Tiszai, "Friendship, Solidarity, and Mutuality Discovered in Music," in this collection.

39. Barthes, "Music's Body," 261.

40. Estelle R. Jorgensen, *In Search of Music Education* (Urbana: University of Illinois Press, 1997), 30.

41. Babbette E. Babich, "*Mousike Techne*: The Philosophical Practice of Music in Plato, Nietzsche, and Heidegger," in *Between Philosophy and Poetry: Writing, Rhythm, History*, ed. Massimo Verdicchio and Robert Burch, Textures—Philosophy/Literature/Culture Series (New York: Continuum, 2002), 171–180, as cited in Deanne Bogdan, "Betwixt and Between: Working through the Aesthetic in Philosophy of Education: George F. Kneller Lecture, Conference of the American Educational Studies Association, Savannah, Georgia, October 30, 2008," *Educational Studies* 46, no. 3 (May–June, 2010): 307–308. For the importance of music education as a "participatory process," see Yob, "There Is No Other"; and Younker, "Inquiry-Based Learning."

42. Edward Said, *Musical Elaborations*, Wellek Library Lectures at the University of California, Irvine (New York: Columbia University Press, 1991), 105; Lawrence Kramer, *Classical Music and Postmodern Knowledge* (Berkeley: University of California Press, 1995), 17.

43. See Deanne Bogdan, chaps. 5, 6, and 7 in Deanne Bogdan and Stanley B. Straw, eds., *Beyond Communication: Reading Comprehension and Criticism* (Portsmouth, NH: Boynton-Cook/Heinemann, 1990); and Deanne Bogdan, *Re-educating the Imagination: Towards a Poetics, Pedagogy, and Politics of Literary Engagement* (Portsmouth, NH: Boynton-Cook/Heinemann, 1992).

44. Marcia J. Citron, *Gender and the Musical Canon* (Cambridge: Cambridge University Press, 1993); Karin Pendle, ed., *Women and Music: A History* (Bloomington: Indiana University Press, 1991); Lucy Green, *Music, Gender, Education* (Cambridge: Cambridge University Press, 1997); and Charlene Morton, "Feminist Theory and the Displaced Music Curriculum: Beyond the 'Add and Stir' Projects," *Philosophy of Music Education Review* 2, no. 2 (Fall 1994): 106–121.

45. Toni Morrison, *Playing in the Dark: Whiteness and the Literary Imagination*, William E. Massey Lectures in the History of American Civilization (Cambridge, MA: Harvard University Press, 1992), 16.

46. Widening the canon is integral to Yob's "wide-angle view" and its relation to there being no Other; Yob, "There Is No Other."

47. Morgan Neville, dir., *The Music of Strangers*, with Yo-Yo Ma and the Silk Road Ensemble (Los Angeles: Tremolo Productions, 2015), documentary film.

48. Northrop Frye, *The Critical Path: An Essay on the Social Context of Literary Criticism* (1971; Bloomington: University of Indiana Press, 1973), 66; Jack Burton et al., *The Music of Strangers: Curriculum Guide*, Journeys in Film (Los Angeles: Participant Media, Silk Road, Educating for Global Understanding, in Partnership with the University of Southern California Rossier School of Education, 2016), http://www.journeysinfilm.org.

49. See Anthony J. Palmer and André De Quadros, eds., *Tanglewood II: Summoning the Future of Music Education*, foreword by Wynton Marsalis (Chicago: GIC Publications, 2012).

50. The Juno award is made annually for artistic and technical excellence in Canadian musical arts; it is named for Pierre Juneau, first president of the Canadian Radio-Television and Telecommunications Commission and former president of the Canadian Broadcasting Corporation; Christos Hatzis, *Going Home Star: Truth and Reconciliation*, music by Christos Hatzis, featuring Tanya Tagaq, Steve Wood, the Northern Cree Singers, and the Winnipeg Symphony Orchestra, conducted by Tadeusz Biernacki, and the Royal Winnipeg Ballet, directed by André Lewis, Toronto, Centrediscs Naxos, 2017.

51. Hatzis's acceptance of the Juno Award is cited in Jennifer Liu, "Interview, Christos Hatzis: Classical Music Caught in the Crossfire of Conflict," *Musical Toronto* (blog), April 11, 2017, https://www.ludwig-van.com/toronto/2017/04/11/interview-christos-hatzis-classical-music-caught-in-the-crossfire-of-conflict.

52. See McConnell and Laird, "Nourishing the Musically Hungry"; Patricia Parr, *Above Parr: Memoir of a Child Prodigy* (Toronto: Prism, 2016); see also Reaching Out through Music, accessed September 8, 2019, http://www.reachingoutthroughmusic.org/; Panel discussion, "Social Justice Arts Education: Opportunities, Challenges, and Contradictions," Centre for Media and Culture, University of Toronto, October 4, 2016.

53. Frye, *Spiritus Mundi*, 121.

54. Nontraditional instruments used in the orchestra are tar, ethnic Ukrainian flutes, jaw harp, sitar, spoons, esraj, tabla, kambélé, n'goni, tamanin, balafon, djembe, doum-doum, oud, lyra, bouzouki, Greek baglama, cajón, conga, timbales, dranyen, piwang, yang chin, bamboo flute, hulusi, xiao, panpipe, and ocarina. The orchestra has performed its original music in concerts across Canada and the United States, and its first CD is now a reality. Instruments and performers are listed on the back cover of KUNÉ, *KUNÉ—Canada's Global Orchestra*, Royal Conservatory of Music, Universal Music Canada, 2018, compact disc.

55. Pierre Elliot Trudeau, "Remarks at the Ukrainian-Canadian Congress, October 9, 1971," in *The Essential Trudeau*, ed. Ron Graham (Toronto, ON: McClelland and Stewart,

1998), 145–146; Mervon Mehta, email message to author, December 6, 2016. The kind of "interpersonal intimacy" that this orchestra members must have experienced as they lived, ate, and worked together over many months resonates with Eleni Lapidaki's notion of "irreducibility." See Lapidaki, "Contemporary Trust and Intimacy." Also, the "multiplicity of music education practices" endemic to this group would work toward breaking down the "dominance of Anglo-American music education"; Kertz-Welzel et al., "A Humanistic Approach." The New Canadian Global Orchestra acts as a bulwark against colonialism in that, despite its being initiated by a Canadian "settler" arts administrator, it came into being by dint of the musical and political imagination of someone who "allowed [himself] "to be tuned *by* the world" (emphasis in the original); see Emily Howe, André de Quadros, Andrew Clark, and Kinh T. Vu, "The Tuning of the Music Educator: A Pedagogy of the 'Common Good' for the Twenty-First Century," in this collection.

17

A HUMANISTIC APPROACH TO MUSIC EDUCATION

(Critical) International Perspectives

Alexandra Kertz-Welzel, Leonard Tan, Martin Berger,
and David Lines

Introduction

The UNESCO report *Rethinking Education: Towards a Global Common Good?* challenges scholars in various fields to start envisioning and developing a humanistic approach to education.[1] This seems particularly important in view of globalization, increasing levels of interconnectedness and interdependence, and a rapidly changing technological world. Even the much-touted "twenty-first century skills" are driven to a large extent by economic considerations.[2] Although it is not easy to determine what a humanistic approach to education would be, the report suggests that such an approach is guided by ethical principles supporting peace, inclusion, social justice, and environmental stewardship. It also stands against exclusion, intolerance, violence, and discrimination. Overcoming the hegemony of Western-derived thinking, embracing alternative ways of knowing, offering everybody access to education, and utilizing technology to facilitate lifelong learning are also significant aspects. A humanistic approach to education is the foundation for implementing the common good. But it would need to be applied to various subject areas, including music education, thereby opening a discourse about what various professions value and how they could address the challenges globalization poses.

How might music education transmit humane values to the young? And how might a humanistic approach to music education that is informed by diverse philosophical and educational systems look like? In this chapter, we draw on a multiplicity of international perspectives. Notions such as the African *ubuntu*, German *Bildung*, or the Confucian *ren* can help to propose guidelines for envisioning a humanistic approach to music education.

This chapter starts with considerations from New Zealand (David Lines), followed by perspectives from South Africa (Martin Berger), Germany (Alexandra Kertz-Welzel), and Asia (Leonard Tan). The final section presents general reflections on how international perspectives can enrich the search for a humanistic approach in music education.

Toward Humanistic Music Education in Aotearoa New Zealand

David Lines

As a "first world" Western country, Aotearoa New Zealand shares many features of music education with other similar countries across the world. One pressing trend is an increasing economic rationalism in the school curriculum, with an associated narrow focus on literacy and numeracy skills.[3] Within a context of an economic and vocational orientated education system, general music—which refers to "music for all" and general access to music learning—is positioned alongside a wide range of learning areas and other highly regarded "important" curriculum subjects, such as reading, writing, and mathematics.

In the most recent curriculum revision of primary school music, music was paired with sound arts in a revised, future-thinking arts curriculum.[4] However, because of limited opportunities for music teacher training and increased curriculum pressure in schools, many general teachers have shied away from teaching music in the classroom. As Linda Webb notes, this has left a gap between the expectations of curriculum policy and the teaching reality of primary music teaching in schools.[5]

Within music education, there are discourses that express how music is thought about, conceived, practiced, taught, and learned. These include humanistic music education, performance-orientated education, specialized music education, general music education, and community music education. In Aotearoa New Zealand, we also have Māori music education and a new kind of Māori humanism that links to "ancient values but is versed in a contemporary idiom."[6]

Although some specialized discourses tend to offer music education specifically for a select, privileged few, counternarratives exist in New Zealand society that provide music education with more humanistic potential and opportunities for alternative concepts of humanistic music education. A thread of resistance remains, made possible through a commitment to biculturalism that holds some hope for a future, humanistic, and sustainable music education. Aotearoa New Zealand is a postcolonial, bicultural nation, with a built-in duty to honor its bicultural citizens including the indigenous population, a fact written into law in the Treaty of Waitangi. As such, the indigenous people—Māori—have an influence on the nature and provision of music in the curriculum.

For instance, the early childhood curriculum *Te Whāriki* is centered around a series of bicultural themes that reflect Māori humanistic values: *Mana Atua* (well-being), *Mana Whenua* (belonging), *Mana Reo* (communication), *Mana Tangata* (contribution), and *Mana Aotūroa* (exploration).[7] These rich, humanistic, and sustainable concepts hold much value for music education of early years.

This curriculum provided a space for a recent early childhood research project called MAPS (move, act, play, sing), which brought community artists in music, dance, and drama into early childhood centers to work with teachers in art-making experiences.[8] The supportive and sharing ethos of this project helped early childhood teachers work through their fears of arts teaching and enabled them to initiate arts learning events themselves, sometimes for the first time.

Māori and Pacific Island arts expression can be a collective means of group performance that communicates meaningful human values and cultural identity. Kapa Haka, a well-known Māori performance genre, for instance, "puts into practice a key Māori concept, *whakawhanaungatanga*, which is the notion of strengthening the individual through shared community activities."[9] The creation of Kapa Haka initiatives and education has served to enable and inspire young Māori, rejuvenate Māori language, and create a decolonized space for art-making and resistance and the affirmation of a political voice.[10]

Despite the ongoing issues affecting music education, indigenous values about the arts and music form a strong block of resistance. These values continue to open discursive spaces for a music education that embodies a caring ethos. The power of the indigenous voice in the Aotearoa New

Zealand context shows us that a more humanistic music education can continue to flourish.

Singing *Ubuntu* and Creating Identity: Choral Singing and Humanistic Music Education in South Africa

Martin Berger

In 1994, a time (around three hundred years) in which music education in South Africa provided a means of consolidating segregation came to an end. Since ethnic groups were brought together by the segregation laws of apartheid, being divided into "white" and "nonwhite" became a principle for learners from the beginning of their educational lives.

After the collapse of the system in 1994, social and political leaders in South Africa were intent on laying the foundations of a unified nation, which should be achieved with the help of an inclusive education system that incorporates indigenous philosophical concepts as well. Among the many concepts to be found, the idea of *ubuntu* seems to be of specific value. Originating from the Nguni languages, the term *ubuntu* is used in many sub-Saharan languages to define the relation between an individual and a group. Christian Gade explains the different possibilities to define *ubuntu* in a very comprehensive way. *Ubuntu* describes a person as individual only because of a specific relation to other individuals: "*umuntu ngumuntu ng-abantu*: a person is only a person through their relationship to other persons."[11] While written sources prior to 1950 mainly define the word as a human quality, it gradually developed toward an understanding of an African humanism, a philosophy, an ethic, and a worldview. This phenomenon happens alongside the political freedom movements of the 1950s–1980s in Africa.

The principles of *ubuntu* are therefore deeply entrenched in a search toward African dignity and identity, and this cannot but influence African music educators' perception of education philosophy. *Ubuntu* involves "aid giving, sympathy, care sensitivity to the needs of others, respect, consideration patience, and kindness" and has a strong moral quality: receiving obliges to give back to the community and to share.[12] *Ubuntu* can be seen as a concept of fundamentally valid principles, which are good in and of themselves and which must be acted on by everyone if human behavior is to observe the moral law: "The African voice in education . . . is the voice of the radical witness of the pain and inhumanity of history, the arrogance of modernisation and the conspiracy of silence in academic disciplines towards what is organic and alive in Africa. It is the voice of "wounded healers" struggling against many odds to remember the past, engage with the present, and determine a future built on new foundations."[13]

Despite the consensus that there is a need for what Philip Higgs calls an "African Renaissance,"[14] new philosophical concepts for music education are still lacking rigor, since postcolonial debate in the past decades focused mainly on decolonizing as a precondition to achieve societal progress. Kofi Agawu argues that the concept of the autonomous individual as we know it from a Western point of view is unknown in most African cultures, the process of deconstruction would therefore automatically lead into growth.[15] Achille Mbembe mourns the "long dogmatic sleep"[16] that sub-Saharan Africa has faced during colonial times and calls on Africa to "face up to itself in the world": "We should first remind ourselves that, as a general rule, the experience of the Other, or a problem of the "I" of others and of human beings we perceive as foreign to us, has almost always posed virtually insurmountable difficulties to the Western philosophical and political tradition. Whether dealing with Africa or with other non-European worlds, this tradition long denied the existence of any "self" but its own."[17] Higgs, however, mentions "the epistemological question that centers around the debate of whether there is, in fact, an indigenous African way of knowing, and if so, what the implications for educational theory, research, and practice would be."[18] The critical point is whether further development of a philosophy will be possible without the perspective of intercultural encounter as a counter pole. "Indeed, in Africa, music has always been a celebration of the ineradicability of life, in a long life-denying history. It is the genre that has historically expressed, in the most haunting way, our raging desire not only for existence, but more importantly for joy in existence—what we should call the practice of joy before death."[19]

The predominant way of musicking in South Africa is singing, specifically singing in choirs, which facilitates and offers possibilities for bridging ideas across the society. Timothy Sibanda's analysis of Oliver Mtukudzi's music as a vehicle for sociopolitical commentary can serve as an example of the extent to which song and meaning are interwoven in the African context: "You don't get to sing a song when you have nothing to say."[20] Philosophies need their analogy in education if they strive for societal impact. Singing together in an African context has always been an expression of *ubuntu*: choirs as places to share knowledge, tradition, education, and art. Here might be the intersection where philosophy and music education meet, creating a fertile soil for the rise of an "African humanism," based on *ubuntu* and song.

The German Perspective: *Bildung* Revisited

Alexandra Kertz-Welzel

Many educational systems have ideals of education that are the result of their philosophical or religious traditions. For Germany and many Northern European countries, this ideal is *Bildung*. While English terms such as formation or cultivation only capture some of its aspects, *Bildung* represents the ideal image of humanity, which the nineteenth century envisioned, its core meaning still applicable today. *Bildung* describes the goal of schooling as educating self-determined, mature, and critical human beings who make significant contributions to the welfare of the society and its people.[21] The Christian origin of the term *Bildung*, which was created by the Christian mystic Meister Eckhart (1260–1328), underlines one of the most basic principles of this Christian image of humanity: if the soul is divine, education is about uncovering the true inner self and developing it through education.[22] By recognizing the god-likeliness of oneself and other's souls, moral principles such as commandments become important, guiding a meaningful life that respects others and contributes to the welfare of the society. Although *Bildung* was secularized and transformed over time, some of its core meanings have remained the same, for example, the trust in everybody's power of reason and the task of shaping it through education, thereby enabling a free and fair society for all. What made *Bildung* so fascinating was the fact that it aims at gaining knowledge and skills in specific areas, but also envisions a cultivation of character, fostering the whole personality and its ethical development. German philosopher and educationalist Wilhelm von Humboldt (1767–1835) created the notion of *Bildung* that is still most common today, even though it has been transformed.[23] In the revised versions, *Bildung* has international "counterparts" in terms of liberal education, critical pedagogy, including concepts linking democracy and music education, although it is no simple concept.[24] However, what makes *Bildung* a compelling notion regarding a humanistic approach to music education is the fact that it represents an ideal image of humanity, which is guided by respect, reason, and ethical principles.

Arts and music were supposed to play a significant role in the process of *Bildung*, as indicated in Friedrich Schiller's (1759–1805) *Letters on the Aesthetic Education of Man* (1791).[25] Through aesthetic experiences, he argued, the arts can "humanize" people by reconciling their inner drives such as reason and emotion. The arts were thought to balance our inner powers, thereby helping to shape our personality and character in a way supporting the development of the ethically responsible, acting persons we were supposed to be. While Schiller wrote his *Letters* during the French Revolution and its aftermath, shocked by the terror of an originally positive liberation of the oppressed being turned into a violent dictatorial regime, he searched for the reasons of this development and thought to have found them in human nature. His vision of utilizing the arts for creating a better world empowered educators, artists, and scholars to develop different approaches of aesthetic education. Schiller's ideas inspired German music education at various times, particularly in the last decades of the twentieth century, to create the approach of *musikalisch-aesthetische Bildung* (aesthetic education).[26] At its core is the notion that music education is about *Bildung* in terms of utilizing the power of music and aesthetic experiences to facilitate the formation of musical abilities, but also balancing reason and emotion. Thereby, music education supports the development of the individual personality, honoring ethical principles as foundation for a humane society. However, while from an Anglo-American perspective, aesthetic education is one of the most contested notions in music education, from the German point of view, there is no problem at all.[27] The notion of aesthetic experience is based on the trust in the power of music to support individual musical and personal development, as exemplified in many psychological studies.[28]

When considering humanistic music education from the German perspective, the notion of *Bildung* is the main point of reference. Educating mature and self-determined people who contribute to the development of a just society for all is a vision that is in some regards close to the notion of social justice that is popular in music education today.[29] This also indicates that, in view of globalization, it might be time to overcome outdated discourses such as the North American rejection of aesthetic education. It is crucial to redefine what the transformative and reconciling power of music means for the global music education community today, particularly with regard to humanistic music education.

From *Ren* (仁) to *Ren* (人): Toward a Confucian-Inspired Humanistic Philosophy of Music Education

Leonard Tan

In this section, I unpack the Confucian concept of *ren* (仁)—the highest of all virtues in Confucianism.[30] Commonly translated as "humanity," "humane," "good," and "benevolence," *ren* occurs more than one hundred times in the *Analects*. *Ren* (仁) has the same sound as 人(*ren*)—"humans" or "people." This section is titled "From *Ren* (仁) to *Ren* (人)" as a reminder that the ethical virtue of *ren* (仁) ought to result in virtuous actions for other humans (*ren* 人).

The character for *ren* (仁) consists of two parts: while the left refers to "person" (亻), the right is the character for the number "two" (二), indicating that at least two persons are needed in order for a person to be *ren*.[31] People who are *ren* are thoroughly relational in their thoughts and actions. When asked about *ren*, Confucius's immediate response was when one goes out to one's front gate, "behave as though you are receiving important visitors."[32] For Confucius, *ren* is first of all exemplified in something as ordinary as receiving a guest. Rather than engaging in a theoretical explanation of what *ren* is, Confucius shows us what a *ren* (仁) person should *do* as a person (*ren* 人), that is, treating each guest with utmost respect. Such an emphasis on actual doing, rather than abstract theorizing, is a distinctive aspect of Chinese philosophy. Later in the same passage, Confucius tells us: "Do not impose upon others what you yourself do not want."[33] Like what to do, what not to do is again about the others.

Since being *ren* involves being thoroughly relational with others, it is socially contagious; the presence of *ren* persons can inspire others to be like them. Confucius teaches his disciples to be close to those who are *ren* and dwell among people who are *ren*.[34] Since *ren* is infectious, who one acquaints with is important, with Confucius's caution to befriend only those who are *ren*. Indeed, learning to be *ren* appears to be more a vicarious affair than one that is explicitly taught or talked about.[35] While Socrates might have been rather happy to engage in a philosophic dialogue to more fully understand the precise nature of *ren*, Confucius rarely spoke about *ren*.[36] In fact, Confucius saw no use for craft in speech and once said that those of glib speech are rarely *ren*.[37] On the contrary, the person who is *ren* is slow to speak and to be reticent is to be close to *ren*.[38]

In short, a humanistic philosophy of music education, one that is based on the Confucian concept of *ren*, is one that is a thoroughly relational and social concept. As Herbert Fingarette puts it, "For Confucius, unless there are at least two human beings, there can be no human beings."[39] Alone on a deserted island, a person cannot be *ren* because there is no context for being one; being *ren*, then, is fundamentally about being *ren* (仁) toward other *ren* (人: people). Confucian *ren* emphasizes actual doing rather than arriving at a theoretical definition of *ren*, is socially contagious, and prioritizes action over vacuous words.

In its emphasis on relationality, active doing, and a social construal of ethics, Confucian *ren* lends support to group-based forms of music education such as traditional large ensembles. To rephrase Fingarette's statement for my purposes here, "For Confucius, unless there are at least two musicians, there can be no musicians." When playing the flute alone, there is just so much that one can learn. When playing with a stand partner, flute-playing takes on a different dimension: one learns to play in time, in tune, and so on, with another person. When playing with the full orchestra, flute playing assumes even greater sophistication as one listens actively, engages in give-and-take, and strives to achieve collective beauty and harmony in a "community of shared meaning" akin to a Confucian utopian society.[40] Were a stand partner to go sharp at a concert, one does not insist on an absolute pitch standard, but adjusts accordingly in order to preserve the larger aesthetic beauty, thus putting into action, the kind of kindness and empathy emphasized by Confucian *ren*. While all these demands of playing in an orchestra aim toward aesthetic goals, they are ethical ones as well; they parallel the challenges of humans living together. Making music with others in an orchestra, therefore, may be seen as putting Confucian *ren* into aesthetic practice; conversely, Confucian *ren* offers an ethical theory by which the aesthetic practice of traditional large ensembles may be illuminated. Through large ensembles, Confucian *ren* (仁) is actualized for humans (*ren* 人); as the title indicates, "From *Ren* (仁) to *Ren* (人)." Although articulated more than two thousand years ago, Confucian *ren* continues to inspire us to exercise kindness, respect, and sincerity to others, and shape a better future for humanity.

Conclusion

The presented perspectives from New Zealand, South Africa, Germany, and Asia exemplify the educational ideas that are important in the respective countries. They suggest some main points of reference for a humanistic approach in music education. Values such as respect, dignity, well-being, belonging, kindness, or a caring ethos characterize such approaches. The most striking aspect might be the fact that, contrary to the most common Western belief in individual autonomy, the South African *ubuntu* and the Chinese *ren* indicate that there is a special link between an individual and society. The society somebody belongs to seems to play a significant role in helping people to become who they are supposed to be. While constructing individual identity solely through belonging to a specific society might be challenging for our Enlightenment-inspired notion of the autonomous subject, we need to acknowledge that in many parts of the world, this idea is paramount.

A humanistic approach in music education classrooms might vary in respective countries, depending on specific approaches, methods, and curricula. It might sometimes be implemented best in general music education as in Germany, in choral singing as in South Africa, or it might concern a specific approach to music making in large ensembles as described regarding Asia. If a humanistic approach to music education is guided by principles that are connected to a respective society and its culture, it might look different in various countries. The perspectives from New Zealand underline the multiplicity of music education practices that can help in implementing respect, dignity and well-being.

What international perspectives on humanistic music education can certainly offer is a lesson on diversity. We need to acknowledge diverse ways of learning and knowing and should not be scared by the variety of perspectives. However, there are also ideas that connect us. As the UNESCO report states, from a global perspective, we could be united by the vision of education as a common good. Music education as a subject that celebrates the diversity of cultures and the power of transformative aesthetic experiences is certainly a significant part of this endeavor. The four international perspectives presented in this chapter illustrate this. One notion supporting education as a common good is, as the UNESCO report mentions, sustainability.[41] Learning to think beyond our immediate needs and to take into account the interests of future generations is important for transforming societies. Music education offers many opportunities for students to get to know sustainability or learning how to implement it regarding musical cultures, lifelong learning, or environmental stewardship.[42] Sustainability is, as the UNESCO report states, a key term to support the common good and education as a common good worldwide.

It would be the task of the global music education community to learn to utilize the worldwide diversity of educational ideas, particularly as related to music education theory and practice. This would also mean overcoming the often nonreflective dominance of Anglo-American music education and moving toward a culturally sensitive perspective in international music education.[43] Acknowledging diversity and practicing tolerance or inclusion is a significant part of a humanistic approach in music education. Ideas from various educational traditions can support developing an international humanistic approach to music education, helping music education fulfilling its promise to foster the development of a just society, which has been an important vision for music education since antiquity.

ALEXANDRA KERTZ-WELZEL is Professor and Department Chair of Music Education at Ludwig-Maximilians-Universitaet, Germany. She is author of *Globalizing Music Education: A Framework* and coeditor of *Patriotism and Nationalism in Music Education*.

LEONARD TAN is Assistant Professor of Music at the National Institute of Education of Nanyang Technological University, Singapore.

MARTIN BERGER is Head of Choral Music Education at Stellenbosch University, South Africa.

DAVID LINES is Associate Professor of Music Education at the University of Auckland, New Zealand. He is coauthor of *Intersecting Cultures in Music and Dance Education: An Oceanic Perspective*.

Notes

1. UNESCO, *Rethinking Education: Towards a Global Common Good*? (Paris: UNESCO, 2015), http://unesdoc.unesco.org/images/0023/002325/232555e.pdf.

2. On the twenty-first-century skills, see Leonard Tan, "Confucius: Philosopher of Twenty-First Century Skills," *Educational Philosophy and Theory* 48, no. 12 (2016): 1233–1243.

3. Janet Elaine Mansfield, "The Arts in the New Zealand Curriculum: From Policy to Practice," (PhD thesis, University of Auckland, New Zealand, 2000).

4. Ministry of Education, *The New Zealand Curriculum* (Wellington: Learning Media, 2007).

5. Linda Webb, "Music in Beginning Teacher Classrooms: A Mismatch between Policy, Philosophy, and Practice," *International Journal of Education and the Arts* 17, no. 12 (2016), http://www.ijea.org/v17n12/.

6. Miraka Szaszy, Anna Rogers, and Miria Simpson, *Te timatanga tatau tatau, Te ropu wahine Māori toko i te ora: Early Stories from Founding Members of the Māori Women's Welfare League* (Wellington: Bridget Williams, 1993), 7.

7. Ministry of Education, *Te whaariki: He whaariki matauranga mo nga mokopuna o Aotearoa Early Childhood Curriculum* (Wellington: Learning Media, 1996).

8. David Lines, Chris Naughton, and John Roder, *Move, Act, Play and Sing (MAPS): Exploring Early Childhood Arts Teaching and Learning Strategies and Concepts through Community Arts Interventions* (Wellington: Teaching and Learning Research Initiative, 2013), accessed August 19, 2017, http://www.tlri.org.nz/tlri-research/research-completed/ece -sector/move-act-play-and-sing-maps-exploring-early-childhood.

9. Te Oti Rakena, "The Voices of Warriors: Decolonising the Māori Voice" (paper presented at the ISME Community Music Activity Commission, Corfu, Greece, July 2012).

10. Ibid.

11. Christian B. N. Gade, "The Historical Development of the Written Discourses on Ubuntu," *South African Journal of Philosophy* 30 (2011): 318.

12. E. D. Prinsloo, "Ubuntu Culture and Participation Management," in *The African Philosophy Reader*, ed. Pieter Hendrik Coetzee and Abraham P. J. Roux (London: Routledge, 1998), 42.

13. Philip Higgs, "African Philosophy and the Decolonisation of Education in Africa: Some Critical Reflections," *Educational Philosophy and Theory* 44, no. S2 (2012): 38.

14. Philip Higgs, "The African Renaissance and the Transformation of the Higher Education Curriculum in South Africa" *Africa Education Review* 13, no. 1 (2016): 88.

15. Kofi V. Agawu, *Representing African Music: Postcolonial Notes, Queries, Positions* (New York: Routledge, 2003).

16. Achille Mbembe, *On the Postcolony* (Berkeley: University of California Press, 2003), 3.

17. Ibid., 14, 2.

18. Ibid., 52.

19. Ibid., preface.

20. Timothy S. S. Sibanda, "'You Don't Get to Sing a Song When You Have Nothing to Say': Oliver Mtukudzi's Music as a Vehicle for Socio-political Commentary," *Social Dynamics—A Journal of the Centre for African Studies* 30, no. 2 (2004): 36.

21. Betty Anne Younker, "Inquiry-Based Learning: A Value for Music Education with Aims to Cultivate a Humane Society," in this collection.

22. Bernhard Schwenk, "Bildung," in *Paedagogische Grundbegriffe*, vol. 1, ed. Dieter Lenzen (Reinbek: Rowohlt, 1989), 208–221.

23. Hans-Christoph Koller, *Bildung anders denken. Einfuehrung in die Theorie transformatorischer Bildungsprozesse* [Thinking differently about *Bildung*. Introduction to the theory of Bildung as transformative process] (Stuttgart: Kohlhammer, 2012).

24. Lars Løvlie and Paul Standish, "Bildung and the Idea of a Liberal Education," *Journal of Philosophy of Education* 36, no. 3 (2002): 317–340; Ilan Gur-Ze'ev, "Bildung and Critical Theory in the Face of Postmodern Education," *Journal of Philosophy of Education* 36, no. 3 (2002): 391–408; Paul G. Woodford, *Re-thinking Standards for the Twenty-First Century* (London: University of Western Ontario Press, 2011).

25. Friedrich Schiller, *On the Aesthetic Education of Man*, ed. Elizabeth M. Wilkinson and Leonard A. Willoughby (Oxford: Clarendon, 1967).

26. Alexandra Kertz-Welzel, "Revisiting Bildung and Its Meaning for International Music Education Policy," in *Policy and the Political Life of Music Education*, ed. Patrick Schmidt and Richard Colwell (New York: Oxford University Press, 2017), 107–121.

27. Hanne Rinholm and Øivind Varkøy, "The Changing Concept of Aesthetic Experience in Music Education," *Nordic Research in Music Education* 14 (2012): 9–25.

28. Susan Hallam, "The Power of Music: Its Impact on the Intellectual, Social, Personal Development of Children and Young People," accessed September 21, 2019, http://static1 .1.sqspcdn.com/static/f/735337/25902273/1422485417967/power+of+music.pdf.

29. Cathy Benedict, Patrick Schmidt, Gary Spruce, and Paul Woodford, *The Oxford Handbook of Social Justice in Music Education* (New York: Oxford University Press, 2015).

30. *Analects* 4.6, 6.30. See Roger Ames and Henry Rosement, *The Analects of Confucius: A Philosophical Translation* (New York: Ballantine, 1998), 90, 110.

31. Roger Ames, "Confucianism and Deweyan Pragmatism," *Journal of Chinese Philosophy* 30, nos. 3–4 (2003): 403–417; Leonard Tan, "Reimer through Confucian Lenses: Resonances with Classical Chinese Aesthetics," *Philosophy of Music Education Review*, 23, no. 2 (2015): 183–201.

32. *Analects* 12.2. See Ames and Rosement, *The Analects*, 153.

33. Ibid.

34. *Analects* 1.6, 4.1. See Ames and Rosement, *The Analects*, 72, 89.

35. *Analects* 15.10. See Ames and Rosement, *The Analects*, 186.

36. *Analects* 9.1. See Ames and Rosement, *The Analects*, 126.

37. *Analects* 5.517.17. See Ames and Rosement, *The Analects*, 96, 207.

38. *Analects* 12.3; 13.27. See Ames and Rosement, *The Analects*, 153, 170.

39. Herbert Fingarette, "The Music of Humanity in the Conversations of Confucius," *Journal of Chinese Philosophy* 10, no. 4 (1983): 331–356.

40. Charlene Tan and Leonard Tan, "A Shared Vision of Human Excellence: Confucian Spirituality and Arts Education," *Pastoral Care in Education* 34, no. 3 (2016): 156–166.

41. UNESCO, *Rethinking Education*, 20.

42. Alexandra Kertz-Welzel, "Sustainability and Music Education: Philosophical Considerations," (paper presented at the 11th International Symposium on the Philosophy of Music Education [ISPME], University of Thessaly, Greece, June 7–10, 2017).

43. Alexandra Kertz-Welzel, *Globalizing Music Education: A Framework* (Bloomington: Indiana University Press, 2018).

18

TOWARD THE DISCOVERY OF CONTEMPORARY TRUST AND INTIMACY IN HIGHER MUSIC EDUCATION

Eleni Lapidaki

THIS CHAPTER EXPLORES THE PREMISE THAT HIGHER MUSIC education needs to fight feelings of ineffectiveness, apathy, ignorance, and detached reflection—shared by individual students and teachers—especially in the face of recent mass refugee migrations and practices of authoritarian populist mobilization.[1] One manifestation of these feelings in our liberal educational institutions is the desire to transcend the limitations of the living experience and the longing for immediate contact among individuals across educational, social, and political divides and borders.

First, this chapter explores new perspectives on our understanding of sociomusical contexts of nearness (or the "oral being-together" of proximity), unpredictability, and power relations in higher music education.[2] These are also important qualities of music interactions and thus expand the notion of openness to communities and the Other that characterizes a current trend of music institution reforms and policy initiatives in Greece and elsewhere, as will be expounded in the next section. Furthermore, the chapter discusses how the emphasis on measurability, standardization, and homogenization these reforms incur may steer the music teaching profession further away from music education's long-standing goals in favor of administrative and standards-based classifications that "base educational accountability on economic advantage."[3]

Building on this framework, the chapter proposes that contemporary intimacy and trust can help us reimagine "the pillar of learning to live together," one of the four pillars of learning, that best reflects, along with the pillar of learning to be, "the socialization function of education," according to the UNESCO publication *Rethinking Education: Towards a Global Common Good?*[4] It is worth noting, however, that while the writers of *Rethinking Education* have been concerned with "developing an understanding of other people and an appreciation of interdependence" in this line of thought, they have paid little attention to the significance of intimacy.[5] This notion may amend the UNESCO publication's discussion of cultural diversity as it can help us articulate and recognize new levels of complexity, fullness, and the multidimensionality of lived realities.[6] More specifically, I will argue for the adoption of a politics of intimacy that aims toward a more nuanced and less reductionist higher music education that understands the oral being-together of proximity as a site that in instances of crisis allows Others to continue to express themselves when watched without the fear that their vulnerabilities will be taken advantage of.

In this context, I will briefly describe the widening participation in the creativity-based program Community Action in Learning Music (CALM) as a pointed and unique form of reimagining the community-building potential of higher music education, which is based on intimacy and trust.[7] CALM is devised to help students—both in the university and in neglected Greek and Cypriot learning communities—to enrich their experiential learning through a student-teaching-student approach.

The chapter concludes with a call to use research in higher music education to understand complex changing, vibrating, and fluctuating intimacies that might open new and more comprehensive ways of thinking about the complexities and contradictions that exist. As the late Irish poet and Nobel laureate Seamus Heaney said when interviewed by Henri Cole, "You have to grow into an awareness of the others and attempt to find a way of imagining a whole thing."[8]

Higher Music Education and Openness to Communities

In the face of the refugee crisis and the success of authoritarian populist mobilization efforts, the potential of openness to communities in higher music education that characterizes a current trend of music institution reforms and policy initiations in Greece and elsewhere appears problematic. More specifically, music institution reforms and policy initiatives treat education as a "learning management system" that is "ultimately about serving the needs of institutions, not individual students"—disguised in the language of socially equitable ways of learning.[9]

Furthermore, in the context of the refugee crisis, we are constantly confronted with the question, What can we do for the refugees? Nevertheless, we have seen that our liberal institutions appear to be insufficient to respond to the challenges that have arisen with the flows of refugees and migrants. The refugees have risked their lives in hazardous journeys to escape certain demise, only to often find themselves trapped in precarious conditions in refugee camps. At the same time, the European Union is struggling to balance their immigration and asylum policies between a professed commitment to upholding human rights and growing pressures from increasingly popular and vocal nationalistic movements. As Nikita Dhawan put it, "How do we instrumentalize these inherited, flawed tools, such as 'human rights,' in order to promote and protect vulnerable individuals and groups for whom these tools were not originally intended?"[10] And with regard to our music education students, as normative practices of everyday bordering, "a form of sorting through the imposition of status-functions on people and things,"[11] have seeped into universities, the question might be, How can higher music education help students become effective in the real world, to help facilitate a change?

If we agree—paraphrasing the late Bennett Reimer—that the nature and value of music education for all people are determined by the nature and value of their interactions with and through music, then "music education—like people's music interactions—cannot be catered, delivered, or taught inside a norm."[12] In other words, communicative practice in communal contexts plays a significant role for music interactions as well as music education. Hence, "one might say that without communal contexts music education in higher institutions would somehow have to exist without a relationship to the people next to them, or without the 'oral' being-together of proximity and immediacy."[13]

The idea of the oral being-together of proximity with and through music interactions is based on a more recent discourse toward the reexamination and deconstruction of musical experience that places it within the context of issues of borders, freedom, and "the ways political power gives advantages to some people while failing others."[14] Although educational practice and research suggest that the purpose of educational institutions is to socialize and integrate students into society, the issue of borders still exists as an economic or functional issue. What exists are contexts of economic utilization or educational contexts designed to impose status-functions, which are "mostly being applied unjustly by imposing on, or colonizing non-dominant cultures."[15] Boris Groys wrote, "Every action that is directed towards the stabilization of the status quo will ultimately show itself as ineffective—and every action that is directed towards the destruction of the status quo will ultimately succeed."[16]

Access to and experience of this oral being-together of proximity requires slowability, incalculability, serendipity, and unpredictability, which are important qualities not only for music interactions but also for the biotope of music learning and teaching, qualities that the neoliberal system does not know how to control.[17] This also concurs with what the Danish philosopher and theologian Knud Løgstrup suggested when he noted that "the other person be given ample time and opportunity to make his or her own world as expansive as possible."[18] Regarding music education, T. Ray Wheeler explains Løngstrup's ethical issue about slowability and boundlessness as follows: "That is, allowing our students to explore how a particular knowledge, skill, or social interaction changes them as a person: how it impacts their individual world. This concept is at the heart of good teaching."[19]

Moreover, the insistence on the importance of slowability, unpredictability, and unexpected outcomes of human interactions is a matter of reconstructing the homogenous, normative, and measurable mastery-based teaching, learning, creating, and assessing.[20] This presupposes that we understand the abovementioned temporal qualities in education as part of the human interaction side of teaching that is characterized by Jacques Derrida's notion of "aporia" (uncertainty or paradox) and Hannah Arendt's notion of the "frailty of human affairs."[21] Building on this framework, the rest of the chapter proposes reimagining the possibility of education on the basis of contemporary intimacy and trust that can serve as the basis for a new kind of learning community.

Intimacy

The interconnection of the oral being-together of proximity, unpredictability, and power—essential for music interactions and, thus, for higher music education—implies the relationship that individuals embrace with themselves as "self" beyond boundaries as they want to transcend their own selves to be continuous—not just rub shoulders—with the selves of other people.[22] Along these lines, the adoption of interpersonal intimacy is considered as an approach that is able to embrace more nuanced and less reductionist notions of how higher music education may connect with, become part of, or be totally detached from our sense of individuality and communality. This is what Roscoe Mitchell, one of the most important composer-improvisers of our time as well as a major musical thinker, said concerning the importance of individuality for music creativity: "I don't stand to benefit when everybody is just trying to be like everyone else. All of us are highly individualized beings."[23]

It is worth noting, however, that while recent music education philosophy has reflected on hospitality and the Other in relation to community, cosmopolitanism, and participatory music making, it has paid scant attention to the significance of intimacy in this line of thought.[24] In this context, intimacy is considered as a "primary internal coherence" among individuals or groups of individuals.[25] It is an approach to proximity and unpredictability that in instances of crisis allows Others to continue to express themselves without the fear that "they are watching us, and if they see our vulnerabilities they will take advantage of them."[26] As the late African American author and documentary filmmaker Toni Cade Bambara said in her keynote at the Journey across Three Continents film festival in Detroit, on March 13, 1987, "To be entrapped in other people's fictions puts us under arrest. To be entrapped, to be submissively so, without countering, without challenging, without raising the voice and offering alternative truths renders us available for servitude. In which case, our ways, our beliefs, our values, our style are repeatedly ransacked so that the power of our culture can be used—to sell liquor, soda, pieces of entertainment, and the real deal: to sell ideas. The idea of inferiority. The idea of hierarchy. The idea of stasis: that nothing will ever change."[27]

In the same vein, this is what the Greek art critic Despoina Zefkili wrote in *Third Text* in relation to Dokumenta 14, Germany's renowned modern art exhibition, which takes place every five years in Kassel, Germany, and in 2017 ran in two cities for the first time in its history (Kassel in the north of Europe and Athens in the south): "Indeed, lots of local artists and critics feel the pressure of this foreign body in the city [Athens]. A body that, nevertheless, exercises the power of a big institution, although it identifies with the oppressed subjects, emphasizes the poetics of the body, and adopts the role of the ignorant ('We are ignorant' said the artistic director of Dokumenta 14, Adam Szymczyk, at the opening of the Public Program) or even the role of the victim (self-victimisation as a way to cope with local criticism, which has been exercised in very problematic conditions)."[28] Zefkeli's article precisely describes a space of nearness of a small marginalized local art scene to a foreign mega-institution to which the need for intimacy appears pertinent as it "challenges colonial and orientalist mechanisms."[29] More specifically, intimacy helps us articulate the complexity of spaces of nearness as greatly as we live it and unpack well-established concepts such as openness, narrative, story, and "giv[ing] voice to the others" or the multiple identifications that are used too much, too often, not only by curators of the dominant or "revolutionary" Dokumenta 14 but also by philosophers of music and arts education.[30]

For through intimacy something other than mere one-dimensional information is being transmitted—something more intangible yet more real. As the video artist Tavi Meraud writes, "Intimacy is that sphere of reality that is not quite the real of the mundane given, and yet could be considered to exude a more intense reality."[31] To understand recent social and political transformations concerning the notion of borders—educational and political—one needs to focus on aspects of interpersonal relations, such as intimacy, that are still important for individuals within the spaces of proximity because they allow for new contents to be sought in our contemplations about a mutually understood exchange with the Others, when the Others feel like showing vulnerabilities that express nuances and thus becoming who they are.

Therefore, intimacy in higher music education can offer the advantages of collectivity without neglecting the needs of the individual as it takes the individual away from identity politics as well as educational, economic, and administrative clusterings. As Lauren Berlant rightly put it, intimacy exceeds the boundaries of what is sanctioned by institutions, creating "much more mobile processes of attachments" that might enable a reimagining of hegemonic fantasies of the normative.[32]

At this point, I should make clear what I do not mean by *intimacy*. It does not simply concern dimensions of music education taking place at spaces of proximity, which are socially constrained to the self and a few known or like-minded others. On the contrary, what is most at issue in the encounter with intimacy is the coexistence of the concomitant components of "curiosity, vulnerability, empathy, and, perhaps most importantly, a recognition of irreducibility" in the proximity of self to the Other.[33] One might say that the mutual willingness to bend together toward or immerse oneself in each other's differences is the foundation of intimacy.

Moreover, this coexistence of curiosity, vulnerability, empathy, and recognition of irreducibility, which make the meaning of intimacy multivalent and vague, is what can serve as a kind of sifter through which certain problems of the intersection of the oral being-together of proximity, unpredictability, and power relations can be examined more carefully or brought into light. For instance, in spaces of intimacy, according to Julia Obert, when curiosity is not accompanied by vulnerability (a willingness to lay oneself "undone by each other," using Judith Butler's words), then the desire to "know about the Other's world" can very easily turn out to be a desire to consume or a desire to have.[34] Similarly, one might say that vulnerability without curiosity can become self-centeredness and narcissism. Obert writes with razor-like accuracy that intimacy can be framed "as a kind of epistemology: it enables us to know our own coordinates, but only insofar as the constantly shifting geometry of our world's Others allows."[35]

Therefore, the element most crucial to intimacy is this: that intimacy cannot exist without the acceptance that one can never fully feel another's suffering, although one thinks that one is devoted to learning about the Other, caring for the Other, or/and laying oneself undone by the Other. This realization of irreducibility expresses a genuine desire of an intimate response—instead of fixity—that reaches beyond educational, political, or gender-based reductions and boundaries. As Sarah Ahmed claims, "the over-representation of the pain of others is significant in that it fixes the other as the one who 'has' pain, and who can overcome that pain only when the Western subject feels moved enough to give."[36]

Trust

Trust as an ethical and political orientation to the Others, even to the closest of friends, can help us acknowledge and accept (as discussed above) recognition of irreducibility that defines the limit or condition of an intimate relationship in the proximity of self to the Other. Thereby, trust in the Other is considered as central to developing interconnections across difference and thus can serve as a self-encouragement to stimulate openness to unpredictable or unfolding circumstances. In relation to music education, one might also say that trust in students stimulates them to put their preconceived ideas about music teaching and learning at risk, especially when

confronting themselves with people they are unfamiliar with and to reflect on the experiences and feelings that made them take risks. This is how
Løgstrup defines trust from an ethical perspective that appears germane to
education:

> Trust is not of our own making; it is given. Our life is so constituted that it
> cannot be lived except as one person lays him or herself open to another per-
> son and puts him or herself into that person's hands either by showing or
> claiming trust. By our very attitude to another we help to shape that person's
> world. By our attitude to the other person we help to determine the scope and
> hue of his or her world; we make it large or small, bright or drab, rich or dull,
> threatening or secure. We help to shape his or her world not by theories and
> views but by our very attitude toward him or her. Herein lies the unarticulated
> and one might say anonymous demand that we take care of the life which trust
> has placed in our hands.[37]

Furthermore, trust is related to the political empowerment of "institutional
nonentities" or those "who have no specific capacity," what Jacques Rancière called "the power of anybody."[38] According to Rancière, democracy
is "a form of dis-identification, and also a form of trust in the capacity of
anybody with no specification."[39] Along these lines, I believe that we should
aim toward the empowerment of the collective capacity of those who lack
specific capacity not only in politics but also in education.

With regard to higher music education, in order to exemplify how
the trust in the emancipatory potential of students' creative practice can
construct an intimate space that directly influences the relation between
different forms of "we" and "you," I will briefly discuss the widening participation, creativity-based, sustainable (since 2000) music educational program Community Action in Learning Music (CALM), which I coordinate
at the Department of Music Studies, School of the Arts, Aristotle University
of Thessaloniki, Greece. CALM utilizes a student-teaching-student participatory process that can be considered as a bridge where music teaching
and learning meet in a direct and fascinating way. More specifically, music
education students at the music department, on the one hand, who are not
yet members of the institutionalized group of music teachers, and students
of approximately more than 150 neglected schools and learning communities, on the other hand, who are deprived of having their own voices heard
through formal music education, expression, and participation, teach each
other and learn from each other.[40]

These schools and communities are mostly located in economically
disadvantaged areas, urban or provincial, and their student body by and

large is predominately comprised of children of economic immigrants and refugees. More specifically, each semester twenty to twenty-five students in their fourth or fifth year enroll in my course "Music Education," which encompasses CALM in the kernel of its syllabus. These students create teams of two to four students. For one semester, each student team adopts a class at a high-risk school or community in order to explore musical and pedagogical pathways that engage all participants in meaningful music making. At this point, it should be noted that the university students are not confined by mentor teachers' practices, since the schools and communities where they themselves choose to go do not have music teachers. As Dorothea Anagnostopoulos, Emily Smith, and Kevin Basmadjian claim, "for our part, we viewed the mentors as limiting interns' learning-to-teach opportunities and promoting ineffective practices."[41]

Empowering students from the university and students from the high-risk schools and communities to build intimate encounters with each other via the music creativity that collectively takes place in the classrooms—without the fear that they are being watched and judged by their familiar teachers—gives them the opportunity to become open to experiences that effectively unsettle them from time to time and to invent modes of music interactions that transgress the standards and norms of conventional educational encounters.[42] Moreover, when teaching each other, students are challenged to move across formally distinct areas of both social and educational hierarchies. As Vicki Lind so rightly argues: "When students perceive they are 'doing' a service rather than learning alongside their community partners, they often see themselves as being at the top of the social hierarchy. In contrast, programs that are built upon the fundamental belief that communities are 'asset rich' and that learning is reciprocal can reinforce the concepts of equality by allowing students to see and value those around them."[43]

Concluding Remarks

This chapter is a call to utilize our practice and research in higher music education to understand complex, changing, vibrating, and fluctuating intimacies that might open new ways of thinking about the complexities and contradictions that exist on the common ground of proximity shared by different people or different forms of "we" and "you," especially in the face of recent mass refugee migrations and authoritarian populist mobilization attempts. Intimacy and trust help us, on the one hand, to see very different types of actors or processes of collectivization that emerge and, on the other, to realize that the concept of the common good should be far more responsive to differences and nuances. According to Boris Groys, "we no longer believe in universalist, idealist, transhistorical perspectives and identities. The old materialist way of thinking let us accept only roles rooted in the material conditions of our existence: national-cultural and regional identities or identities based on race, class, and gender. And there are a potentially infinite number of such specific identities because the material conditions of human existence are very diverse and are permanently changing."[44] This implies that the common good should not stunt or distort the mutually understood exchange with the Others—especially in instances of crisis—when the Others cannot show their vulnerabilities that express nuances and thus become who they are, out of fear that they are being watched and that their vulnerabilities will be taken advantage of. Thus, the development of knowledge that is considered by the writers of *Rethinking Education* as a common good—along with humane education— would acquire new kinds of participatory educational processes as well as research approaches to diversity that promote intimacy and trust. To act in a spirit of intimacy and trust as a constant responsibility to the Other helps educators to confront "the common fate" of individual human beings that is stamped by "the radically contingent, transitory, precarious conditions of their existence," as Boris Groys wrote.[45]

Simply telling and researching stories and histories in higher music education research is not enough. The idea that we believe that the Others live life in a straight line, like a story, a narrative, seems to me to be restrictive and, more than anything, a kind of intellectual convenience disguised in the language of socially equitable ways of "learning about" or "giving voice" to the Others. We can only learn when time (as unpredictability) and space (as the oral being-together of proximity and immediacy) are colliding into a kind of explosion of pure intimacy and trust, while all around there are borders, identifications, clusterings, and crises. As Nick Cave put it so brilliantly, "I feel that the events in our lives are like a series of bells being struck and the vibrations spread outwards, affecting everything, our present and our futures, of course, but our past as well."[46]

Music education, like music interactions, cannot change the world. However, by providing opportunities to experience the complexity of intimate spaces of proximity of the self to the Other, music education can help all students to briefly connect with the Others' finer selves, which are endearing, frail, unpredictable, frightened, noncompliant. And perhaps that will give them consolation, encouragement, and—more importantly—time to become who they are.

ELENI LAPIDAKI is Professor of Music Education in the Department of Music Studies at the School of the Arts at Aristotle University of Thessaloniki, Greece.

Notes

1. For a nuanced discussion about authoritarian populism, see Pippa Norris and Roland Inglehart, "The Authoritarian-Populist Challenge," in *Cultural Backlash: Trump, Brexit, and Authoritarian Populism*, ed. Pippa Norris and Ronald Inglehart (Cambridge: Cambridge University Press, 2019), 443–470.
2. Luis Jacob, "Communities between Culture-by-Mouth and Culture-by-Media," *Public* 3 (Spring 2009): 90, http://pi.library.yorku.ca/ojs/index.php/public/article/viewFile/30388/27915.
3. Betty Anne Younker, "Inquiry-Based Learning: A Value for Music in Education with Aims to Cultivate a Humane Society," in this collection.
4. UNESCO, *Rethinking Education: Towards a Global Common Good?* (Paris: UNESCO, 2015), 40, http://unesdoc.unesco.org/images/0023/002325/232555e.pdf.
5. Ibid., 39.
6. Ibid., 16, 66, 29.
7. For a detailed discussion about the Greek interdisciplinary project CALM, see Eleni Lapidaki, Rokus de Groot, and Petros Stagkos, "Communal Creativity as Sociomusical Practice," in *Creativities, Technologies, and Media in Music Teaching and Learning: An Oxford Handbook of Music Education*, vol. 5, ed. Gary E. McPherson and Graham F. Welch (Oxford: Oxford University Press, 2018), 56–73.
8. Seamus Heaney, "The Art of Poetry No. 75," *Paris Review* 144 (Fall 1997), http://www.theparisreview.org/interviews/1217/the-art-of-poetry-no-75-seamus-heaney.
9. Jim Groom and Brian Lamb, "Reclaiming Innovation," *EDUCAUSE Review* 49, no. 3 (May/June 2014), http://www.educause.edu/visuals/shared/er/extras/2014/ReclaimingInnovation/default.html; Justin Reich, "Techniques for Unleashing Student Work from Learning Management Systems," *Mindshift*, February 13, 2015, https://ww2.kqed.org/mindshift/2015/02/13/techniques-for-unleashing-student-work-from-learning-management-systems/.
10. "But Who Is 'They'? Roundtable Discussion with Manuela Bodjadžijev, Nikita Dhawan, and Christoph Menke," *Texte zur Kunst* 27, no. 105 (March 2017): 34–61, https://www.textezurkunst.de/105/tzk-105-roundtable/.
11. For a comprehensive discussion about institutional borders and bordering, see Anthony Cooper and Chris Perkins, "Borders and Status-Functions: An Institutional Approach to the Study of Borders," *European Journal of Social Theory* 15, no. 1 (November 2011): 57. According to the authors, "Bordering as a process is a form of sorting through the imposition of status-functions on people and things, which alters the perception of that thing by setting it within a web of normative claims, teleologies and assumptions. Bordering is,

therefore, a *practical* activity, enacted by ordinary people as well as (nation) states, to make sense of and 'do work' in the world."

12. Bennett Reimer, *A Philosophy of Music Education: Advancing the Vision*, 3rd ed. (Upper Saddle River, NJ: Prentice Hall, 2003); Eleni Lapidaki, "Uncommon Grounds: Preparing Students in Higher Music Education for the Unpredictable," *Philosophy of Music Education Review* 24, no. 1 (Spring 2016): 69.

13. Lapidaki, "Uncommon Grounds," 69–70.

14. Franziska Schroeder, "Network[ed] Listening—Towards a Decentering of Beings," *Contemporary Music Review* 32, nos. 2–3 (2013): 218.

15. Julia C. Duncheon and William G. Tierney, "Changing Conceptions of Time: Implications for Educational Research and Practice," *Review of Educational Research* 83, no. 2 (June 2013): 256.

16. Boris Groys, "On Art Activism," *e-flux journal*, no. 56 (June 2014): 14, http://worker01 .e-flux.com/pdf/article_8984545.pdf.

17. Lapidaki, "Uncommon Grounds," 70.

18. Knud Løgstrup, *The Ethical Demand* (Notre Dame, IN: University of Notre Dame Press, 1997), 27.

19. T. Ray Wheeler, "Toward a Framework for a New Philosophy of Music Education: Løgstrup as Synergy between the Platonic and Aristotelian Perspectives in the Music Education Philosophies of Bennett Reimer and David Elliot" (PhD diss., University of North Texas, Denton, TX, 2006), 170.

20. Panagiotis Kanellopoulos, Eleni Lapidaki, Patrick Schmidt, and Lauri Väkevä, "Knowledge-Power/Mastery-Institution" (panel presentation at the Ninth International Symposium on the Philosophy of Music Education, Teachers College, Columbia University, New York City, June 5–8, 2013).

21. Simon Critchley, *Ethics, Politics, Subjectivity: Essays on Derrida, Levinas and Contemporary French Thought* (London: Verso, 1999), 108; Hannah Arendt, *The Human Condition*, 2nd ed. (Chicago, University of Chicago Press, 1998), 181.

22. Julia C. Obert, "What We Talk About When We Talk About Intimacy," *Emotion, Space, and Society* 21 (November 2016): 25.

23. Catherine Despont and Jake Nussbaum, "Ecstatic Ensemble: Original Music and the Birth of the AACM," *Intercourse Magazine* 3 (2015): 51, http://www.akamu.net/file/AACM _Intercourse.pdf.

24. See for example Janice Waldron, Roger Mantie, Heidi Partti, and Evan S. Tobias, "A Brave New World: Theory to Practice in Participatory Culture and Music Learning and Teaching," *Music Education Research* (June 29, 2017): 1–16, http://www.tandfonline.com/doi/full /10.1080/14613808.2017.1339027; Jacob Axel Berglin and Thomas Murphy O'Hara, "Working with Transgender Students as a Humane Act: Hospitality in Research and in Practice," in this collection; Lauren Kapalka Richerme, "Uncommon Commonalities: Cosmopolitan Ethics as a Framework for Music Education Policy Analysis," *Arts Education Policy Review* 117, no. 2 (2016): 87–95, doi:10.1080/10632913.2015.1047002. See Tia DeNora, "The Role of Music in Intimate Culture: A Case Study," *Feminism and Psychology* 12, no. 2 (2002): 176–181.

25. Steven Pinter and Greg Nielsen, "Intimacy and Cultural Crisis," *Canadian Journal of Political and Social Theory* 14, nos. 1–3 (1990): 69.

26. Museum of Contemporary Art Chicago Talk: "Art and Life" (panel discussion with Hilton Als, Jaqueline Stewart, and Michelle M. Wright, October 1, 2016), https://mcachicago .org/Stories/Audio/Art-And-Black-Life.

27. Toni Cade Bambara (keynote presented at the Journey across Three Continents Film Festival, Detroit, March 13, 1987), quoted in Pearl Bowser, Jane Gaines, and Charles Musser, eds., *Oscar Micheaux and His Circle: African-American Filmmaking and Race Cinema of the Silent Era* (Bloomington: Indiana University Press, 2001), xiv.

28. Despina Zefkili, "'Exercises of Freedom': Documenta 14," *Third Text* (February 2017): 1, http://thirdtext.org/domains/thirdtext.com/local/media/images/medium/Exercises_of_Freedom.pdf.

29. Ibid., 4.

30. Ibid., 3; see also Jeni Fulton, "How Documenta 14 Failed Everyone but Its Curators," *Sleek Magazine*, July 3, 2017, http://www.sleek-mag.com/2017/07/03/documenta-14-kassel. See, e.g., Pamela Burnard, Valerie Ross, Helen Julia Minors, Tatjana Dragovic, and Elisabeth Mackinlay, eds., *Building Interdisciplinary and Intercultural Bridges: Where Practice Meets Research and Theory*, BIBACC 2016 International Conference (Cambridge, UK: BIBACC, 2017), http://bibacc.org/wp-content/uploads/2016/08/Building-Interdisciplinary-and-Intercultral-Bridges_compressed-updated-v_4.pdf.

31. Tavi Meraud, "Iridescence, Intimacies," *e-flux journal*, no. 61, (January 2015): 10, http://worker01.e-flux.com/pdf/article_8993792.pdf.

32. Lauren Berlant, "Intimacy: A Special Issue," *Critical Inquiry* 24, no. 2 (Winter 1998): 284.

33. Obert, "What We Talk About," 26.

34. Ibid., 28; Judith Butler, *Precarious Life: The Power of Mourning and Violence* (London: Verso, 2004), 24.

35. Obert, "What We Talk About" 31.

36. Sara Ahmed, "Collective Feelings: Or the Impressions Left by Others," *Theory, Culture and Society* 21, no. 2 (April 2004): 35.

37. Løgstrup, *Ethical Demand*, 18.

38. Jacques Rancière and Christian Höller, "The Abandonment of Democracy," *Documenta 12 Magazine (Education)*, no. 3 (2007): 21.

39. Nikos Papastergiadis and Charles Esche, "Assemblies in Art and Politics: An Interview with Jacques Rancière," *Theory, Culture and Society* 31, nos. 7–8 (2014): 31.

40. Lapidaki, de Groot, and Stagkos, "Communal Creativity," 56–73.

41. Dorothea Anagnostopoulos, Emily R. Smith, and Kevin G. Basmadjian, "Bridging the University-School Divide: Horizontal Expertise and the 'Two-Worlds Pitfall,'" *Journal of Teacher Education* 58, no. 2 (March/April 2007): 140.

42. For examples of music creativity by students from the university and the high-risk schools and communities, see http://calm.web.auth.gr/StudentsPage/students_Intro.html, accessed July 22, 2017; Lapidaki, "Learning from Masters of Music Creativity. Shaping Compositional Experiences in Music Education," *Philosophy of Music Education Review* 15, no. 2 (Fall 2007): 93–117.

43. Vicki R. Lind and Constance L. McKoy, *Culturally Responsive Teaching in Music Education* (New York and London, Routledge, 2016), 117; also see Lisa Garoutte and Kate McCarthy-Gilmore, "Preparing Students for Community-Based Learning Using an Asset-Based Approach," *Scholarship of Teaching and Learning* 14, no. 5 (December 2014): 48–61.

44. Boris Groys, "Entering the Flow: Museum between Archive and Gesamtkunstwerk," *e-flux journal*, no. 50 (December 2013): 1, http://worker01.e-flux.com/pdf/article_8976476.pdf.

45. Ibid., 9.

46. Mark Mordue, "Nick Cave. The G2 Interview," *Guardian* (US edition), May 4, 2017, https://www.theguardian.com/music/2017/may/04/nick-cave-death-son-struggle-write-tragedy.

CONCLUSION

On Making Music Education Humane and Good: Gathering Threads

Estelle R. Jorgensen

In her latest book, *School Was Our Life*,[1] Jane Roland Martin reflects on the musical experience led by Beatrice Landeck, known to music educators as compiler and author of folk song collections and editor of the Making Music Our Own series, published by Silver-Burdett. Landeck taught music in a New York City elementary school where music and the other arts played a central role in a progressive educational approach. This experience was so valued by her students that seven or eight decades later, they still treasure and sing her collection of school songs, recite poems they memorized as children, and reminisce about their teachers. Connected by bonds of friendship and shared experience, they feel fortunate to have attended this school. How I long to be a teacher who might have such a long-term impact.

In this book, our writers have reflected critically on what it might mean to make music education humane and good, and on various means whereby these objectives might be undertaken. In drawing some of the important threads, I ask the following: What can be learned collectively from our authors about humane music education and the common good? What shall all those involved in the work of music education do to make it humane and good? How might the approaches of our authors make a difference to the practice of music education?

Notice that I bring the value of the "common good" into music education itself rather than think of it as outside music education *for* the common good. I do this because music education is something that lies within the power of music teachers to influence. Randall Allsup refers to this reality using Montaigne's notion of looking "under our feet." Beginning with what we (individually and collectively) think and do is a starting point for the practice of humanity and goodness in music education. Still, as Iris Yob suggests, this close-up view of our immediate situation is transcended by a broader view of the predicament in which all the members of the human family dwell in respect of our common humanity, mortality, physicality, and mentality. In this radically inclusive view, and notwithstanding our diversity, Yob suggests, there is no Other. We are all together in the reality of the preciousness of our humanity and the multiplicity of our beliefs and practices.

What Does It Mean to Make Music Education Humane and Good?

The choice of published UNESCO texts as a touchstone for our authors' reflections is particularly ironic in the present political moment. International perspectives are arguably even more important when nation-states withdraw from international organizations and treaties and espouse nativist and extremist policies that undermine attempts to foster international understanding and world peace. These realities open the possibilities for wars and conflagrations, slavery, tyranny by totalitarian and authoritarian regimes, and ecological destruction of the planet. Although Hanne Rinholm and Øivind Varkøy urge values of humility, sobriety, and temperance in making utilitarian claims for music, they argue that music is good for being human and that music education needs to engage the "big issues of life" in ways that manifest ethical values of hope, identity, and authenticity. Their reminder of the limits of music education is reinforced by Allsup's worry that it may be easier to embrace the mantra of diversity than to accept diversity when it does not align with a set of values that one has internalized. The import of an international conversation such as this opens the prospect of differing value sets and the possibility of disjunctions, tensions, and conflicts regarding matters of what is good, what is common, and what is humane. Collectively, our writers present a radical view of diversity that encompasses the entirety of humanity in all its plurality and difference and the implication of self in this difference. Paradoxically, to take a radical view of diversity does not necessitate that each person takes a radically relativist ethical position. All human beings are important and precious and need to be free to make their own ethical and aesthetic decisions grounded in faith and moral traditions. Our judgments are based on values that we have internalized and seek to express. Practically speaking, as teachers, we prioritize both the music to be studied and the instructional means whereby people come to know that music according to values to which we are committed. Rather than supposing a monolithic hegemony of specific educational means and ends, *Rethinking Education* invites readers to contemplate general values of humanity and commonly held conceptions of goodness as inimitably humane educational values that ought to be shared by all human beings, irrespective of the diverse goods to which we may be directed or the specific ways in which these values are expressed.

A crucial problem, discussed by Kevin Shorner-Johnson, is the shortsightedly Western linear view of educational progress in the UNESCO report—and the privileging of this view and failure to acknowledge cyclical views of time as commonly understood by African, Native American, and Eastern societies, among others. Shorner-Johnson reminds us of the violence wrought by so-called technological progress in recent centuries and the sense of "disconnection" and "disruption" in human relationships as a result. In his view, music educators in the West need to learn from other world views that privilege the present moment, the cyclicality of the natural world, the possibility of renewal, and the spirituality of experience. Ambiguity feeds imagination and fosters diversity, and this temporal and social diversity needs to better balance individual ways of being. This more holistic and even ecological view of music education benefits from international insights from West and East, North and South, and when they are accounted for, the musical and educational changes are likely to be profound. As Ebru Tuncer Boon's case study of the Gezi Park resistance in Turkey illustrates, music potentially disrupts society and the physicality of its vibrations constitutes a potent social and societal force. In analyzing the mutuality of music and protest, Boon shows the impact of music on an ecological and political resistance movement and the effect of the resistance movement on the emergence of diverse artistic and musical expressions. She envisages nothing less than a metamorphosis of music, education, and society.

Central questions of what is meant by the "common good" and "humane" music education are broached by Yob in her introduction and chapter, "There Is No Other." The central paradox of this book consists in the claims of global thinking about music education that presupposes the welfare of everyone on the one hand and the value of difference and diversity on the other. Yob offers a solution to this dilemma in the metaphor of perspective in her "close-up" and "wide-angle" views. This very useful metaphor illustrates the tensions that emerge from differences between thinking in generalities and thinking in specificities. For Yob, it is necessary to think of a nested perspective in which the wide-angle perspective on humanity and music education also includes the close-up view of differing thoughts and practices. (This proposition reminds me of some of my earliest writing about music education, in which I emphasize the importance of differing levels of generality in our thought about music education and the principle that resolving dilemmas in social events such as music and education is often a matter of differing perspectives on them.) As for what is meant by "humane" music education, Yob draws on the humanistic and humane approach echoed in the various incarnations of the UNESCO document. She points to notions of the value of all human life, the claims of respect, dignity, equal rights, justice, diversity, and a sense of community and solidarity for the common good (wide-angle view) while also fostering and sustaining the social and cultural diversity of all dwellers on planet earth (close-up view). In pointing to the inextricability of the common good (understood as common goods) and humane education, Yob notes that while both notions have a social justice "edge," the common good serves as an ideal and humane education serves as an important means of reaching toward it. Notwithstanding the problematical character of these ideas, it is difficult to imagine the common good without a humane education. Each reinforces the other.

What Shall All Those Involved in the Work of Music Education Do to Make It Humane and Good?

Music educators are practically minded. Writers in the two middle sections of this book, "Pedagogy and Teacher Preparation" and "Educating Others for the Common Good," provide specific examples of practical ways to make music education humane and good. The focus shifts from teaching approaches and preparing teachers to undertake a humane music education in part II to broader considerations of how to educate others for the common good in part III. Writers in both parts illustrate beautifully Yob's "close-up" and "wide-angle" views by simultaneously considering specific ideas or situations and thinking more generally about them. In pedagogical situations such as piano studios, music teacher preparation programs, prisons, special education situations, and multicultural music classrooms, we see humane teaching at work. Christine Brown's reflection

278 | Humane Music Education for the Common Good

on humane principles of studio teaching, Betty Anne Younker's use of an inquiry-based approach in music teaching, Joseph Shively's principles of humane music teacher preparation, and Emily Howe, André de Quadros, Andrew Clark, and Kinh T. Vu's cases of teaching music in prisons, special education situations, and multicultural music classrooms provide an array of ways, means, and principles for teaching humanely. Our writers are not content simply to describe their cases; they also provide critical and analytical perspectives on them and on the UNESCO documents to which they respond. Although they would go about teaching in multiple ways and espouse differing principles that guide their work, their perspectives are unified by a pervasive concern for the people at the heart of music education and an effort to make the music education that they offer emblematic and expressive of the ends of fostering humanity and goodness. This paradoxical multiplicity in unity is evident in their expressed hope to practice this humanity and goodness in a myriad different ways and situations. Their examples illustrate how music teachers from antiquity onward have sought to cultivate humanity and goodness in their teaching and through their teaching and thereby cultivate dispositions toward these values in their students. Focusing on principles and practices, these cases offer windows into what may be done practically by teachers to make music education humane and good.

Focusing on learners and their needs and the contexts in which music education is undertaken provides other lenses on a humane pedagogical situation. The community music learning described by Luca Tiszai, opportunities for cultural diversity in vocal education portrayed by Emily Good-Perkins, parallels in the Suzuki method and humane education described in the UNESCO documents observed by Blakely Menghini, the ecological approach to sacred music proposed by Mary Thomason-Smith, and hospitality to transgendered students advanced by Jacob Axel Berglin and Thomas Murphy O'Hara all suggest myriad possibilities for humane education to be taught by and taught to students. They see educational possibilities in contexts well beyond music education traditionally construed as school music in communities, music studios, and places of worship. They illustrate the importance of reaching learners wherever and whenever they may be found and of devising multiple formal and informal ways to reach them.

Thinking about these examples drawn from around the world and advocated by people who are passionate about creating a humane world of music education and, through music education, contributing to the common good, I am struck by the fact that wherever we teach and learn music, in whatever contexts we undergo music education, and whatever our specific musical and educational objectives, wherever people are central to our work and life, humane music education may thrive. Since these writers have offered evidence of an array of differing ways to approach music and to do this humanely, it is imperative to genuinely embrace and welcome the differences in specific objectives and methods. Each one of these writers brings an important perspective to bear. A reader may resonate more with one than another. Yet it is undeniable that encouraging every music teacher to pursue his or her passion opens possibilities for transformative music teaching and learning. Fostering diversity rather than uniformity in music education aims and methods frees music teachers and learners to come to know and do music in ways that best fit specific settings and individual and communal aspirations. In fostering this diversity of practice, paradoxically, our authors illustrate how it is also possible, at least generally speaking, to approach humane music education that a plethora of ways that seek common goods.

How Might the Approaches of Our Authors Make a Difference to the Practice of Music Education?

In responding to this important question, our writers make several theoretical and practical suggestions. Among these, Johnnie-Margaret McConnell and Susan Laird build on Laird's earlier philosophical writing on musical hunger to posit a human need for musicking and the imperative to satisfy it. Many students are not in school music classes, and those who are too often find the experience dissatisfying. Humane music education requires satisfying musical hunger. It is imperative to regard music education as an essential aspect of a well-rounded education rather than a "frill" that is available at the margins of general education or only to the few who can afford it. It is imperative to open the doors of music education and welcome everyone with a musical desire (whether it be latent or already known) to participate in making and taking music. Rather than one monolithic and grand house, it may be helpful to envision homes of music of various sorts, with a myriad teachers and students with different aptitudes, desires, and needs, and the possibilities of visiting one home or another or moving from one to another. Hospitality to difference, as Berglin and

O'Hara urge us to consider, needs to be paramount in our musical villages. Rather than thinking exclusively of human-made objects, as dwellers on planet earth, we might also take an ecological view of the sort advanced by Thomason-Smith. The musical homes we construct need to be in harmony with the wider environment, as other sentient creatures such as animals and even plants are also responsive to musical sounds.

Deanne Bogdan opens the prospect of a holistic education through music as feeling and thought are bound together inextricably in literature and music. Her ideas, resonant with Shorner-Johnson's, bring the Other into a space and time in which otherness disappears—what a wonderful metaphor for music education! Musicians and educators have long realized that the artificial although useful distinctions between cognitive, affective, and psychomotor domains need to be made whole again. Music constitutes, for Bogdan, a powerful opportunity to make people whole again. Moreover, coming into the presence of another's music, becoming acquainted with it, and being able to do it, like the other arts, myths, and rituals that humans have created, reveals the other's humanity. Greater understanding, emotional and physical connectedness to another's music ultimately, for Bogdan, dissolves otherness and opens to greater musical and artistic community and solidarity.

Alexandra Kertz-Welzel, Leonard Tan, Martin Berger, and David Lines suggest that music educators can study models of music education already in existence. Drawing on the perspectives of Germany, Singapore, South Africa, and New Zealand, respectively, they illustrate ways that music educators are seeking to create humane music education for the common good. I have called the study of models of music education the "demonstration effect" because of the potency of models and demonstrations of music education for music teachers, their musical and educational colleagues, and members of society at large. Models are especially effective because of the ways that they illustrate more abstract theoretical or philosophical principles and prompt others to want what they do not presently have. Throughout this book, our writers have provided examples of ways to undertake humane music education for the common good, at least as it is perceived by nation-states, communities, schools, churches, temples, mosques, and synagogues, and music teacher associations. That models or examples are drawn from around the world is important in regarding different societies (as the human beings who comprise them) as having value. Doing this dignifies the societies in which models or examples are found, and instances the importance of thinking through the ways that humane music education can be conducted divergently. One society may learn from another while also considering the specific ways in which what is done elsewhere might be done differently here.

It is also important to consider the gaps and errors in the UNESCO document that need to be addressed and that have been alluded to by contributors to Part I of this book. In the concluding part IV of this book, Eleni Lapidaki considers values of intimacy and trust that she finds to be absent from *Rethinking Education*. Her feminine perspective is important in documents that may be read by some to constitute a quite masculine view of education. With an expansive vision that moves ever outward to encompass the world, music educators can miss the importance of feminine values that focus inward and that highlight the intimacy and trust of familial bonds. Lapidaki's views resonate particularly with the subjectivity and vulnerability of Bogdan's notion of the musical dissolution of the Other, with Shorner-Johnson's ecological view of humane music education, McConnell and Laird's concern about the need to satisfy human hunger for music, and Allsup's admission of the vulnerability of openness to difference and the imperative of openness to others. Indeed, the personal writing by all the chapter authors highlights the importance of human subjectivity in musical making and taking and in a humane musical education.

In sum, our writers espouse a musical education for human flourishing, about and for people. Such a person-centric view of musical education in its myriad forms and manifestations is radical and paradoxical in that it is also about the music and the rest of life. How shall music education and the people involved with it flourish? If we posit the radical idea that there is no Other, our writers suggest that it is possible to see the many and the one through "close-up" and "wide-angle" lenses. We may begin at the ground at our feet, seek to express humanness in our teaching, and open our hearts to the needs, interests, and desires of our students. Collectively, we may foster the host of means whereby students can come to know music. We may aspire to love our students and live in ways that evoke goodness. And we may hope that our influence ripples out to infuse the wider society of which we are a part.

ESTELLE R. JORGENSEN is Professor Emerita of the Jacobs School of Music at Indiana University and Contributing Faculty Member in the Richard W. Riley College of Education and Leadership at Walden University, Minnesota. She is the author of numerous titles, most recently, *Pictures of Music Education.*

Note

1. Jane Roland Martin, *School Was Our Life: Remembering Progressive Education* (Bloomington: Indiana University Press, 2018).

INDEX

tolerance, 42, 80, 81, 84, 88, 90, 143, 258
transformation, 1, 6, 43, 86, 94, 117, 148
transgender, 8, 11, 199–214
trust, 11, 97, 99, 175, 176, 177, 193, 253, 254, 261–273, 281
truth, 19, 22, 30, 33, 37, 49, 82, 83, 87, 181, 235, 240

ubuntu, 59, 249, 251–53, 257
United Methodist Church, 189, 190, 192, 193, 194
universal, 3, 24, 26, 31, 32, 46, 71, 153, 186, 200
utopia, 3, 7, 55, 256

values, 6, 8, 19, 26, 29, 31, 32, 34, 45–49, 80, 82, 84, 86, 87, 90, 92, 95, 96, 97, 99, 110, 111, 113, 115, 116, 117, 119, 123, 127, 128, 143, 153, 162, 186, 187, 188, 189, 190, 191, 193, 196, 200, 209, 219, 221, 233, 237, 242, 249, 250, 257, 265, 275, 276, 277, 278, 281
vibrations, 66–74, 270, 276
violence, 3, 9, 23, 24, 27, 54, 55, 57, 60, 61, 115, 122, 161, 163, 248, 276
vocal, 35, 60, 113, 117, 121, 159–169, 200, 209, 263, 278; education, 10, 149,

158–171; pedagogy, 160, 163–168. *See also* classroom: and vocal: education; music: teacher education
voice, 1, 25, 57, 94, 136, 149, 151, 160, 161, 162, 165, 166, 168, 185, 190, 191, 204, 206, 209, 224, 225, 234, 250–51, 265, 266, 270

welfare, 1, 4, 6, 9, 17, 58, 143, 201, 224, 253, 276
well-being, 3, 5, 8, 18, 24, 26, 30, 67, 97, 160, 176, 189, 196, 227, 233, 250, 257
Western, 7, 44, 59, 101, 164, 166, 167, 174, 244n29, 248, 249, 252, 257, 267, 276; art, 36, 335, 237; music, 84, 101, 121, 159, 162, 221. *See also* art
whakawhanaungatanga, 59, 250. *See also* Māori: values
whole, 11, 22, 23, 25, 72, 109, 175, 180, 199, 200, 204, 206, 262, 280; body, 147; child, 181, 182; cosmos, 74; heart, 115; human being, 6, 42, 154; human experience, 195; human family, 4, 9, 22; human species, 94; person, 42, 172; personality, 144, 253; society, 146, 151; world, 7, 30, 31